Frank C. Robertson and Beth Kay Harris are seen autographing copies of former books, *Soapy Smith: King of the Frontier Con Men*, written by both authors in collaboration, and *The Towns of Tintic*, written by Mrs. Harris alone.

Frank C. Robertson has written more than a hundred Western novels and the much admired autobiographical work *A Ram in the Thicket*. He was a founder of the Western Writers of America and has served that organization as president. Besides his many books, he writes a popular newspaper column, "The Chopping Block," and operates a large cherry farm in Utah.

Beth Kay Harris was born in Utah and grew up in the Tintic mining area, which she so vividly recreated in her *The Towns of Tintic*. Educated at Brigham Young University, she lives in Provo, Utah, with her husband, an officer of U. S. Steel, and their three children.

BOOM TOWNS
OF THE GREAT BASIN

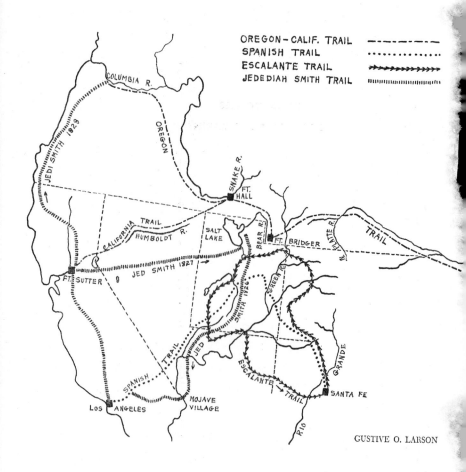

GUSTIVE O. LARSON

Early Trails Across The Basin

BOOM TOWNS
OF THE
GREAT BASIN

Frank C. Chester Robertson
and Beth Kay Harris

SAGE BOOKS, DENVER

Sage Books are published by
Alan Swallow, 2679 So. York St., Denver 10, Colo.

Contents

Introduction

The Great Basin has been a unique feature of the American Scene. At the beginning it was scorned as The Great American Desert; even today it is scorned by many who think some of its people enjoy too many liberties, but its activities have been as wide and varied as any part of the Western frontier.

Geographically it is a rough triangle with its three largest cities Salt Lake City, Reno, and Las Vegas as the anchor points. It is the only large section of land in the nation without drainage. Once most of it was covered by an ancient lake, of which only Great Salt Lake remains. Its rivers disappear in the land instead of seeking a way to the ocean. The Las Vegas area is drained by the Colorado, but its ethnic relations with the basin are too close for it not to be connected.

Name any phase of pioneer life and the Great Basin has known it. It had Indians and Indian wars. It had those intrepid explorers, the trappers. It was a highway for the covered wagon era. Part of it was the scene of the most successful colonization in the history of the country, and under the most adverse conditions. It knew the whoop of the cowboy and the trail driver, and above all it knew those argonauts of the second phase of Western history, the prospectors. It endured the worst hardships, and has settled into civilization. If a thing could be done the people of the Great Basin did it.

We have not attempted to write a complete history of the basin, but enough to show how, and why, it was conquered. We have tried to chronicle some of the life of every epic, from the first Spanish explorers, and the sedate, feet-planted-on-the-ground respectability of the Utah Mormons down to the free and easy life of the gambling population of Reno and Las Vegas.

Almost every settlement was in some sense a boom town because in each people created something that was not there before. All towns were based on hope and energy and effort. Everybody who came to the Great Basin were boomers, though there was a wide variance in their objectives. We have selected as best we could those that were either spectacular or typical.

If we have stressed the mining era overmuch it is because it was the most dynamic of all. Many of the mining towns are ghosts, but few of them are content to stay quietly in their graves. The prospector and the miner supplied the nation with gold and silver, copper, lead, and zinc, and other minerals when these were sorely needed. They were good men, and bad. They were extremes of selfishness and generosity. Their lives were hard, and necessarily reckless, but their deeds were heroic.

So, too, were the lives of the Mormon pioneers who brought industry and stability into the basin. They never considered Salt Lake City a boom town, but it was the most important one of all. It sprang up almost overnight into a full grown city, and its influence extended over the entire basin. To leave it out of the boom towns of the Great Basin would be like leaving the head off a portrait.

Neither was Las Vegas a geographical part of the Great Basin, but it was blood brother to the others and so must be included.

Salt Lake City, Las Vegas, Virginia City and the Comstock, Reno and the Washoe, and many more: these were names to stir the minds and imaginations of men. We have tried to write of them all with sympathy, compassion, and above all with admiration.

Many people have helped us in securing material for this book. We are especially indebted to the staffs of the Utah State Historical Society, and the Nevada State Historical Society, and to Mr. Stanley Adams of the Carson City Library for their courtesy and helpfulness. To Mr. Ira A. Lutsey, Technical Editor, University of Nevada, for permission to use Nevada Bureau of Mines Bulletin Number 57, by Grant H. Smith. To Nell Murbarger, Marietta M. Mariger, and Mrs. Ella Cain, for permission to draw material from their books, the latter through her publisher, Fearon Publishing Company, of San Francisco. We are grateful to Harolds Club of Reno, for allowing us access to their two volume series on Pioneer Nevada. Also, to Caxton Printers, the *Salt Lake Tribune*, and the *Utah Farmer*. We also wish to thank Mr. Howard Cox, of Manti, Utah, and Mr. William Brooks of St. George, Utah, for stories from their personal recollections.

FRANK C. ROBERTSON
BETH KAY HARRIS

CHAPTER ONE

The Background

While the Founding Fathers of the Republic were signing the Declaration of Independence in 1776, two Catholic priests and their retainers were having the first white man's look at the Great Basin. Father Silveste Velez de Escalante and Father Francisco Atanasio Dominguez left Santa Fe, New Mexico, July 29, 1776, in search of a direct route to Monterey, California. They passed through the western part of what is now Colorado, and turned west along the southern flank of the Uintah mountains, the only important mountain range in the West that runs east and west, and in September they came down Spanish Fork canyon to Utah Lake, connected to Great Salt Lake by a sluggish river later named the Jordon by the Mormon pioneers, but the discouraged priests turned south and returned to New Mexico.

An earlier explorer, Captain Garcia Lopez de Cardeñas, may have seen a little of the basin from the south rim of the Grand Canyon in 1540, but it is too improbable to be counted on.

Other Spaniards ventured farther, among them a party led by Manuel Mestas in 1805, and another by Lagos Garcia and Mauricio Arze in 1813, which made contact with the Indians of central Utah, and taught them the Christian religion, and how to make a profit by raiding the weaker tribes and selling their captives into slavery.

Some of these explorers worked their way north as far as Tintic and opened mines, some of which were discovered when the mines were opened up in that district in 1869-70, but they left no written record of their presence.

It is certain that there were prehistoric people in the basin, for in caves west of Promontory Point, and near Wendover, Nevada, are artifacts many feet deep that date back for centuries, indicating a higher culture than that enjoyed by the Indians when the white men came.

The man most responsible for the discovery of the Great Basin never saw it. That was General William H. Ashley. But again we can't be sure, for four trappers from the John Jacob Astor party of 1811-12 broke away from the main party, and may possibly have seen the Great Salt Lake. Ashley was looking for fur, and in his company were many of the most intrepid mountain men of the West, among them such as Jedediah S. Smith, William L. Sublette, David E. Jackson, and James Bridger. Sent on ahead by Ashley, a party of his men led by William Sublette reached Cache Valley in northern Utah.

One of the number, young Jim Bridger, floated down Bear River in a bullboat and was reputedly the first white man ever to see Great Salt Lake. One of Bridger's later favorite stories was that he came upon a herd of buffalo snowbound on the side of a mountain, killed and dressed them all, and that when the spring thaw came the carcasses rolled down into the lake and were so pickled in the briny water that they kept the Mormons from starving to death twenty-three years later—a story categorically denied by the Mormons.

About the time Bridger was coming down Bear River a Hudson's Bay man named Etienne Provot was descending the Weber river from the camp of Peter Skeen Ogden, and he may well have been the first to see the lake. The city of Provo, Utah, was named in his honor. The first man to circumnavigate the lake was undoubtedly Joseph R. Walker.

General Ashley descended the treacherous Green River by boat as far as present day Green River town in Utah, but soon sold out his interest to Smith, Sublette, and Jackson. In 1826 Jedediah Smith journeyed southward to California, and although he had little to do with the great basin proper became more widely known as an explorer than any of his fellows.

Trappers of the Hudson's Bay Fur Company, the American Fur

Company, and the Rocky Mountain Fur Company were soon established on the streams emptying into Salt Lake, but they were dismayed by the barren wastes to the westward, and for a time the great basin lay virtually unexplored.

The mountain men held rendezvous at various places each year to trade and celebrate what they thought of as civilization.

Fort Hall to the north was a growing concern in the early thirties, but it must share honors as being the first semi-permanent settlement in the vicinity with Fort Roubidoux. Neither was technically in the great basin, but on its fringe, but from the tops of the Uintah Mountains a portion of the great basin could certainly have been seen.

Antoine Roubidoux established his fort near the present Ute Indian town of Whiterocks. There is said to be a monument to mark the location of the old fort, but one of us tried to find it and failed. However, Jake Cuch, an old personal friend who is the son of a Ute chief, told us the old fort was about a mile from Whiterocks, and that the site is marked by what he called "a pile of rocks." According to Mr. Cuch, Indian tradition has it that Roubidoux sold whiskey to the Indian men and debauched and enslaved the women until the Utes finally rebelled and burned the fort. By a little stretching of geography and the imagination Fort Roubidoux might be called the first settlement in the Great Basin.

Five years later Phillip Thompson and David Craig established Fort Davy Crockett in Brown's Hole, in northeastern Utah, which name was quickly changed to Fort Misery, described as "the meanest fort in the West." Many years later Brown's Hole was the main hideout for the notorious Wild Bunch outlaws led by Butch Cassidy, and has maintained its isolation until now, an isolation soon to be shattered by the building of the Flaming Gorge dam on Green River. Brown's Hole is now known delicately as Brown's Park, but it is not technically in the great basin.

The first fort west of the Wasatch Range, which placed it definitely in the Great Basin, was built by Miles Goodyear on the present site of Ogden, Utah, in 1844, which he called Fort Buenaventura. It was purchased by the Mormons in 1848.

Meantime, the Great Basin was being explored. In 1832 there appeared on the scene the most controversial figure of that part of the West in the person of Captain B. L. E. Bonneville, on leave of absence from the United States Army. Ostensibly, he was looking for furs, but some believed he was on a secret military mission having to do with the Oregon country. His personal explorations were puny and his imagination large, but his adventures were believed by Washington Irving who wrote them down for posterity and Bonneville has enjoyed fame quite beyond his deserts.

Bonneville, who had the habit of being a little late on most occasions, established a fort on Green River, just about the time the trappers had stopped congregating at forts in favor of the rendezvous at whatever place they found convenient, and the trappers contemptuously called Bonneville's place Fort Nonsense. But Bonneville did bring wagons farther west than they had ever been brought before. His competitors made it tough for him, and his penchant for claiming more than he had accomplished did not add to his popularity. He tried to name Great Salt Lake, which he never saw, Lake Bonneville, but the name didn't stick.

History did, however, give Bonneville's name to the great Pleistocene lake that had once covered nearly half of the Great Basin; honor enough, perhaps, since had justice been done it would have been named after its first explorer, Joseph Reddeford Walker, one of Captain Bonneville's lieutenants. But Walker's name has been perpetuated by Walker Pass and Walker River in California, and Walker Lake in Western Nevada.

At Bonneville's request, Joe Walker, with a strong party, explored Great Salt Lake, then headed out across the desert toward the Pacific Ocean. Apparently Hudson's Bay had already penetrated part of the basin for when Walker reached the Humboldt there were trappers there who called it Ogden's River, but Walker pressed on, leading the first party ever to traverse the Great Basin from east to west. Walker's trip to California and return is one of the great sagas of the West, but has no place in this narrative except to mention that he was the first real explorer of the Great Basin.

Edward Rose, Jim Bridger, and others had trapped many of

the streams for beaver, and during the next seven or eight years it became widely known to the trappers, although it was never the best beaver country in the West.

About this time John Charles Fremont came into the basin, following his usual custom of discovering country with which other men had been long familiar. Fremont sent Kit Carson on ahead to discover the Great Basin, following the tracks which Walker had made several years earlier. Fremont, however, had the backing of the government which made his explorations official, a practice followed as long as there was any land left which the tourists couldn't reach.

Even in this century government surveyors announced the "discovery" of Bryce Canyon, although Ebenezer Bryce had been living there for many years, and its existence was known to practically every Mormon in southern Utah. But Bryce and the others did not publish an official document, and the only report Bryce is known to have made of it was his classic remark: "It's a hell of a place to lose a cow."

So, it devolved upon Fremont to make maps and write descriptions of the country. Like Bonneville he was not too apt about names, for, ignoring the men who had been in the Great Basin, he named its largest river, the Humboldt, after a German scientist who never saw the river, or had any intention of ever seeing it.

In the summer of 1841 the first emigrant train bound for California, the Bartelson-Bidwell party which had left the Oregon trail and circled Great Salt Lake to the north, took the first prairie schooners across the Great Basin, and with that move, though there was no permanent settlement as yet, civilization had set in. The Great Basin was still considered a desert rivaling the Sahara, and no one dreamed of the treasures that lay beneath their feet as the paths to glory were being beaten.

Only the small, rabbitskin-clad "Digger" Indians along the wagon roads, who had already clashed twice with Joe Walker, had a premonition that the white men had come to stay, and they were to see the game and the forests of pine nuts on which they lived destroyed. The history of the Great Plains was being slowly reenacted.

13

The full terror and treachery of the Great Basin did not strike the nation until the ill-fated Donner party crossed in 1846. George and Jacob Donner were well-to-do farmers in the East who were lured by tales of the fantastic fertility of the valleys of California, and they collected a number of others of like mind and wended their leisurely way westward. Had they followed the usual route to Fort Hall and down the Raft River Cut-off to the Humboldt they would have been all right.

Unfortunately they contacted a well meaning but careless adventurer named Lansford W. Hastings, who had been across the route and written an alleged Guide Book. Listening to Hastings' siren voice, the Donners were persuaded to leave the main trail and take a presumably shorter route around the south side of Great Salt Lake.

They made good enough time until they left the Weber River and had to spend twenty hard days making a road up East Canyon and down Emigration, and their labors were to help the first party of Mormons a year later. Crossing the desolation where Salt Lake City was later to stand, they touched the lake and paused near present day Grantsville to rest their animals.

Going on, they struck the forty-mile-wide Bonneville Salt Flats. On a portion of those flats numerous automobile speed records have been set and broken. They had no water except what they could carry and it was soon exhausted. The sun beat down on the glistening salt and their oxen mired in the muck. They were forced to abandon everything they could, including some of the wagons. Over a hundred years later Charles Kelly, Utah historian, painfully followed their tracks in the salt and found many of the thrown away articles, including old ox-bows, wagon tires, and log-chains, all heavily encrusted with salt.

Some of the stronger men walked on ahead to near present-day Wendover and returned with water, or all would have perished. Privation, anxiety, and discontent caused feuding to break out. The Donners were good men, but not leaders. Gradually James Reed emerged as the strong man of the party, but at a crossing of the Humboldt he killed a man named Snyder who had struck Reed's wife with a whip while he and Reed were fighting. Many

14

of the party wanted to hang Reed, but his friends succeeded in getting the sentence reduced to exile, and he was forced to leave the train in the desert without food or gun, articles which his daughter succeeded in getting to him in the night.

The divided, quarreling party became snowbound near Donner's Lake and spent a winter on the verge of starvation. They killed and ate their animals, including the rawhide. One at least, and perhaps more, practiced cannibalism. Injury and sickness plagued them; there are few more ghastly episodes in the annals of the West. Forty-five survived, thirty-seven died.

Some of the men tried to cross the Sierras; some failed, some succeeded, and some died. One who made it had to eat his dead companion, but the worst cannibalism was back at the camp.

When Adolph Sutter at Sutter's Fort learned of their extremity, he sent out rescue parties, one of which included James Reed who had miraculously made it through, and the weakened survivors were saved.

Word of the tragedy eventually swept the nation, but the land-hungry pioneers were not to be deterred, though it made them scurry across the Great Basin with all possible haste. But the next year a durable people who were looking for a refuge rather than riches were on their way across the plains. It was the Mormons who were to transform the Great Basin.

CHAPTER TWO

Salt Lake City

The event which touched off the first permanent settlement of the Great Basin occured June 27, 1844, at Carthage, Illinois, when a mob raided the jail there and brutally assassinated the founder, president, and prophet of the Church of Jesus Christ of Latter-day Saints, commonly known as the Mormon Church.

Joseph Smith had been in hot water ever since as a fourteen-year-old boy he had announced that he had been personally visited by God and His Son, Jesus Christ. Later, Smith claimed to have been visited by an angel named Moroni, last survivor of a white race which had inhabited both American continents. Moroni had shown young Joseph some gold plates containing the history of that race, and the ancestors of the American Indians, which had been hidden for centuries in a hill called Cumorah, near Palmyra, New York.

Smith claimed to have translated the golden plates into English (The Book of Mormon) by miraculous means, and April 6, 1830, he organized his church with six members. (It now boasts nearly two million.) He sent out missionaries and the church grew rapidly in numbers. From the first Smith was subjected to considerable persecution. He led his people westward to Kirtland, Ohio, and built a temple; but peculiar financial difficulties caused him to send scouts ahead to Missouri, and the main body of the church followed them. Stating that it had been revealed to him that the Garden of Eden had been located at Independence, Jackson County, Missouri, Smith promised his people that they would build a temple from which Christ Himself should reign, and that they would build up the Central Stake of Zion.

Religious, political, and economic disputes with the people of Missouri soon ensued until there was virtually a state of civil war. One of the leading Mormon Apostles, David W. Patten, was killed in the battle of Crooked River, October 24, 1838, along with Patterson O'Banion, and others were wounded.

A worse affair, the Haun's Hill Massacre, which was to have repercussions in the Great Basin years later, occurred six days later, on October 30, 1838. An angry mob attacked a group of Mormons at Haun's Mill, killed nineteen of them, some children and old men, and wounded fifteen others. The Mormons buried the dead bodies in a dry well and fled for their lives.

Joseph Smith and other Mormon leaders were imprisoned for a time, but managed to escape, and the Saints moved to Illinois, where they built a city called Nauvoo which became the largest and most prosperous in the state; but they soon encountered the same prejudice and enmity they had met with in Missouri.

The Mormons voted as a unit, and at the time of his death Joseph Smith was a candidate for President of the United States. He also introduced the practice of polygamy, though it was not publicly avowed until eight years after his death. There was trouble almost from the first as the natives saw nothing but menace in this united and industrious people, and they would not believe that he was in daily communication with God.

A newspaper called the *Expositor* was started in Nauvoo by a group of Mormon apostates, which so enraged the Mormons that they destroyed the press after a single edition had been printed. Joseph Smith, his brother Hyrum, Patriarch of the Church, and two associates, John Taylor and Willard Richards, were arrested and taken to Carthage jail where the Smith brothers were assassinated.

It is not the purpose of this book to go into the merits of the controversy, but the conflict became more bitter until it became evident that the Mormons would have to leave Nauvoo. Some Mormons maintain that Joseph Smith had had a vision of his people moving to the Rocky Mountains, while others insist that they moved blindly and without a planned destination. However that may be, the leadership fell upon Brigham Young, the most titanic figure the Great Basin was ever to know.

Young gathered his people for a mass emigration. He established an advance base at Winter Quarters, near Council Bluffs, Iowa, and personally led the first company of pioneers to the shores of Great Salt Lake, following the route of the Donner party. Advance scouts entered the valley July 22, 1847; the main body arrived July 24.

When he had his first view of the Great Basin, Brigham Young exclaimed, "This is the place!" Water was turned out on the thirsty soil and ground plowed to raise a crop. The Mormons had come to stay, and stay they did, even though later threatened by a United States army. In the years that followed, thousands of Mormons, many of them destitute, crossed the plains in what was America's largest and most successful attempt at colonization.

Brigham Young made himself absolute dictator and established rigid discipline, a thing made possible because his followers believed that the mantle of Joseph had fallen literally upon his shoulders, and because they believed themselves the Chosen People of the Lord. Their hardships, especially for those who came in the handcart companies, were incredible.

Though that part of the Great Basin was then Mexican territory, Brigham Young organized all of it, and much more between the foot of the Rockies and the foot of the Sierras, into the state of Deseret, with himself as governor, and applied for admission into the Union. The country had passed from Mexico to the United States by the Treaty of Guadalupe Hidalgo, February 2, 1848, before a convention and election could be held, but Deseret (meaning Honey Bee, from the Book of Mormon) was rejected. It was designed to be a sanctuary for the Saints, and continued to function until Utah was admitted as a territory in April, 1851.

Brigham Young had Joseph Smith's revelation authorizing polygamy incorporated into the official Doctrine & Covenants, and himself set the example by marrying at various times twenty-seven wives. One of his first problems was dealing with the Indians, and he pronounced the dictum that, "It is cheaper to feed than to fight them," and Utah had a minimum of Indian troubles. One of his first acts was to abolish the traffic in slaves by which they had been doing a profitable business with the Mexicans.

On the way across the plains Brigham Young talked with anyone who knew the country, among them the famous trappers Jim Bridger and Black Harris. Bridger is said to have told Brigham that he would pay a thousand dollars for the first bushel of corn that could be raised, but if the promise was ever made it was one Bridger had no intention of keeping for he was well aware that Miles Goodyear had already raised corn and other vegetables at his fort, forty miles north of Salt Lake.

Had one Mormon leader had his way the Saints would never have stopped in the Great Basin. In 1846 Samuel Brannan, who was later to play a prominent part in the development of California, brought a colony of Mormons around Cape Horn in the ship *Brooklyn;* after many tribulations he landed at the Mexican town of Yerba Buena, now known as San Francisco. Completely taken by the fertile country, Brannan galloped eastward as soon as he heard that Brigham Young was on the way. The two men met at Green River and Brannan made his pitch to have the Saints journey on to California.

Nothing could shake Young's indomitable purpose. When Brannan told him how wonderful California was, Brigham replied that he was looking for a country so poor that no one else would want it, where his people would be let alone. In California he foresaw a repetition of the old hassles in Missouri and Illinois. He wanted to be free from the "Gentiles," as all non-Mormons were called, and he was determined to develop an entirely self-sustaining community.

Sam Brannan exhausted his eloquence in vain, and after a few weeks spent in Salt Lake Valley quarreled with Brigham and returned to California to fame, fortune, and ultimate poverty.

Salt Lake City was established as a God-fearing, law-abiding town with none of the fanfare and boisterousness so prevalent with all other boom towns—though that was a condition not long to exist.

Other towns sprang up all over Utah as Brigham sent out

colonies to wherever water was available for irrigation. These, too, might be called boom towns, since most of them sprang into existence almost overnight, but the most exciting thing that ever happened to them was an occasional Indian scare, or the bishop taking an additional wife. For social and religious reasons and for protection from the Indians, they were all laid out alike in a neat pattern. The people lived inside the towns and worked the farms that lay on the outskirts. It was said that many of them feared they would become so pure that they would be taken up bodily to heaven as was the ancient City of Enoch.

Unfortunately for the Mormons, the dust had scarcely settled over the tracks made by their first wagons when the hated Gentiles began to invade Zion. Sam Brannan had participated in the discovery of gold, and when he came down to San Francisco from Sutter's Fort to ride through the streets waving his hat and yelling, "Gold! Gold! Gold!" he was unwittingly dooming Brigham Young's dream of splendid isolation.

The Mormons had scarcely squared away for their grim fight for survival when the gold-mad Forty-Niners were using Salt Lake City as a halfway house. The Mormons resented it, but Heber C. Kimball, second in command to Brigham, prophesied that in a short time they would be able to buy goods in Salt Lake cheaper than they could in New York or St. Louis, and he was soon proven right. Salt Lake City became a graveyard for the worn-out animals and broken-down wagons of the Forty-niners, who wanted only fresh animals to get them to where they could pick gold off the hills, and the Saints knew how to drive a hard bargain. As the Saints saw it, the only good thing about the stampeders was their haste to coninue their journey, and their willingness to sacrifice their outfits and supplies.

The Forty-Niners helped the Mormons to survive during those first troublesome years of toil and hardships, but the Mormons give more credit to the seagulls which inhabited the islands of Great Salt Lake. When one year their small fields were threatened by an invasion of crickets, the seagulls came soaring in from the lake and devoured the insects, an event that is commemorated by a bronze statue of a seagull on the temple grounds that is still one of the sights of the city. But the next year the Saints planted more acres and there were more crickets than the seagulls could handle. Many of the Mormons were reduced to digging sego roots for survival.

Then the streets resounded to the tread of alien footsteps, but Brigham Young had one advantage: perfect discipline. He could call any of his people on a mission to do anything he wanted done.

So determined was he to preserve the unity and isolation of his people that he ordered his scholars to create a new alphabet for use of the people of Deseret, though it was never widely accepted. But as fast as he could get around to it he took steps to provide culture for his people. He established a university. Work was begun on the great temple with its All-Seeing-Eye that was to take forty years for its completion. He built the dome-shaped Tabernacle with its mighty pipe organ that is still the pride of Mormondom, and he built the Salt Lake Theater, the finest in all the West, that was torn down a few years ago to make way for a service station, bringing loud cries of protest from both Mormon and Gentile throats. He built Social Hall, now also gone into limbo, and he travelled the length and breadth of his domain urging thrift and hard work and establishing home industries.

The Forty-Niners came and went, leaving the Saints richer for their brief stay. They could buy "Valley Tan" whiskey distilled by the abstemious Saints, but Brigham kept his town pure, and Salt Lake City grew rapidly in size and importance.

Elders were called to establish a colony in Utah's Dixie at St. George, in the southern part of the territory, and cotton was grown so that the people could make and wear their own clothes. They grew grapes to make wine which the Saints were not supposed to drink.

Lead was discovered at Beaver, and iron near Cedar City in the south part of the territory, but their products were used only for manufacturing articles needed by the Saints and were not exploited commercially. It was in the minds of many Mormons that fortunes could be more quickly come by prospecting for gold in California than the hard life they were living, but Brigham answered them with the same arguments he had used against

Sam Brannan. Only by eschewing mining could the Saints be held together and Zion established in the valleys of the mountains. He held his people, and for as long as he lived continued his opposition to prospecting and mining, even after it was demonstrated that his own country was rich in mineral.

Meanwhile, the storm clouds were gathering. Young was absolute master of his own people, both by virtue of his presidency of the church, and his governorship of the territory; but judges of the Supreme Court and a secretary of the territory were sent in from outside, and they were Gentiles. Not only did they form the nucleus of an alien population, but from the first they waged a crusade against Brigham's power, and against what they called Mormon immorality.

Polygamy was now an avowed institution, even though from the first the male population exceeded the female. It was far less common than was generally supposed, and it is claimed that at no time did more than four per cent of the men have plural wives; but that minority numbered most of the leading men of the church and of the scattered communities. The Mormons claimed they had a constitutional right to practice their religion in any way they saw fit. For forty years the legal battle raged, and it was a mark of distinction for a man to have gone to the penitentiary for having more than one wife. The story of polygamy is a long and involved one, but it finally ended when in 1890 President Wilford Woodruff issued a Manifesto bowing to the law of the land; the alternative was disfranchisement and confiscation of church property.

In 1856 the Mormons were having other troubles. There was a drouth, and an infestation of locusts, and on the heels of that came the hardest winter they had ever known.

Though Brigham Young had been reappointed governor, his term was coming to an end, and opposition to his reappointment was growing. Another effort to achieve statehood in 1856 had failed. Charges and counter charges were being made. Territorial Secretary Almon W. Babbit was killed by Indians on his way to the East. Associate Justice Leonidas Shaver died of a sudden heart attack, and there were a number of other violent or sudden deaths, all of which were charged to the Mormons without proof. It was alleged that Governor Young had burned the Territorial records, and an Indian Agent tried to incite the Indians against the Mormons.

Though Chief Justice John F. Kinney was fair and friendly toward the Mormons, his two associates, Judges William W. Drummond and George P. Stiles, were not. Stiles was an apostate Mormon, and Judge Drummond was accused of living in open adultery. Salt Lake City was torn by strife, and the fate of Mormonism hung in the balance.

By the light of history it appears that the carpet-baggers who were trying to take over the territory were actuated not so much by righteous hatred of polygamy as by frustration at their inability to break the ranks of Mormon solidarity.

Wild reports of rebellion were carried to Washington and President Buchanan ordered General Harney to take the field and crush the rebellion. Harney was succeeded by Colonel Albert Sydney Johnston. A bloodless guerilla war of a sort ensued in which Mormon scouts under red-whiskered Lot Smith burned two wagon trains loaded with provisions for the army, took the wagonmasters prisoner without firing a shot, burned wagons and supplies and drove the cattle back to Salt Lake. As a result the army was halted at Fort Bridger for a miserable winter while the Mormon boys rode home in triumph. The chief financial sufferers were the firm of Russell, Majors and Waddell, later promoters of the Pony Express, who owned the wagon trains and supplies and were never reimbursed by the government.

While the Mormons fortified Echo Canyon, Alfred Cumming was appointed governor to succeed Brigham Young and peace negotiations initiated by Colonel Thomas L. Kane, an old friend of the Mormons, got under way, but it was an agonizing winter for all concerned.

The Nauvoo Legion had come intact to Utah under General Daniel H. Wells, and while the crippled army was limping into Fort Bridger the Legion was building breastworks and piling up rocks to roll down into Echo Canyon if the army tried to get through. Any military strategist can see how easily the fortifications could have been outflanked, but it was most impressive to new Governor Cumming when he arrived in the spring; made more impressive since he was taken through in the night where he could look up and see men marching around hundreds of camp-fires on the canyon rim. What he did not know was that these were the same men keeping pace with him and marching around each campfire as they came to it. What he supposed to be two or three thousand men were no more than one hundred and fifty.

Governor Cumming arrived in Salt Lake in early April, 1858, and was cordially received by Brigham Young and other Mormon officials. The only fighting the Mormons proposed to do was a delaying action to let the people move out, leaving a scorched earth behind them. This movement was already under way. According to the historian Bancroft, thirty thousand people had left their homes in northern Utah for Provo and other settlements. Only a few guards remained to set fire to the city if the army proved hostile.

Salt Lake City became a ghost town while the Mormon leaders and the two peace commissioners, Powell and McCullouch, sent out by President Buchanan, negotiated an agreement that was extremely distasteful to fire-eating General Johnston.

The comic opera war was soon over, but the friction continued to exist as long as the army was in Utah. Brigham Young would never have called any of the towns he founded a boom town; the very words were anathema to him, for they implied imper-manence, and what the Mormons built they built to last. Utah had its boom towns, but almost without exception they were Gentile dominated.

Every Mormon town was carefully planned. It was laid out on the square with wide streets and four lots to the block. The people were encouraged to build good houses and barns, and to milk cows and raise gardens. Partly for social reasons and partly as a defense against Indians, all the people lived in the towns and their farms were on the outskirts.

Such towns can be seen all over Utah today, but a new kind of boom is threatening to turn many of these peaceful hamlets into virtual ghost towns, for the Great Basin has become a fortress of national defense, and is dotted with air and missile bases. A great new steel industry has arisen in Utah, and the people are flocking to the cities and a life far different from what it was in Brigham's day.

The Mormons now deny that they are a peculiar people, though they still think of themselves as a chosen one, but some of the old ones privately express their fears that Zion may yet be overwhelmed by the world. Prosperity, they fear, may weaken them where poverty could not.

It was the Mormons, those first pioneers to settle the last remaining part of the Great American Desert, who built the first roads. They made the Pony Express possible, and they furnished many of the men and much of the material to build the first telegraph line, and they helped immeasurably to connect the first continental railways. They at first opposed mining for sound and sensible reasons, but mining has brought more wealth to the Great Basin than any other source. Now oil and uranium are still proving that the wealth of this once thought to be worthless land lies below the surface.

Mining created most of the boom towns, which bloomed, harvested their one crop, and for the most part died. The miners, unlike the organized and disciplined Saints, were lusty individualists. Their towns grew helter-skelter and willy-nilly, and contributed little to the culture of the country, but while they lived they were full of boisterous, roaring life. The miners were tough, and their deeds are worthy of commemoration.

In the space of little more than a hundred years the Great Basin made history as fast as it was made anywhere, and is still making it. Along the paved highways one can see modern cities and towns, prosperous ranches, herds of cattle and sheep, and the air is crowded with airplanes, while here and there jeeps follow the old trails of the prospectors and their burros, and maybe there will be new boom towns—for the Great Basin is still a land of mystery and paradox.

It is a land which some love with fanatical devotion, and others hate with equal zeal. It is a land of contrast; of fertile farms, and grim forbidding mountains and deserts; of ultra-modern industry, and gaunt ghost towns harboring only memories of vanished dreams.

But the greatest contrast of all is that while the easternmost of its two states is so puritanical that even the drinking of a cup of coffee may bring one into social disrepute, and drinking liquor is considered a sin, the westernmost neighbor is the only state in the Union where gambling is legalized, and its towns are for the most part wide open.

The two states touch at a little town called Wendover. On one side of the town you may gamble to your heart's content, and the huge figure of a cowboy points your way to a casino with a never wearying hand. But a few feet away you could be arrested if you tossed a nickel in the air and bet another nickel that it would come down heads or tails. This is the Great Basin.

CHAPTER THREE

Camp Floyd

One of the causes of the Mormon War which made negotiations so difficult was the Mountain Meadows Massacre of 1857—a thing the Mormons have tried diligently to forget, and is part of what one Utah writer and lecturer calls, "Utah's forty years of historical amnesia."

A wagon train known as the Fancher party, of about 140 persons, was, with the exception of fewer than twenty children considered too young to talk, treacherously wiped out after they had been induced to give up their arms under promise of safe conduct. The deed was done under the excitement of war hysteria, although all Mormons now agree that it was inexcusable.

Included in the Fancher party from Arkansas were a few Missourians whom the Mormons believed had been implicated in the Missouri persecutions, including the Haun's Mill massacre, and the Missouri "Wildcats," as they called themselves, were abusive to the Mormons on their way through the settlements. It was rumored that the emigrants were poisoning the springs, though the rumor was later proven baseless.

Another rumor was that an army from California was coming to join Johnston's army from the East to destroy the Mormons. Indians were incited against the emigrants, but when the Fancher party put up too stout a resistance the local Mormon leaders felt impelled to take a hand.

James H. Haslem was ordered to ride to Salt Lake City and ask Brigham Young for instructions, and he made the ride there and back in the record time of six days, returning with written instructions from Young to let the emigrants go in peace. Whether Haslem arrived back after the massacre or before it is still a subject of some dispute, but the preponderance of evidence indicates that he was too late.

Brigham Young must be acquitted of any connection with the crime, which could only hurt his church, but it is also certain that he knew who the guilty parties were and made no effort to punish them. He must have known that the cattle, wagons, and goods of the slaughtered emigrants had been distributed to the Indians, and the *missionaries*. In a letter to Jacob Hamlin, who took over the care of the rescued children, although he was not present at the massacre, occurs this significant sentence: "In regard to the cattle you should control them and use them for the best interest of both the missionaries and the Indians; the Indians should be encouraged in keeping and taking care of stock."

Nearly twenty years later John D. Lee, the alleged leader of the massacre, was executed for his crime by being shot by a firing squad at the site of the massacre. All the participants had been sworn to secrecy so it would have been hard to collect evidence, yet John D. Lee, an adopted son of the prophet, reported to him in person in less than a month after the massacre, and filed a written report with him November 20, 1858. (*The Mountain Meadows Massacre*, by Juanita Brooks, Stanford University Press, 1950.) It would appear that the official attitude of the church was strictly negative. Whoever was responsible, it was a colossal blunder and did the church injury when it was already in grave disfavor.

The peace negotiations were begun in April, and already the Mormons had moved out. Brigham Young was distrustful of any promises made by the government, and rumors were rife that he would again conduct a mass migration of his people. Nobody knew exactly where he would go, but the name most mentioned was Sonora, Mexico. But one thing Brigham made clear: if forced to leave his enemies would find nothing but scorched earth ahead of them. For more than three months men stood by to burn Salt Lake City and surrounding towns, while their families rested uneasily in Provo and towns farther south. It seems now that

28

Young's threat to leave the territory was a bluff, and his real purpose was to isolate the army from his people. In that he was successful.

The army was allowed peaceful entry on condition that it did not stop in the city. It marched through the deserted streets, crossed the Jordan River, remained in camp there a few days, then marched southward into Cedar Valley, stayed for a time at what is now the hamlet of Cedar Fort, then went into permanent quarters at Camp Floyd. The town that grew up around it blossomed and boomed into a metropolis of 7,000 people who were that many thorns in the side of Brigham Young. Camp Floyd became the second largest city in Utah.

Governor Cumming, who by his patience, tact, and fairmindedness kept the negotiations going, deserves a higher place in history than has been accorded him. Brigham Young willingly accepted the authority of Governor Cumming, but it was a tongue-in-cheek acknowledgment, since he knew that although Cumming had a right to govern the arid acres—"which nobody else wanted"— Brigham himself had, and always would have, complete control of the people. Governors came and went, but until his death in 1877 Brigham Young was the real ruler whose word was law.

The peace commission from Washington had brought a full pardon for the Mormons, but Young and his two counsellors, Heber C. Kimball and Daniel H. Wells, were offended at being pardoned for a rebellion they insisted had never been a fact, but they admitted having burned the wagon trains so they reluctantly accepted the pardon for that. They also declared their loyalty to the Union and the constitution, and in that they were one up on General Johnston and Secretary of War Floyd, who were already planning to join the Confederacy in case the South seceded. Floyd's purpose it is now abundantly clear in sending the army to Utah was to get it out where it couldn't be used against the South when the war began.

At the time, however, General Johnston followed up the peace treaty with a proclamation assuring the Mormons that they would be protected in person, rights, and peaceful pursuit of their vocations. To this Governor Cumming added a declaration that

Federal and Territorial laws would be strictly enforced, and so, in July, 1858, Johnston was permitted to march through the city.

An army correspondent, watching the entry of the troops, wrote: "The utter silence of the streets was broken only by the music of the military bands, the monotonous tread of the regiments, and the rattle of the baggage wagons." George "Beefsteak" Harrison, a cook with the army, said that, "Salt Lake was as still as a cemetery when they marched in." He saw only two people, a man riding a sorrel mule, and an old lady who peeped out of a window blind at the troops.

Still suspicious of the army, the Mormons did not return to the city until the coming fall. General Johnston kept his promise, but the army brought a new way of life into the territory, a way cordially disliked by the Mormons.

By 1860 a town of 7,000 had grown up around the army post, most of them soldiers, army employees, and camp followers. There were gamblers, soiled doves, and the usual number of riff-raff. The contrast between Camp Floyd and the Mormon towns could not have been greater, yet the money-minded Mormons were able to extract a profit from it.

It was estimated by Bancroft that until the coming of the army there was not $3,000 hard cash in the territory, but the army had plenty of it. The camp afforded a market for Mormon produce, and there were always supplies they could buy or trade for. The Mormons bought cheap and sold dear, and there was an ever increasing traffic between Camp Floyd and Salt Lake City, though relations were seldom friendly.

Most of the buildings at Camp Floyd were of adobe bricks which the Mormons made in nearby pits, and since most of the houses in Salt Lake were made from these sun-dried bricks the Mormons were master builders with the material, and building the houses in Camp Floyd was an added source of revenue. The soldiers were resented, but the wealth they contributed was welcomed.

In time some of the riff-raff overflowed into Salt Lake City, and Brigham watched helplessly as his city began to know the kind of corruption he had feared from the first the Gentiles would bring.

There were so many saloons on Main Street that the thoroughfare became known as Whiskey Street. The historian T. B. H. Stenhouse notes that during a part of 1859 there was a murder every week in Salt Lake. Lawlessness was rampant, but trade flourished.

Not all the people of Camp Floyd were lawless, and a number of soldiers and teamsters joined the Mormon church, married Mormon girls, and their descendants are among the most respected in Mormon country. Beefsteak Harrison settled in Springville and for years ran a restaurant that catered to the carriage trade from Salt Lake. James Davids, from New York, married an Indian girl for whom Anson V. Call had traded a sack of flour to save her life and raised as his own daughter. Both James Davids and his wife became respected pioneers of Idaho.

The Mormons having put an end to the slave traffic, the warlike Utes were left with a number of captured children on their hands, so to realize on their property they gave the Mormons the choice of buying the slaves or seeing them put death before their eyes. James Davids played a prominent part in assisting his father-in-law, Anson V. Call, to establish Call's Landing on the Colorado river, one of the few Brigham Young ventures which didn't turn out successfully. A few boats did ascend the river, being pulled up the canyon in some places by winches and cables fastened to eye-bolts driven into rocks along the bluffs, but today the ruins of Call's Landing lie buried beneath the waters of Lake Mead.

Among the tougher followers of Johnston's army was William Clarke Quantrill, later to become infamous as leader of Quantrill's Raiders prior to and during the Civil War. His most famous exploit was the murder of more than a hundred people at Lawrence, Kansas, but at Camp Floyd Quantrill was an army cook.

Another "badman" who was seen around Camp Floyd was Bill Hickman, former Mormon and self-confessed "Destroying Angel." When Hickman was at Camp Floyd he had been repudiated by the church, and his numerous wives taken from him. Sylvanus C. Waddell told of being attacked at Camp Floyd by a badman he knew as Des Hickman, but Waddell knocked Hickman down with

31

a chair and took his gun away from him. Later Hickman hit Waddell between the shoulders with a rock. Friends offered to protect Waddell if he would kill Hickman, but Waddell declined.

Encounters between the soldiers and the Saints were of common occurrence during Camp Floyd's heyday. The two could not be kept apart. Once Parley P. Pratt, a Mormon Apostle, had written of Zion: "All is quiet—stillness. No elections, no police reports, no murders, no wars in our little world . . . . It is the dream of the poets actually fulfilled."

But soon Brigham Young was shouting angrily at his enemies, "Bring on your civilization! Whore houses for the women and grog shops for the men." (Maurine Whipple's, *This Is the Place: Utah.*) And the detested civilization came, with all the things he had dreaded. It could all be found on Whiskey Street.

There were many clashes. An instance that was typical will suffice. A young Mormon named Howard Spencer was herding cattle at the Spencer-Little ranch in Rush Valley, west of Camp Floyd, when a detail of soldiers under Sergeant Ralph Pike arrived to cut hay for the fort and ordered young Spencer to remove his cattle. Upon being told by Spencer that the cattle couldn't be moved until morning, Pike struck the youth over the head with a gun barrel, inflicting a near fatal wound which affected him mentally the rest of his life. This occurred March 22, 1859, and on August 11, while the trial was in progress, Spencer encountered Pike on Main Street in Salt Lake City and shot him in the presence of a military guard. Pike died a few days later.

Spencer made his escape, and a few days later some of the Camp Floyd soldiers raided the little Mormon settlement of Cedar Fort, six miles to the north, burned haystacks and sheds, and shot at those who tried to put out the fires, though no one was killed or wounded.

The Mormons appealed to General Johnston who offered to send a guard to protect the settlement, though rendering the promise useless by adding that he could not control the soldiers while Spencer was still at large.

The Mormon view of the inhabitants of Camp Floyd is given by Orson F. Whitney, in Whitney's *Popular History of Utah.*

"Banded together for rapine and acts of violence, they have stolen large herds of horses and mules. Many of these men, maddened by intemperance, or rendered desperate by losses at the gaming tables, or by various other causes, have shed each other's blood in frequent conflicts, and secret assassinations. These lawless and bloody deeds are committed by them almost daily with impunity, and when their atrocity and frequency shook the public mind, it has become a custom with a certain set of people to exclaim against the people of Utah; but it is an injustice to impute the acts of these desperadoes to the community in general. With an equal show of justice might they be attributed to the inhabitants of the States and Territories whence these men have so recently emigrated."

At one corner stood Brigham Young, and at the other Albert Sydney Johnston, and between them was Governor Alfred Cumming, vainly trying to keep the peace. Cumming was a man of fairness and good will, and he might have succeeded had it not been for the misguided ardor of some of the imported judges. He was the object of abuse from Johnston, who accused him of trying to protect the people Johnston would have liked to destroy.

Judge Charles E. Sinclair opened his court at Salt Lake City with the statement that he would not recognize the presidential pardon, and urged the grand jury to indict the Mormon leaders for treason. Judge John Cradlebaugh opened court at Provo with a hundred soldiers in attendance. When the citizens protested, Cradlebaugh summoned eight more companies. Governor Cumming requested General Johnston to remove the troops and was refused. The governor was left in the unenviable position of having his authority flouted by both the army and the people, for although Brigham Young recognized Cumming's authority the people themselves would take orders only from Brigham Young. Eventually, the U. S. Attorney General delegated power over all ordinary troop dispositions to the governor, but the friction continued.

Judge Cradlebaugh was determined to fix the guilt for the Mountain Meadows massacre, but he had, as one writer claims, the ability always to put his worst foot forward, and his arrogance

33

nullified his usefulness. His Mormon grand jury naturally refused to return indictments against the leaders of the church, and bitterness between Camp Floyd and Salt Lake City increased.

The coming of the army had ended the splendid isolation Brigham Young had hoped to achieve, and during the troublesome years the army was always a factor. With the beginning of the Civil War the army was withdrawn from Camp Floyd; General Johnston went home to join the Confederacy and meet a hero's death on the battlefield. A Colonel Smith took over for a short time and was succeeded by Colonel Phillip St. George Cook, who had commanded the Mormon Battalion during the Mexican War and was their good friend. But a greater foe to Brigham Young than Johnston had ever been was soon to come.

Camp Floyd, though the name had been changed to Fort Crittenden, because Floyd was considered a traitor, was far from dead. Before Johnston's departure Russell, Majors and Waddell had got the Pony Express going and Camp Floyd became one of the most important stations on the entire route. Salt Lake City was the division point, but Camp Floyd was an important jumping off place on the Western division.

Just beyond Camp Floyd lay Faust's ranch at the foot of Lookout Pass, and beyond that were the warlike Piutes who liked nothing better than to kill the pony boys, most of whom, on that most dangerous part of all the Pony Express route, were Mormon boys. The manager of that division was Major Howard Egan, Mormon frontiersman and scout. Egan's deeds of daring are legion, but he was glad to have the protection of the soldiers at Camp Floyd. In a battle in Nevada the soldiers defeated the combined Piutes, Bannacks and Shoshones, and in that one action justified for the first time their presence in Utah. Oddly enough, General Johnston and Brigham Young never met. The general did not believe in personal diplomacy.

Perhaps no better contemporary summation of the significance of Camp Floyd exists than was written by Horace Greeley who passed through there on his widely publicized tour of the West.

"The camp," wrote Greeley, "was formed of low and neat adobe houses, generally small." (The lumber for roofs and finishing had

34

been supplied by Brigham Young and his son-in-law from the only canyon opening into Salt Lake Valley which abounded in timber fit for sawing. The profit on the lumber was probably over $50,000, the price being seventy dollars per thousand feet, delivered. The total cost of the military post to the government, was about $200,000. (Whitney's *Popular History of Utah.*)

Whitney further quotes Horace Greeley: "Very general is the inquiry in the army, why were we sent here? And why are we kept here? What purpose does it subserve, beyond enriching contractors and Mormon magnates, at its own cost and that of the Federal Treasury? Every article eaten, drank, worn or in any manner bought by the soldiers, costs three to ten times its value in the States. . . . I have not so bad an opinion of the Mormons as that entertained by the army. While I consider the Mormon religion, so called, a delusion and a blight, I believe many of its adherents . . . to be pure-minded, well meaning people; and I do not believe that Mormons generally delight in plunder and murder. . . . But I concur entirely in the conviction of the army, that there is no use in its retention here under existing orders and circumstances. . . . A suspicion that it is kept here to answer pecuniary ends is widely entertained. It is known that vast sums have been made out of its transportation by favored contractors."

By 1861 most of the soldiers had been ordered elsewhere. As an echo of the hard feeling that had existed some of them encountered a couple of Mormon men in Echo Canyon, William and James Hennifer. At the instance of Assistant Surgeon Edward Covey and Lieutenant Ebenezer N. Gay, William Hennifer was stripped of his clothing and beaten nearly to death. Covey had been arrested in Salt Lake City for riot and assault, and Hennifer was one of the officers who had taken him into custody.

The Mormons are an adaptable people, proud and independent. Though bitterly resenting Camp Floyd and the presence of the army, they did not hesitate to use it in any way that resounded to the profit and glory of Zion. And it was profitable. They were able to take contracts from the army, and to sell their produce for spot cash, but the greatest windfall of all came when the camp was abandoned in the early Sixties. The profits associated with war surpluses were not strange even then.

Whitney has this to say: "Before the post was abandoned immense stores of provisions and army supplies were offered for sale by the military authorities, and disposed of at an enormous sacrifice. Goods worth four million dollars, were sold for one hundred thousand. Far-sighted buyers made their fortunes. Great quantities of arms and ammunition, which could not be transported, were destroyed by direction of the War Department."

Among those "far-sighted buyers" were the Walker brothers who by the profits of that sale became mining kings, merchant princes, and bankers of Utah. Good Mormons at the time of the sale, it is reported that they fell into apostasy because of a reluctance to pay tithing on their gains.

A little light on how that auction was conducted was thrown on the matter by Alexander Toponces, a French trader, freighter, and rancher who came into the valley with Johnston's army. He says in his Rememiscences that there was a story current among the soldiers how General Johnston and Smith, his chief of staff, acted when they learned that the peace commissioners, L. W. Powell, ex-governor and senator-elect from Kentucky, and Major B. McCulloch, had brought official word from Washington that there should be no fighting. Johnston took off his hat with the insignia on it, threw it on the ground, stamped on it, and said, "Damn such a government. Here we have starved and froze all winter, and now that we have got these fellows right where we want them they are going to get off without shedding so much as one drop of blood. Damn such a government!"

Toponce didn't know if the story were true or not, but thought it reflected the attitude of the army officers who three years later sided with the South.

Just before the auction Toponce had charge of a herd of 1900 horses and mules in Bingham and Butterfield Canyons, so it might be said that he knew his mules.

"Most of the stuff brought ridiculous prices. Colonel Carter, a storekeeper from Fort Bridger, bid in 200,000 pounds of side meat at a quarter of a cent a pound.

36

"One man had contracted to deliver 31,000 sacks of flour at 30 cents a pound. He did actually deliver 2,000 sacks, but the Department paid him for 30,000 sacks, and then advertised it for sale again and he bought the 30,000 sacks at auction, paying only one cent a pound. The 28,000 sacks he never saw at all.

"I saw big government wagons, complete with bows, covers, neck yoke, double-trees, stretchers and chains for six mules sold at $6.50. One Payson man bought a score of them at $6.50 apiece.

"When they got around to selling the government mules, the main wagon boss in charge called me in and said, 'Alex, you know these mules pretty well. Here are some numbers. The ones, two twos, two three and so on. You go into the corral and match up the mules in spans and put the numbers on their headstalls, so we can sell them in teams.'

"The mules he pointed out were a lot of 100 little mules that the army had picked up at Fort Laramie when the army was coming out. They were culls and little scrubs . . . and they were in the same corral with a lot of big, rangey mules they had bought in Missouri at fancy prices.

"When the auctioneer got ready for the mules they led out the span of little ones marked No. 1 and sold them, and who should be there bidding for them but my old friend Ben Holladay (The stagecoach king). He bought that team for $40.00, and they were put back in the corral and number 2 came out, and Holladay bought them. . . .

"Then I made a discovery; every time a team of those little mules were sold to Ben Holladay someone would take the numbers off their headstalls and change them for the numbers of the big Missouri mules.

"So all day long they sold little mules. Nothing but little mules came out of the corral, and as fast as they were sold someone traded the numbers for the numbers of the big mules. Ben Holladay bought nearly all that were offered at $30 to $40 a span. Some of these mules he bought two or three times. So I decided to buy some myself. Ben glared at me but he would not bid against me and I got most of my mules at around $30. I bought twelve altogether.

37

"But I noticed that when my mules were turned back into the corral no one changed the numbers, so after a while I went in and changed them myself. No one made any objection. They did not dare to. I knew too much."

Toponce relates that he sold one of his twelve mules for $500.00. It was a champion pacer and saddle mule. He sold one team for $500.00, and undoubtedly came out well with the others.

That giveaway auction was a fitting climax to the brief but stormy life of Camp Floyd. Conceived in trickery by men who cared little about the loyalty or morals of the Mormons, but who wanted to aid the South in the oncoming struggle between the states, it had no real justification for being, and accomplished nothing except the enrichment of the Mormons the army was supposed to conquer, and of a few speculators like Ben Holladay.

Where Camp Floyd once stood is now a quiet little Mormon farming community called Fairfield, and the inhabitants evince little interest in the fact that their village was once the home of seven thousand as tough citizens as ever haunted the West. All that remains of history is a Pony Express monument, one restored building, and the old army cemetery just south of town where lie buried some seventy odd soldiers and camp employees of old Camp Floyd. Until a year ago they lay in neglect with tumbleweeds rolling over the bare level ground. It was surrounded by an iron fence, with a granite monument in the middle. But now each grave has a gravestone, very few of which, probably, are above the right people.

Few if any of them died in battle, but in a roster that was finally recovered occurs this simple notation after many of the names: Killed. It is the opinion of some that quite a few may have been shot by sentries because they were drunk and couldn't remember the password.

It is not much to look at today, but at one time Camp Floyd rivaled Salt Lake City as the most important town in the Great Basin.

CHAPTER FOUR

Corinne — The Burg on the Bear

At one time after the stormy days of Camp Floyd, a bellicose little town of three thousand people near the mouth of Bear River boldly challenged the mighty power of the hierarchy at Salt Lake City, and called itself the Gentile capitol of Utah. To its enemies it was "The Burg on the Bear."

Towns seldom spring out of the earth without reason. The immediate excuse for Corinne's existence was the coming of the railroad, but its roots went far deeper than that.

With the influx of Gentiles to Salt Lake City, Mormon antagonism grew. Brigham Young wanted to hold his people together, and the Gentiles wanted to penetrate. Brigham, the Lion of the Lord, fought back. Gentile merchants had the goods, but the Mormons had the buying power; so, Brigham instituted a boycott. Faithful Mormons were not supposed to trade at Gentile stores, and the Gentiles were hit where it hurt most—in their pocketbooks. Some hung on, some were ruined—and some moved to Corinne.

In 1858 a reformation swept Zion. Meetings were called, and the Saints arose and confessed their sins, and were rebaptized. Some of them, it is alleged, confessed to sins they had never committed, such as adultery and tobacco using, so great is the power of suggestion. But it gave them a feeling of purity, and a corresponding feeling of contempt for the wicked Gentiles.

Not all Mormons agreed with the boycott, for they found trading with the Gentiles profitable. A counter reformation which demanded the right of the Saints to think for themselves set in in the late Sixties, led by William S. Godbe and Elias L. T. Harrison, publishers of the *Utah Magazine*. That reformation, though it had political repercussions, was short-lived and ineffectual for it was a revolt against Brigham Young's power and dissenters were quickly excommunicated. The natural gathering place for sedition was Corinne, but religious differences alone could not have made Corinne the hell-raising little town it was during its brief career. Only the coming of the railroad could have done that, and Corinne was the nearest town to Promontory where the first continental railroad was joined.

The Union Pacific railroad was building west from Omaha, and its goal was Humboldt Wells, Nevada, while the Central Pacific was driving just as hard to the east from California, and its hoped for destination was Green River, Wyoming. Recklessly, they laid parallel grades for two hundred miles, though the rails finally touched at Promontory, a few miles west of Corinne, on May 10, 1869.

The Central Pacific was built largely by Chinese labor, the Union Pacific by the Irish; and a rowdier lot than the Paddies has never been known. The temporary camps or towns at railhead were known as Hell on Wheels, and not the least of these was Corinne. Unlike the others it did not fade away when the railroaders folded their tents and disappeared. One of those to the west of Corinne was Blue Creek, but because of their transitory nature few of them had permanent names, and such designations as Deadfall, or Hell's Half Acre, sufficed.

Few towns have ever had such diversified reasons for existing as Corinne. The railroads were one, the schism between Mormon and Gentile was another, and the third was the discovery of gold in Montana.

During the Sixties the towns of Bannack and Virginia City, Montana, were booming, and the closest metropolis was Salt Lake City. From their beginning there was much freight and passenger traffic between Virginia City and Salt Lake City, a traffic that was greatly shortened by the coming of the railroad. Instead of Salt Lake, the jumping off place for the Montana commerce became Corinne. Its streets were lined day and night by cumbersome freight wagons and passenger coaches.

40

Promontory, where the rails had met, was out in the desert and a wholly impractical place to build a town. The Gentile masters of Corinne hoped that their town would be chosen as a permanent junction of the railway systems, but an agreement was reached by which the Central Pacific used the Union Pacific tracks into Ogden, which then became the junction city.

Brigham Young, who had been sulking in his tent because the transcontinental line had missed his city—though he had accepted some contracts to help build it—at once became busy building a branch line from Ogden southward. A contemplated line into Montana got only as far as Cache Valley in northern Utah, though eventually such a line was built north from the Oregon Short Line when it reached Pocatello, Idaho, thus dealing the final death blow to Corinne.

But during those few years Corinne prospered as a freighting town, and the Gentiles strove mightily to make it the real capitol of Utah.

The Burg on the Bear was a far cry from the gentle City of the Saints. It had row upon row of saloons, perhaps as many as fifty, and a corresponding number of houses of ill-fame. It had its quota of badmen and its deeds of violence. The railroad had brought prosperity to the country, and the welding of the iron band across the continent gave Corinne its brightest hour. For one day Corinne practically moved to Promontory.

The roads were supposed to meet May 9, 1869, but there were unavoidable, perhaps, delays and mix-ups so the 10th was the historic day. Except for the squabbles, the lines could have been joined two weeks earlier. While a whole nation waited with bated breath for the sound of a silver maul striking a golden spike that was to be carried over the wires, the delay wasn't made known in San Francisco and Sacramento and those two cities enjoyed an extra, if premature, day of celebration.

Ten miles of track was laid by the Union Pacific in a single day in order to keep its date, but Alex Toponce, who was there and gave a vivid description of the proceedings, says one hundred feet had to be laid the morning of the celebration.

An official photographer was supposed to be there to take a

picture of the event for posterity but somehow missed connections and his place was taken by C. R. Savage, Utah's first pioneer photographer. Mr. Savage's was the only picture taken, and it was a gem, but unfortunately is not the one the public is familiar with, which shows a lot of dignified and solemn faces, some of whom were not even there, and one of whom had been dead for several years. Savage's picture was of an hilarious, rollicking celebration which did not please Leland Stanford, president of the Central Pacific, who had another artist paint the picture over more in accordance with Mr. Stanford's idea of what was fitting and proper.

Mr. Stanford's displeasure can be readily understood since he was the one supposed to drive home the golden spike in the laurel tie; but perhaps due to the nature of the celebration, he swung powerfully—and missed. Mr. Durrant of the Union Pacific did no better, to the great delight of the Irish and Chinese laborers who were accustomed to swinging a sledgehammer. Jack Casement, the builder of the Union Pacific, stepped up and drew cheers of acclaim from the bystanders when he hit the spike. Meantime, a frustrated telegrapher managed to get off a message announcing the union of the railroads, the first click of his instrument being mistaken in some quarters for the sound of Stanford's mallet striking the seven-inch gold spike—that spike, by the way, was made from twenty-three twenty dollar gold pieces.

Savage's photograph shows bottles of whiskey being passed around, and there were "ladies" in the picture, said ladies being mostly Sisters of Joy from nearby Corinne. Since Corinne was there practically in mass, it is not to be wondered that the scene was not quite as decorous as Mr. Stanford would have liked. The Reverend Todd, from Pittsfield, Massachusetts, who was there to confer the proper air of piety, does not appear in Savage's picture, though he is in the revised version, and the ladies from Corinne are not. Corinne has never received the credit that is its due for livening up the proceedings.

The Hell on Wheels towns were an irreverent bunch. Once aristocratic former governor Pico of California stopped off at one of the hell towns west of Corinne, but the Mexican Grandee was robbed the same as anybody else.

Sometimes the boys played a little rough. While the rivalry between the railroad construction gangs was at its height, the Irish played crude jokes on their Chinese competitors, and kidnapping them was a favorite form of sport. At one of the camps, said to have been called Cosmos, where the crews were working side by side building parallel grades, the Irish blew up a box-car containing a number of Chinese workers. Unable to see the joke, the Chinese retaliated in kind, which led the bosses to patch up a peace treaty.

After Promontory, Corinne boomed. Because of the struggle over polygamy the Gentiles secured a rather firm hold on the government of the territory with a succession of carpet-bagger governors. Politics was under control of what the Mormons contemptuously called "the Ring," with headquarters at Corinne. Allied with them were the apostate Godbeites, though the latter never repudiated polygamy.

There, too, for a time, lived General Patrick E. Connor, the arch-enemy of Brigham Young. Connor had come into Utah in 1862 and established Fort Douglas on the foothills overlooking Salt Lake City. Though more diplomatic than General Johnston, he was an avowed enemy of the Mormons. Scoffing at Brigham Young's attempt to stop mining, he encouraged it with every means within his power, and became known as the father of Utah mining. He was undoubtedly Brigham's most determined and successful opponent. For years he kept a cannon trained on Young's residence, and the wary Brigham kept constant watch on the fort through a spy-glass. General Connor was the patron saint of the Gentiles.

In one two weeks period 500 houses and tents went up in Corinne. After the completion of the railroad the town had more than three thousand people, who ate cheaply in those days. Old records reveal uninflated prices that would gladden the hearts of consumers today. Here is a list:

20 pounds of beef sold for $1.40.
9 pounds of bacon, 90 cents.
5 pounds of cabbage, 10 cents.

Oysters were ten cents a can.

Overalls, 75 a pair.

Brooms, 25 cents each.

At Promontory Summit Tom Brown and his family ran a combination country store, eating place, and rooming house. The restaurant was kept for the men who ran the engine helper crews and the passengers who traveled on the trains. Each day a message would come in from Corinne reporting how many passengers to prepare for and Tom Brown would set to work getting the meals ready. The meals cost 25 to 35 cents, and a month's room and board was $22.50.

Among the colorful characters, aside from General Connor, who lived for a time at Corinne were J. W. Guthrie, banker, known all over the West as Guthrie of Corinne; Colonel House, former Pony Express rider and friend of Buffalo Bill Cody; Stage owner E. P. Johnson, later Grand Master of the Masonic Lodge of Utah. Unquestionably, Ben Holladay, greatest stage operator of them all, made frequent stops at Corinne.

Freighters to the Montana gold field amassed small fortunes operating out of Corinne, among them being Alex Toponce who owned a ranch at Call's Fort on the road between Corinne and Brigham City.

When the Oregon Short Line reached Pocatello, Corinne began to wither on the vine, and when the Southern Pacific established a division point at the little Mormon town of Kelton to the west of Promontory, Corinne had its finishing blow. Today, because the line has been shortened by a fill across Salt Lake, Kelton itself has all but vanished, but such is the fate of most boom towns.

For a time Corinne enjoyed a taste of glory as a seaport. Ore from the mines of Tintic and the Oquirrhs had to be shipped to San Francisco by land and then taken by ship to Swansea, Wales, for smelting. With the idea that the ore could be hauled cheaper across the lake than around it, the steamboat, *City of Corinne*, 70 feet long, was put into commission. A second boat, *Kate Connor*, was launched shortly afterward, but neither proved profitable. The mud at the mouth of Bear River grew thicker and deep-

44

er, and the *City of Corinne* settled down there into its final resting place. The *Kate Connor* wound up as a pavilion at Garfield Beach, twenty miles from Salt Lake City on the south side of the lake. Both vessels bore what the Mormons called "The curse of Corinne."

One of Corinne's gambling games was called Free and Easy, in which a single card was placed face down on the table and the customer invited to bet whether the next card turned would be larger or smaller than the exposed card on the table. But a more popular gambling device was known as the Divorce Machine, which was operated by a pair of lawyers named Johnson and Underdunk.

It seems that anyone wishing a divorce need only slip $2.50 into the machine and presto! a divorce was in his hand. The one seeking to sever relations with his mate could even have the job done by proxy. A copy of their ad appeared in the press:

"Divorces secured. Presence not necessary. Fee: $2.50. Address: Johnson and Underdunk, Corinne, Utah. Lawyers."

Many divorces were granted, and many fees collected. The enterprising lawyers drew up a decree stating that the couple were forever separated. If alimony was desired they could put that clause in the decree. Each document bore the signature of a judge.

Of course the practice was illegal, and many who were remarried to other mates after receiving a Johnson and Underdunk divorce found themselves in hot water with the law. (This information from Judge Jones of Brigham City, in *The Bear River Valley Ledger*, December 15, 1927.)

Corinne capitulated, but not without a valiant struggle. The handwriting was on the wall when the junction point of the railroad was moved to Ogden, which eventually made that city the second largest and most influential city in Utah; one well within the Mormon domain. "The Gentile City became the butt of sarcastic editorials, jokes, and ridicule as business institutions migrated to Ogden." (*Utah Guide Book.* W.P.A. Project.)

The citizens of Corinne drew up a memorial to Congress urging a grant of land in Bear River Valley, stating: "It is the only place where a truly American community can be brought into permanent and successful contact with the Mormon population, whose feet have trodden and who hold in their relentless grasp, every other valley in Utah. . . . It is a notorious fact that everywhere in this territory the Mormon prophet and his coadjutors have acquired control of the water courses isssuing from the mountain sides, that can be used for irrigation and of all the canyons that afford any valuable timber within reach of cultivated lands. This monopoly . . . had enabled them to confine immigration to those of their own creed."

A bill giving effect to this petition was introduced in both houses of Congress. In 1870 the *New York World* stated: "Congress proposes removing the capitol of Utah from Salt Lake City to Corinne, which, containing but a few Mormons, is deemed a fitter place to put the military corps in." (*Utah Guide Book.*) The bill was defeated, and the Gentile population of Corinne gradually drifted away.

Today, Corinne is a Mormon hamlet with a store or two and gas stations as conventionalized as in any other small town. The tourist would do well to arrange for a stopping place at Brigham City, or go up the valley to Tremonton, which is booming with new war industry.

Once each year Corinne comes to life when the dignitaries of state, church, and railways go out to Promontory to celebrate the joining of the railroads. May 10th is a big day, and the solemnity of the occasion would be most pleasing to Leland Stanford. But if the ghosts of C. R. Savage, the Irish and Chinese laborers, and the gals from Corinne are still hovering about, there must be levity which the celebrants know nothing about.

CHAPTER FIVE

Bingham

Most visitors to Utah are advised to drive out sixteen miles from Salt Lake City to view "The world's largest open pit copper mine." If the claim is exaggerated, it is not exaggerated much, for it is certainly one of the largest and well worth the seeing. It is the most important remaining mining section of Utah, perhaps in the entire Great Basin, and after many vicissitudes is now owned lock, stock, and barrel by the great Kennecott Copper Company.

Brigham is a one street town in a narrow canyon in the Oquirrhs, called by the poetic, "The Shining Mountains." Once it had a population of eight thousand people, now dwindled to less than two thousand, and in a short while it will have practically none though millions of dollars worth of ore will still be mined.

In 1960 most of the private property was bought by Kennecott Copper Company with the avowed intention of tearing down all the old buildings. Hundreds of men still labor there, but instead of living in the houses perched precariously on the rocky sides of the canyon at the mercy of floods and slides, the men now mostly drive to work from Salt Lake City, Murray, or Midvale, or live in the company-owned model town of Coppertown just below the mouth of the canyon. But the canyon is rich in history.

At the very beginning one encounters the names of those two powerful antagonists, Brigham Young and General Patrick E. Connor, the one determined to prevent mining, the other equally determined to develop it.

The Mormons arrived in Salt Lake Valley in 1847, and in 1848 Brigham Young sent two young Mormons, Sanford and Thomas

Bingham, out to the canyon to farm, and to herd cattle in the abundant timber that grew there then. The Bingham brothers bequeathed little but their name to the canyon, but they may have been the first discoverers of gold in the Great Basin. Sawmills were started and the hills were soon denuded of their trees. The Bingham boys, having little else to do, turned to prospecting, and turned up some nuggets which they dutifully carried to Brigham Young. He ordered them to cover up their find, and forget it. Said he, "Instead of hunting gold let every man go to work at raising wheat, oats, barley, corn, and vegetables and fruit in abundance that there may be plenty in the land." The order was obeyed and the vast mineral deposits of Bingham Canyon slept on for another thirteen years after the Bingham brothers made their discovery in 1850.

In 1863 an apostate Mormon named George Ogilvie picked up some samples in the canyon and having heard of General Connor's interest in mining sent them to him. The lead ore was so rich in gold and silver that elated General Connor issued a letter on War Department stationary informing the public of Utah's wealth, and assuring all comers of the protection of the army, and he turned his own soldiers loose to prospect the neighboring hills. It was these soldiers who made the first real find in Bingham Canyon, and also in Utah's other big camps at Alta, Park City, and Tintic, though a few Mormons had reached the last camp and located claims a little ahead of them, claims which they were to abandon when they heard the stern voice of authority.

This discovery by the soldiers whose names, unfortunately, have been forgotten, started the first mining stampede in Utah, although by that time stampedes in the Nevada part of the basin were common enough.

There was, however, one unique feature about the first Bingham Canyon stampede. Women joined with the men and staked out the Women's Lode, subject to the same conditions as the men.

"Lack of transportation and expense of raw materials," says the *Utah Guide Book*, "almost caused the abandonment of the raw new town." But discovery and development of placer mines in the canyon saved the day. The richest placer was found by one

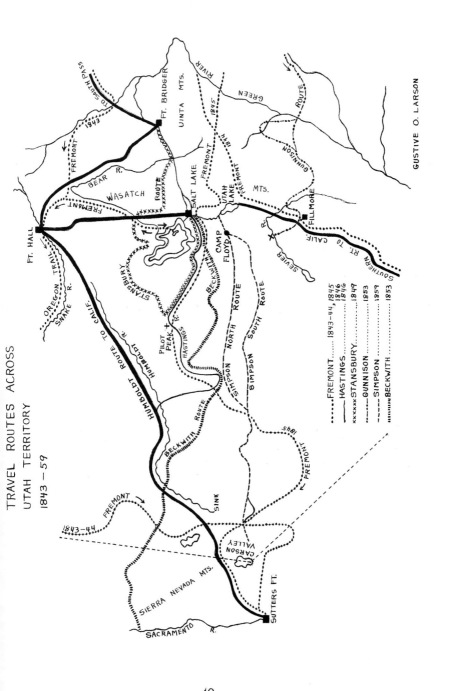

TRAVEL ROUTES ACROSS
UTAH TERRITORY
1843 – 59

GUSTIVE O. LARSON

FREMONT 1843-44, 1845
HASTINGS 1846
xxxxx STANSBURY 1849
GUNNISON 1853
SIMPSON 1859
BECKWITH 1853

49

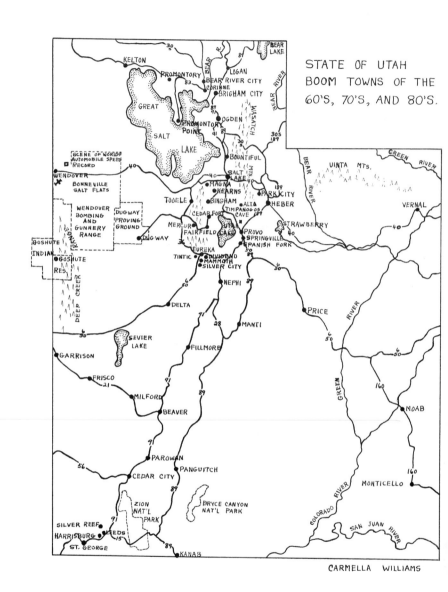

STATE OF UTAH
BOOM TOWNS OF THE
60'S, 70'S, AND 80'S.

CARMELLA WILLIAMS

50

Mine and tailings in the Tintic district, Utah.

This solid concrete shaft sunk by the Chief Consolidated
Mine in Tintic cost one million dollars.

A West Tintic claim.

Gallows frame of the Norway Mine where Joe Fisher was dragged and hanged.

View at the entrance of Pinyon Canyon showing the lime stream at a grand level. Flath of the

View of Tintic's underground workings, showing the timbering of heavy ground.

Jack Finley, inventor of the mucking machine used in the Tintic mines.

Temple Block, Salt Lake City.

Main Street looking north, Park City, Utah.

Silver King Mill, Park City, Utah.

Marsac Mill, Park City, Utah.

Judge Mine, United Park City Mine Company, Park City, Utah.

The great fire of 1898 nearly destroyed Park City. St. Mary's (upper left) was the only church left untouched by the flames. *Courtesy C. W. McCullough.*

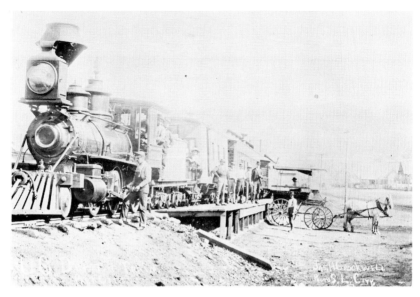

The Johnny W backed up to the passenger coach depot at Park City. Note the fresh air taxicab of the Nineties. *Courtesy C. W. McCullough.*

Ore train with Shay engine brought ore from Crescent Mine to Utah Central tracks. Engineer is Jim Langford, now retired, who graduated to the Johnny W and the D.& R.G.W. run. *Courtesy C. W. McCullough.*

Dan Clay, and called Clay Bar. Clay and his brothers produced $100,000 from it in 1868, and later worked the tailings which paid them from $7.00 to $15.00 a day. In those tailings Dan Clay found the largest nugget ever found in Utah, worth $128.00. By the end of 1868 more than two million dollars worth of gold had been mined, and General Connor was entitled to his chuckle.

Unfortunately, as in many other places, the placer diggings were soon worked out, and by 1870 Bingham seemed to be dying on its feet. Then the Bingham & Camp Floyd railroad was completed, and a boom in lode mining began. Bingham burgeoned from a population of 276 to more than a thousand, and it continued to grow. The Buel and Bateman mill was constructed in the early Seventies and was highly ssuccessful. Bristol and Bateman from Nevada erected the Winnamuck smelter in 1872-73, and lode mining became an established success. The first concentration plant was built in 1874 by A. H. Bemis for treatment of sulphide lead ore, and this gave the camp another boost. There were rich strikes at Yosemite No. 1, Brooklyn, No-You-Don't, Highland Boy, and Boston Consolidated.

Brigham Young saw a rough and rowdy mining camp growing up right before his eyes, but he was old and getting weary, and his successors never put the energy into the fight that he had. By 1900 Bingham boasted thirty saloons, most noted of which were Old Crow and the 16 to 1. Gambling was prevalent and wide open, and fights and killings common, but Bingham has always been a virile town and though the saloons and gambling joints stayed open twenty-four hours a day there were other forms of recreation. Boxing matches were a weekly event and athletic miners hurled powder boxes, broad jumped, and pole vaulted with lead pipes over the mine dumps, since in the narrow canyon there was no other place for such activity. Later, the town moved out a bit, and Bingham is still proud of its baseball and basketball teams.

There was music in the saloons, at first confined largely to mouth organs and jew'sharps played by local talent, but soon every saloon had a piano, and visiting vaudeville troops performed in many of them.

In Bingham as in most mining camps the population was predominantly male, so there were many houses of prostitution. Since segregation in the canyon was manifestly impossible, the respectable women made the best of it, and it was no uncommon sight to see them hanging over the fence gossiping with members of the frail sisterhood. Bingham was a live and let live sort of place.

Bingham had its famous outlaw, one Rafael Lopez, who came to Bingham as a strikebreaker in the camp's first serious labor trouble in 1912 when the Western Federation of Miners struck for a fifty cent raise. Fifty sharpshooters from the National Guard were sent to town, and four hundred local men were deputized and armed. Railroad crossings and mines were drenched in floodlights, and saloons and gambling halls closed. There was the usual hatred of scabs, and they were given a rough time in spite of the fact that the law, as usual, was on the side of the company. But by the end of October half of the men had gone back to work and the company was able to announce that the strike was broken. Some grievances had been corrected, but the union failed to get recognition.

Rafael Lopez stayed on after the strike and leased the Apex mine. The general opinion was that though no great mixer he was well liked. He is said to have been unusually light-complexioned for a Mexican. One November night he beat up a Greek for molesting some girls, and was thrown in jail, which started his hatred for officers of the law.

When Lopez was released, he got into an argument with a fellow Mexican named Juan Valdez. Valdez drew a knife and Lopez shot him. Opinion varies as to whether the quarrel was over a girl, or politics—and it may have been for another reason. At any rate Lopez went home, got his rifle and ammunition and left town. The ground was covereed with snow and four officers trailed him to the west side of Utah Lake. They caught up with him at a ranch and a short but lethal battle resulted. Lopez killed three of the officers with as many shots, and later expressed regret that he hadn't got the fourth man who was the particular object of his hate.

Scareheads appeared in all the newspapers and everyone was

58

on the lookout for Lopez the bandit. Meantime, Lopez returned to Bingham and forced a friend named Stefano to supply him with an extra rifle, ammunition, food, clothing and bedding, which he forced Stefano to carry to the entrance of the Apex mine. Once released, Stefano hurried to the police and guards were sent immediately to the mine. The newspapers blazoned that Lopez was trapped, but no volunteers were found who were eager to go into the mine and risk a bullet from so deadly a shot as Lopez.

The mine was closed, throwing two hundred men out of work, and a plan of campaign decided on. Outlets were sealed off and bales of hay placed at the only remaining entrance. While the barricade was being built shots rang out and one man was killed and another wounded. The law decided that the only way to get the bandit out was to smoke him out. Lump sulphur, damp gunpowder, and cayenne pepper were added to the burning hay, and the fires were kept going for five days and nights, until the officers were sure Lopez could not have survived.

At the end of that time a thorough search was made of the mine, but nothing was turned up except the bandit's extra clothes and bedding. Lopez had disappeared. For years miners searched hopefully for a skeleton in some remote crevice but they found nothing. For years there were rumors that Lopez had been seen at various places, but none of the rumors was ever verified.

Now legend enters the picture. The story goes that Lopez and Valdez were ancient enemies in Mexico, and that Valdez had murdered Lopez's entire family, starting him out on a long quest for vengeance. Lopez is said to have become such a good shot with a rifle that he joined Buffalo Bill's Wild West show as a sharpshooter. Always he searched for his enemy, and finally caught up with him in Bingham Canyon.

There are certain questions that might be asked, such as how long Lopez had known Valdez in Bingham before he forced a quarrel on him, but there is at least one reputable writer who asserts that he has proof for the story.

Whatever the truth may be, Lopez is a living legend in Bingham, and many articles have been written about him. During the early nineteen-twenties William H. Hamby, an Eastern novelist of renown, wrote a prize-winning novel of Bingham called *Manacled Millions,* in which Lopez is a recognizable character. Bingham is justly proud of its bandit.

Few Western mining camps have led a more hazardous existence than Bingham, and at various times in its life it has been the victim of fires, cloudbursts, landslides, and snowslides; the snow lies deep in the Oquirrhs and the slopes are steep. Carr's Fork has been a particular target for slides. In 1926 the little suburb of Highland Boy was virtually destroyed by a snowslide which swept seventeen dwellings and a three-story boarding house from their foundations and buried them under a mass of debris. Thirty-nine lives were lost.

In 1932 a $400,000 fire all but wiped out the town. Those were prohibition days, and stills were popping like firecrackers, flooding the streets with moonshine booze.

In 1930 Bingham suffered another near half million dollar disaster when a cloudburst struck Markham Gulch, burying houses, business buildings, and automobiles. Land, loosened by water, slid down the canyon blocking traffic. Over the years there have been minor disasters, and finally retaining walls were built to lessen the danger. More fire precautions were taken, and Bingham possessed one of the most efficient fire departments in the state.

Bingham had many outstanding characters during its history. One of whom it was proud was Dr. Russell G. Frazier, who had been surgeon-physician with Rear Admiral Richard E. Byrd's expedition to the South Pole. Another beloved citizen was "Doc" Inglesby, a dentist who for a number of years operated a stage line. Doc was a crusty, cantankerous character who leavened his crankiness with a sense of humor. During his last years he operated a motel at Fruita, in the Wayne Wonderland of Southern Utah, where he became an authority on the rare minerals and petrified wood in the area. He had his own lapidary and produced some of the finest specimens of the kind in the entire country. If Doc didn't like the looks of the people who asked for lodgings, he sent them to another motel, but if he liked them but happened to be busy he might invite the lady to go into the kichen to prepare a meal for her family and for Doc.

The real giants of the camp, however, were Colonel Enos A. Wall and D. C. Jackling. The depression of 1893 practically put an end to the gold and silver mining in Bingham, and for a time the camp hovered on the verge of oblivion; but Bingham's fame was to be founded on copper rather than gold and silver. For its development Bingham is indebted to these two men.

There was known to be copper in the hills, but it was low grade, and anyone dabbling with it was supposed to be weak in the head. It was not taken too seriously even after Thomas Weir struck a vein of 18% copper in 1896, and for the first time copper was produced.

Colonel Wall entered the district in 1887, and was immediately struck by the possibilities. According to the stories he inspected an old abandoned tunnel driven by General Connor's men at the beginning of the camp, and there found samples of copper ore which aroused his interest. He set quietly about buying up property he wanted, driving over the country in a buggy with a hired coachman. During the ensuing years he accumulated two hundred acres of ground which others considered so worthless that they called his holdings "Wall's rocks," but he kept up his assessment work and drove 3,000 feet of tunnel in various places on his property. From this property later was to come millions of dollars worth of ore, insuring Colonel Wall's position as one of the great mining magnates of Utah.

Another capitalist who left his mark on Bingham was Samuel Newhouse, whose monuments in Salt Lake City are the Newhouse Hotel and the Newhouse office building. Newhouse was associated with Thomas Weir in the Highland Boy, and they built a cyanide plant in Carr's Fork to extract gold, but the ore called for too much cyanide and the plant shut down after huge losses. While Weir continued digging and discovered the 18% copper, Newhouse went east for additional capital. In 1899 the Highland Boy was merged with the Utah Consolidated. Twelve million dollars changed hands and control passed into the hands of Standard Oil of New York, and John D. Rockefeller became one of the heavy stockholders of Bingham.

Colonel Wall, like Br'er Rabbit, was lying low while trying to find a new process to extract low grade copper profitably. Meeting little but discouragement, he finally sold an interest in his mine and a six month lease to his friend Captain Joseph DeLamar for $375,000. DeLamar now brought two young engineers, Daniel C. Jackling and Robert G. Gemmell, from Mercur to investigate the property.

The two young men completed their report in 1899, and it was revolutionary. It was an analysis of a mining enterprise based on the treatment of low grade ore. Jackling so convinced himself that he bought an interest in the Wall property. He planned to combine mass production methods with scientific metallurgy, and he did revolutionize the copper industry with his successful flotation process, but his theories were not at once accepted. The *Enigneering and Mining Journal* thought it wise to warn investors against "Jackling's Wildcat."

Jackling went on to become president of the open pit Utah Copper Company, and installed concentrating processes which made the company one of the heaviest taxpaying and labor employing corporations in the state of Utah.

One need only to go to the state capitol in Salt Lake City to know what the people think of their most famous mining man. In the place of honor in the rotunda stands a lifesize bronze statue of Daniel Cowan Jackling. D. C. Jackling was born August 14, 1869, at Appleton City, Bates County, Missouri; married Virginia Jolliffe of San Francisco, in 1915. His sketch in *Who's Who* is an American epic of accomplishment.

"Ed. State Normal School, Warrensburg, Mo.; and B.S. and Metall-engr. Mo. Sch. Mines, 1891-92. Asst. prof. chemistry and metallurgist, Cripple Creek District, Colo. 1894-96; in charge condtrn, and operation metall, works of Consolidated Mercur Gold Mines, Mercur, Utah, 1896-1900; organized, 1903, and later president of Utah Copper Co.; (Also, 1940) pres. Nev. Consol. Copper Co., Butte & Superior Mining Co., Mesabi Iron Co., Bingham & Garfield Ry. Co., Gallup Am. Coal Co., Ray and Gila Valley r.r.; v.p. Nevada Northern Ry. Co.; dir, Chase Nat. Bank, Pacific Steamship Co., Braden Copper Co., Granby Cons. Mining, Smelting & Power Co., Ltd., Southern Phosphate corpn.; dir. and chmn., operating Kennecott Copper Corpn."

The sketch lists a large number of other activities of this remarkable man. General Patrick Connor would have been proud of him, for he achieved all the things Connor dreamed of, except ousting the Mormons from Utah, but times had changed in Jackling's day and he got along with the Mormons very well.

Before Jackling's statue was unveiled in the capitol rotunda the place of honor was held by a huge statue of Massasoit by Cyrus E. Dallin, one of the nation's greatest sculptors, a native of Utah. But Massasoit was shunted out into the elements to make way for the successsful businessman. Thus has the Indian always had to give way to the white man.

Steam shovel operation in the Bingham district began in 1907 and has continued ever since. Many big financial deals were made in the early history of the company, but the largest was a merger with Boston Consolidated and Nevada Consolidated in 1910 which created a $100,000,000 copper company. For organizing the merger Samuel Untermeyer, New York lawyer, was paid a fee of $775,000.

Indicating the magnitude of the operations, Bingham and upper Bingham were connected by a 6988 foot tunnel costing $1,400,000, large enough to accommodate one line of auto traffic controlled by signals, with a railed sidewalk for pedestrians which is cement lined, electrically lighted, and ventilated by fresh air ducts.

The camp was greatly benefitted by the building of a standard gauge Denver & Rio Grande Western Railroad branch from Salt Lake City to a point three-quarters of a mile below Bingham. It can now be reached over a well-paved road.

That the camp had other troubles besides the usual ones is indicated by an articles in the *Bingham Bulletin* in 1907: "The farmers of Salt Lake Valley now seem to be as anxious to have the smelters remain as they were a little while ago to give them the 23 sign ('skidoo'). Just so soon as they found their bluff was taken in earnest, there was much hurrying to and from across the valley, and the prospects of seeing the easy money they had been getting from the smelters fade away, did not appeal to the gentleman with a bunch of whiskers on his chin. For the last four years the smelters have paid in damage suits, in and out of court, a half million dollars annually."

The town of Bingham is going, but the mining operations are as great as ever with new and improved methods being constantly introduced. The workers are now all unionized, and the camp has its share of labor troubles. Bingham has produced value running into the billions, even though the copper is low grade. There are still enough gold and silver and other metals to pay a good share of the cost of operations. No one knows when Utah's greatest mineral deposits will be exhausted, but it will have to reach bottom sometime.

Just over the summit of the Oquirrhs is the old smelter town of Tooele, now a great military base, and close by a famous old mining district called Ophir. Nearby stands a quiet little village called Stockton on the Union Pacific from which ore by the train load used to be shipped. To the north of that, hard by the lake, is the sleepy little Mormon town of Grantsville, named after one of Brigham Young's early day Counselors, which is much as it was in those days. The bustle of the mining industry never touched it.

At the north end of the Oquirrhs there was once a smelter town called Garfield. The smelters, fed largely from Bingham, still operate, but the people and the houses are gone. There were never many people at Arthur, but it was there D. C. Jackling put his flotation process into operation and it is still a busy place.

On around the point is Magna, a prosperous little town that is half mining and half farming. Beyond that is booming Bacchus kept alive by government spending. Farther on, south and east of Bingham, is Lark, still populated mostly by miners. All are part of the Bingham district.

From the mountain above Bingham one can easily see the smoke from the great steel mills near Orem. U.S. Steel vies with Kennecott Copper as the greatest private corporation in Utah. Though a small mill operated for some years at Ironton, the big boom in steel came at the beginning of World War II. Thousands of men are now employed there, most of them ex-farmers who quit the farms of Utah Valley in droves to get in on the high wages. Iron comes from the mountains of iron discovered in Iron County many years ago by Brigham Young's scouts, and coal and coke come from the company's own mines in Carbon County on the other side of the Wasatch Range. The railroad runs through the practically ghost town of Soldier Summit from where Fathers Escalante and Dominguez first looked out over the Great Basin.

CHAPTER SIX

Alta

The eastern side of Utah's Long Valley, a disconnected thread of reasonably level land running through the central part of the state, containing most of the arable land in Utah, is bounded most of the way by the rugged Wasatch Range, which in places rises to a height of twelve thousand feet. On either side of that range, like the stirrups of a saddle, were two great mining camps which classify under the name of boom towns.

One, on the western slope in Little Cottonwood Canyon, just across the valley from Bingham, a mere twenty-eight miles from Salt Lake City, was called Alta, perhaps short for altitude, of which it had plenty. The other on the eastern slope, thirty-two miles from Salt Lake City, was Park City. Both with the insistence of a Mark Twain deny that they are extinct, but the old days of glory are gone.

Roving soldier-prospectors from General Pat Connor's army brought them into existence by finding token ore on the surface, which led to discovery of the vast deposits which lay underneath. Both began in the late 1860's. If Park City produced the most ore, Alta raised the most hell. Mount Baldy of the Wasatch raises its majestic dome between them.

Most famous and notorious of the mines of Alta was the Emma, which produced thirty-seven million dollars in silver, and almost brought about a war between the United States and Great Britain. The early history of Alta was the story of the Emma mine. Its history is one of confusion. Even the origin of the name is in dispute.

66

It is generally agreed that the mine was located by two prospectors named Robert B. Chisholn and J. F. Woodman in 1868.
Chisholn, a New York born Scot, worked in the lead mines near
Galena, Illinois, and went to California in 1851. In 1864 he happened to be in an assayer's office in Salt Lake City when a soldier
brought in an ore sample from Little Cottonwood Canyon. Already claims had been filed and it wasn't until four years later,
after the early strikes had been forfeited for non-payment of assessments, that Chisholn formed his partnership with Woodman
and filed on the Emma.

The winters are unusually hard there, and the first winter forced
the partners out. Chisholn returned to his farm near Elgin, Illinois,
hoping to sell the farm, but being unable to do so returned to
Utah with his son William in the spring of '69, having but ten
dollars in his pocket. His partner, Woodman, was equally broke.
Their mine at that time was only eighteen feet deep and full of
muddy water.

The sentimental story of the naming of the mine is that it was
named after Chisholn's daughter Emma, who constantly implored
her brother William to return to "dear little Emma in Illinois."

The less sentimental version is that there was a shady lady in
San Francisco whose first name was Emma with whom one or the
other of the partners was on friendly, not to say intimate, terms,
and the account says the mine was named in her honor.

A New York mine promoter named James E. Lyon was in the
canyon in 1868, and is supposed to have advanced money to the
partners in exchange for a one-third interest in the Emma.

During the first year only a hundred tons of ore was taken from
the mine and Lyon, satisfied that the lode ran in a northwesterly
direction, became discouraged with the prospects and returned
to New York. But in the middle of October, 1869, Chisholn and
Woodman broke into a chamber of solid ore. The discovery had
been made in a direction from the original shaft different from
what Lyon had anticipated.

Forgetting about Lyon, Chisholn and Woodman relocated the
claim and in February, 1870, had it surveyed and entered on the
books of the district. But being without funds they borrowed

money from two former army officers to sink a deeper shaft and get provisions. The new partners were to receive one-sixth of a share each.

Three thousand feet along the ledge was claimed by the Emma Silver Mine of Utah. A month later the partners sold 400 feet of claim to the Walker brothers of Salt Lake for $30,000. The Walker brothers began shipping ore to Great Britain for reduction.

As was to be expected, James E. Lyon returned from New York and brought suit to recover his one-third interest. His chief attorney was U.S. Senator William M. Stewart of Nevada and Comstock fame. Sixteen other lawyers were involved in the case, and things were getting mixed up with the Emma, but they "hadn't seen nothin' yet."

While the case was in litigation, two wealthy promoters named Trenor W. Park and General George Baxter came to Utah hoping to secure an interest. Chisholn claimed they had learned about the Emma from two other sharks who had tried to sell the mine in the East for a million and a half dollars, but had failed. Park was a Vermont lawyer who had done very well at his profession in San Francisco, and had a sound knowledge of mining law.

In March, 1871, Park and Baxter bought an undivided half interest in the Emma for $375,000 in gold. This placed an estimated three-quarters of a million on the whole property.

Lyon secured a temporary compromise agreement on his claim, but by this time Park and Baxter insisted that they had spent a million and a half dollars in development of the mine. Chisholn and Woodman had not put up their percentage of costs and Park and Baxter pressed for a sale. Chisholn and Woodman received small payments in cash, and an assurance that they would receive a sizeable sum contingent on the sale of the mine.

The name of the mine was then changed to the Emma Silver Mining Company of New York. Lyon was assured that he would receive one-sixth of what the mine sold for, less the million and a half Park and Baxter claimed they were out, provided he did not press his claim before November 15, 1871, while a U.S. Patent was being applied for.

English capitalists had become so interested in Western min-

68

ing that it was called mining mania. The promoters of the Emma appeared more interested in getting British capital into the ground than they were in getting mineral out of it. They got a glowing report of the possibilities of the Emma from a Professor Silliman of Yale University who claimed to be a mining engineer. Armed with this, Park and Senator Stewart, the latter presumably representing Lyon, crossed the Atlantic to see what they could do. Failing to interest the regular channels of trade, they turned to local promoters, speculators, and politicians.

Pursuing tried and true Yankee methods they sought out one Albert Grant, known as "Baron" Grant, a promoter with an international reputation, who undertook to introduce the Americans into British financial circles for one-tenth of the stock, once the new company was successfully launched.

The American Minister to the Court of St. James, Major General Robert C. Schenck, was persuaded to lend his name and prestige to the enterprise and bought some of the stock, allegedly paid for by Park and Stewart—though this has never been conclusively proven. But he did issue a supporting statement in the prospectus that was being circulated. That prospectus, issued November 9, 1871, announced the formation of the Emma Silver Mining Company with a capital of one millions pounds in twenty pound shares. One half of this was offered for subscription, and the other half retained.

Included in the board of directors were three members of Parliament, Minister Schenck, Senator Stewart, General Baxter, who was a former president of the New York Central Railroad, and Trenor W. Park—a most distinguished outfit in every way.

The prospectus estimated the net yield of the Emma at 800,000 pounds a year. The profits were to be restricted to 18 per cent per annum until a reserve of 800,000 pounds was accumulated. Within two days the 20 pound shares were selling at a premium of from three to four pounds. The public immediately subscribed for 25,000 shares divided among 2,000 stockholders.

Park immediately took the money paid for those shares and settled with Baron Grant for $170,000. Stewart, supposedly representing Lyon, joined forces with Park and Baxter, and Lyon was alloted $30,000, and a vague promise. Lyon denounced Senator Stewart who, to placate him, paid him $200,000, less $50,000 for legal services for his shares, which Stewart soon sold on the New York market for $15.00 a share. Lyon claimed that Stewart had cheated him out of a million dollars, but could do nothing about it.

With Lyon out of the way the original discoverers, Chisholm and Woodman, were persuaded to sell all their shares at ten pounds a share, less than half the market value, leaving Park, Baxter, and Stewart in control of all the vendor's shares.

The *Engineering and Mining Journal,* of New York, scathingly denounced the promoters and U.S. Minister Schenck. The magazine concluded: "The plan does honor to the shrewdness of the promoters, but not to the judgment of the British public, nor the good taste and delicacy (to use no stronger term) of the American minister."

Schenck's resignation was described as "diplomatic etiquette," with no reflection upon the value of the Emma, which was prospering beyond expectations. Production was being increased and monthly dividends were being paid. At a company meeting March 7, 1872, the chairman stated that silver was coming out of the mine so fast that it seemed likely they would pay 30 to 40 per cent rather than the 18 per cent that had been anticipated.

Still, ugly rumors were being circulated, and Park offered to pay the expenses of the entire board of directors to go to Little Cottonwood Canyon and inspect the property for themselves. Instead, they delegated one of the directors, Brydges Willyams, to act as their representative. Willyams took along G. A. Lawrence, a fiction writer, who upon his return published a book called *Silverland,* for which his publishers paid him a thousand guineas, and paid Willyams all his expenses.

The Emma Silver Mine, Limited, then became involved in litigation with the Illinois Tunnel Company over conflicting claims to the same ground. In April, 1872, workmen for the Illinois company broke into Emma workings, and the manager was forced to block off the opening. Shortly thereafter a cave-in cut the Emma off from that section of the mine, and the Illinois people were left in possesssion.

The case, of course, went to court, the Illinois company trying to prove by "expert" testimony that the disputed area was not a part of the original vein of the Emma. The decision of the Supreme Court of Utah Territory was a victory for the Emma, which held that they could follow their ore vein outside the surface limits of the patent into neighboring ground.

In London, the *Mining Journal* praised "the high-minded sagacity of the American Bench."

During the first year of its existence the Emma distributed $195,000 in monthly dividends, the last of which was distributed December 2, 1872, presumably from earnings of the mine, although Park was suspected of advancing money on ore in transit to keep up the price until he could dispose of his vendor's shares, for a strange thing had happened at the Emma. The supposedly inexhaustible ore body, after producing thirty-seven million dollars worth of ore, had nothing left. An unexpected fault in the earth had simply sliced it off like a butcher's cleaver. Nor has the vein ever been relocated again. For many years a few optimists thought it might be picked up again somewhere in the mountain, but after nearly ninety years it is still lost.

When the news leaked out, the British government and the British people believed that the whole thing had been a gigantic fraud. Half of the stock was owned by people in Glasgow, and indignation meetings were held, and the company was denounced in Parliament. Hotheads demanded war with the United States over the swindle, but fortunately cooler heads prevailed, though it did the already scandal-ridden administration of President U.S. Grant no good.

In alarm, the *San Francisco Mining Journal* reported, "The Emma mine in Utah is probably the best known mine abroad. On the success of this mine depends, in a great measure, the future of Anglo-American mining. For such is its position that should failure ensue small support will again be extended to American mines on the London market."

The shares dropped from thirty-one pounds sterling to practically nothing, and soon were unsalable at any price. An alarmed Congress ordered an investigation, and geologists from Heidelberg and lawyers from London were brought over and 879 pages of testimony was taken. A bulletin of the Mineralogical Society of Utah stated: "America was eventually exonerated of trying to pick the pockets of the British brethren, but indignant growls from across the Atlantic died slowly."

Meanwhile, back at the mine! While the promoters and lawyers of the Emma were dabbling in high finances, Alta had grown to a lusty town of eight thousand inhabitants who worked, fought, drank, bled, and died in typically Western boom town fashion. One hundred fifty men who died violent deaths were buried in Boot Graveyard at the foot of Rustler Mountain, and 110 of them had been killed in two of Alta's twenty-six saloons, The Gold Miner's Daughter and The Bucket of Blood.

Six sawmills operated to furnish timber for the mines and lumber for the buildings. Three breweries were kept going full blast to slake the thirst of the population, and a semi-weekly newspaper, *The Cottonwood Observer,* kept a close tab on what was going on.

The altitude of Alta was nine thousand feet, and Little Cottonwood Canyon is steep. The first ore taken out was wrapped in beef hides and dragged, or "rawhided," out to Tannersville, five miles below, thence to be hauled by ox teams to the railroad at Ogden, where it was shipped to San Francisco and there transferred to vessels for shipment around Cape Horn to Swansea, Wales.

The two most noted madams of the redlight district were Kate Hayes and Alta Nell. One of the claims was called the Kate Hayes and her name was attached to one of the main fissures of the camp. Alta Nell owned and operated a claim which she called her Green Mountain Boy. Alta was shunned by the pious Mormons who lived a scant twenty miles away.

The lost Emma fissure and the Crime of '73, when silver was demonitized, were crushing blows to Alta, and by 1880 the town was all but dying. But during its short tenure of life it had more than its share of joys and troubles. The canyon is peculiarly subject to snowslides, and one of the worst occurred in 1874 when

72

a slide swept down from the Emma Hill, snuffing out the lives of sixty men in buildings on Main Street. The snow was forty feet deep and fire added to the devastation.

September 13, 1871, a fire destroyed Tanner's Hotel, and May 8, 1873, most of Alta was destroyed by fire. It was rebuilt, but August 1, 1878, another disastrous fire wiped out most of the town permanently.

Alta, like other camps, had a large Chinese population who followed the mining strikes as diligently as the white prospectors to whom they were "heathen Chinee," and there was universal prejudice against them as is reflected by an editorial in the *Cottonwood Observer*: "For so young and so small a city we have never seen so many China houses of ill repute. The eternal twang of the China banjo, the sing-song monasyllables and unintelligible jargon of the gamblers of these heathen Chinese are an intolerable nuisance. We can boast a Chinatown here as in all cities of importance where these vile creatures do congregate. Their superstitions exhibited every evening at the doors on the lighting lamps and exhibitors of gestures, low mumblings, and burnt sacrifices to keep 'Auld Clooty' away from them. But the old gentleman is so used to the rites he won't be banished by them and the orgies under his auspices are annoying and disgusting and a disgrace. We wish we were rid of them."

Editors R. Webb and H. Simcocks were leaders in the anti-Chinese crusade, and seemingly had no idea that posterity might judge them as being just as crude and narrow as the aliens they criticized.

Their own idea of what constituted a Christian and civilized town is given in another article. "Two or three lively spars took place in our bars on Sunday last to the great delight of the boys. Although it was fun for them it was bad for the conchs and peepers of the manly art. A little bloodletting is good sometimes the doctors say, so let the blood flow, so long as it doesn't end in anything fatal, and leaden shots do not tunnel through the veins instead of the mines."

The *Observer* also took a keen interest in a trial between Nick Dramer and a Mrs. Simmons, who owned adjoining places of

73

business, described as barrooms. Though Mrs. Simmons had the habit of throwing her filth, as garbage was called in those days, over Nick's fence, and had at one time threatened to blow his head off with a shotgun, she was the plaintiff in the action, for Nick had been ungentlemanly enough to throw the filth right back. She was in the act of throwing it over the fence again, she claimed, when Nick came out with a small pistol and called her bad names, thus treating her "mean and low."

In his defense Nick testified that Mrs. Simmons picked up a rock and threatened to strike him. Then she broke a broom over the fence and did strike him. The testimony of the City Constable appeared to be decisive. Said he, "I'd rather meet Nick anytime than Mrs. Simmons." Mrs. Simmons lost her case.

There were many other mines in the district besides the Emma, though none that made so much history. The ore zone nosed over into Big Cottonwood Canyon to the north, and American Fork Canyon to the south. Some of the better known mines were The Prince of Wales, the South Hecla, the Maxfield Mines, the Albion, City of Rocks, Columbus, Toledo, North Star, Grizzly, Reed & Benson. The Cardiff, a big producer, was developed as late as 1914 and embraced a number of the old workings.

In 1903 colorful George H. Watson got title to thirty-four of the old claims and merged them into the Alta United Mines Company, and for many years Mr. Watson was self-elected mayor and almost the sole inhabitant of the camp. "Making," wrote Maud Robinson in the *Salt Lake Tribune* of March 4, 1945, "regular dashes down the 28 miles to Salt Lake City to his town office and town home to meetings of The Great American Prospectors Association held at Roaring Gulch, alias his town office. The association founded by Mr. Watson on paper is a country wide club on paper which is relaxing the blood pressure of dozens of well known men who have been guests at the mines. It encourages more nonsense than small boy hi-jinks in the way of correspondence among staid and important individuals than has enlivened this land for some time. Magazine editors, political writers, bankers, lawyers, and mining men dutifully turn in their dollar-a-year dues to belong to a club totally without bodily existence. They do it for the sheer joy of writing accompanying scathing letters belittling Mr. Watson, the association 'Scribe.' With much joy he shoots back hotter missiles and uses their dollar for postage. Behind the fun is the serious plan of founding a home for indigent and crippled mining prospectors."

To philanthropist George H. Watson belongs most of the credit for making Alta what it is today—one of the finest winter resorts in the nation—when he signed a deed and presented the land to J. E. Gurr, superintendent of the Wasatch National Forest. The basin at the foot of Mt. Baldy, which rises 11,169 feet, and Rustler Mountain, provides skiing eight months of the year, and is equipped with lodges and ski lifts and every modern convenience.

The government keeps the road open at considerable expense, even to the extent of hiring an expert to start miniature snowslides before they can become big and dangerous, and thousands of automobiles go up and down the canyon where once the miners dragged out their ore in bullhides. Alta has no present need for the millions of dollars worth of gold, silver, lead, copper, and zinc, bismuth and tungsten, which George Watson was firmly convinced still lies untouched beneath the surface.

One story of Alta remains to be told. In the spring of 1873, after the camp had been busy digging tunnels through the snow all winter to reach Boot Graveyard to bury the victims of gunfights in the Gold Miner's Daughter and the Bucket of Blood, a mysterious stranger appeared in town and offered to go to the cemetery and resurrect the dead.

At first it appeared to be a good and kindly thought, but after more mature deliberation the residents decided that it might prove inconvenient to the widows and widowers who had remarried; and those who had inherited property from the deceased were against it from the very first.

To make sure the mysterious stranger did not foul things up, the people of Alta took up a collection and gave the stranger $2500 to leave town. At last reports there had been no resurrection of the dead at Alta.

CHAPTER SEVEN

Park City

Far richer and less turbulent than Alta was the camp of Park City on the other side of the Wasatch. This is not to say that Park City was particularly calm and gentle. Although its first mine, the Flagstaff, was discovered by General Pat Connor's soldiers at the same time others were exploring Little Cottonwood Canyon, the camp was just beginning to boom as Alta was passing out of the mining picture.

While Alta and the Emma mine created a national scandal in the stock exchanges of the world that are long forgotten, there are still mines in Park City that are selling briskly on the market.

In 1848 Parley P. Pratt, a Mormon Apostle, explored a canyon to the east of Salt Lake City, which is still called Parley's Canyon. Over the summit, and some five miles below Park City, he came upon a beautiful little round valley which became known as Parley's Park. Pratt was given a franchise to build a toll road up the canyon. The round valley was granted to two of Brigham Young's Counselors, Heber C. Kimball and Jedediah M. Grant, and a lesser known Mormon named Samuel C. Snyder. Snyder settled there, and the hamlet that grew up at the edge of Parley's Park was called Snyderville.

Just as Alta and the Emma mine were synonymous, so were Park City and the Ontario. In 1872 Herman Budden made the first strike at the fabulous property, though his partner, Rector Steen, is sometimes credited with the discovery. They took in other partners and in August, 1872, sold the Ontario to George Hearst for $27,000, thus bringing in outside capital and starting the great camp on its way, and incidentally helping to lay the foundation of the great fortune that created the Hearst newspaper system.

For many years the Ontario was called the greatest silver mine in the world. Up to 1934 it had produced more than fifty million dollars worth of high grade silver and lead, and had paid fourteen millions in dividends. It is still producing more ore than any other mine in the camp. The old highgrade may be exhausted, but new flotation processes have made it possible to mine lower grade ore profitably.

There were other mines of great importance, and in time the Ontario became part of the great Silver King Coalition company, which itself is now part of the United Park Consolidated company.

For a long time it was believed that mineral could be found only in the vicinity of the Ontario, but an Ontario miner named J. J. Daly became convinced that there were mineral deposits west of the property, and he located the successful Daly mine. About the same time E. P. Ferry, from Michigan, located ore still farther west on the Anchor property, and this became part of the great Daly-Judge mine. Subsequently, J. J. Daly incorporated the Daly-West mine, which became one of the largest of the district.

Two other Ontario miners out prospecting crossed from the Crescent mine down the mountain by way of Woodside Canyon. One of them noticed a piece of black rock protruding from the soil, stuck his pick into it, and discovered that it was high grade ore. More than half a million dollars was taken out there.

This discovery finally led to the opening up of the Silver King properties and made millionaires of David Keith and Thomas Kearns.

Later on the Park Consolidated to the east produced millions of dollars of ore, though it was not so high grade as some of the others. Down below the old Flagstaff on Mt. Baldy is the newest and one of the richest of present day Park City mines, The New Park Mining Company, which is a consolidation of various mines, including the Star of Utah and the Mayflower. Nearby are the

New Quincy and the Naildriver, but the two great companies dominate the scene. The lone prospector is out of luck.

As in many other camps, too much water has been a problem. The Ontario was saved by a costly pumping operation, and a number of long tunnels have been driven which serve the double purpose of development and drainage. Great ore bodies are known to be untouched, and many believe the tunnels will eventually open them up. Park City can legitimately claim to be one of the greatest mining districts of the West. It has seen pick and shovel miners become millionaires, and it can point with pride to the fact that many of the largest and best buildings in Salt Lake City were built with Park City money. Yet Park City has pretty much remained an orphan child.

Like the other mining towns, Park City brought money to the Mormons but never gained their approval, though more Mormons worked in mines there than in the other camps. During the boom years of the last century the population was divided between Catholics and Masons. They took a fierce pride in building schools and churches, but the first Mormons were obliged to hold their meetings secretly.

Samuel C. Snyder built a sawmill at Snyderville and supplied most of the lumber for the district. His brother, George G. Snyder, and his wife, Rhoda, who was known to everyone for miles around as "Aunt Rhoda," built the first boarding house in Park City upon the discovery of the Ontario, and there have always been a few Mormon businessmen in the town.

In 1880 James Schubach started the *Park Record*, the oldest continuing weekly newspaper in the state, which soon passed into the hands of the Raddon family who published the *Record* until it passed into other hands in 1957 upon the death of S. L. Raddon. It was a successful and readable paper from the start. The newcomers had little interest in Mormon church doings and the conflicts pro and con which filled the Salt Lake papers, so they took kindly to their own newspaper which kept them informed on the things that mattered to them.

The town built wooden sidewalks in 1880 and cement ones in 1890. The first settlers came from every part of the nation, and even a few from Salt Lake City. Among the first were the "hot water" miners from Virginia City, Nevada, who for a while had trouble getting used to the cold underground water at Park.

In the late Sixties the people lived in shanties near the portals of the mines, but they found food plentiful and cheap. Rector Steen, co-discoverer of the Ontario, wrote concerning the food prices.

> Flour was $4 and $5 a hundred pounds.
> Bacon was 30 to 40 cents per pound.
> Beef was 25 cents.
> Irish potatoes were 50 cents a bushel.
> Butter was 30 cents a pound.

But tools cost money. Steen wrote that a pick cost $5.00 and a shovel $2.50.

Park City has always tried to live its own life and never tried to win any medals for decorum and respectability. It had its full quorum of saloons. Its red light district was in Deer Creek Gulch. On May 24, 1884, the *Park Record* editorialized, "There is too much promiscuous shooting on the streets at night. The police should be put to work at once so that the disturbers of the peace may be dealt with as they deserve."

Three gunmen who called themselves Tex, Mex, and The Big Nigger, invaded the town during the Eighties and cut quite a swath for a while before they were run out of town. Park would never harbor such characters very long. It also had one of the three lynchings that has disgraced the state. It is related in an article in *Utah Historical Quarterly* of April, 1960, by Dr. William M. McPhee, entitled "Vignettes of Park City." According to the article a dying man accused a Mr. Murphy of shooting him. Murphy was arrested and placed in jail at Coalville, the seat of Summit County. The evidence against him rested mostly on the fact that he had been in the vicinity and that one shot had been fired from his gun, which he maintained had been fired on a hunting trip from which he had just returned. It is said that there was considerable evidence that Murphy was not the guilty man, but a crowd of irate Park City men stole a locomotive and forced the engineer to run them over to Coalville, where they took Murphy out of the jail, brought him back to Park City, and hanged him from a telegraph pole.

The oldest living native son of Park City is Lawrence Berry, eighty years of age, hale and hearty, who has lived there all his life. We are indebted to him for an account of Park City's most famous criminal episode. As a boy of fifteen he saw two young men he knew, Patrick Coughlin and Fred George, enter a stable. Thinking nothing of it, he remained silent. After all these years he feels that had he spoken several lives might have been saved.

The young men had stolen a case of strawberries, and Sheriff Harrington had made such violent threats against them that they decided to leave the country. That night they stole a couple of horses from the sheriff's brother and struck out for Wyoming. They stopped at a sheep camp in Crandall's Canyon, fifteen miles to the north, and the sheriff trailed them there.

In the gunfight Sheriff Harrington was slightly wounded, and the boys went on to Wanship and bought 300 rounds of ammunition. From there they rode to Coalville, up Chalk Creek, and on to the Wasatch flats where they holed up at Palmer's shack for the night, at the head of Duck Creek, a few miles west of Evanston, Wyoming.

Four men surrounded them during the night, and when Patsy Coughlin opened the door next morning he was narrowly missed by a bullet. Coughlin started shooting back while George lay on the floor loading the rifles. Coughlin's second bullet mortally wounded N. E. Dawes, of Evanston, and Constable Parry Stagg, of Echo, was accidentally killed by his companions. The other two men retreated.

Fred George had been wounded in both thighs by a single bullet. Coughlin dug the slug out with his pocketknife, and the boys gave the dying Dawes a drink of water and rode away. A posse from Evanston returned and fired 500 shots into the empty shack. The manhunt was on, and Sheriff Harvey Hardy of Salt Lake assumed command.

The fugitives passed down Ogden Canyon. They were falsely reported to have been seen in Ogden but rode south, passing near Kaysville and Farmington. A posse from Salt Lake intercepted them near Bountiful. After a fusillade of shots the boys escaped and made their way to City Creek Canyon, overlooking Salt Lake City.

In another gun battle Coughlin's horse was killed, but the fugitives escaped over the City Creek-Hardscrabble Ridge and vanished from sight.

They spent the next two days hiding in Mt. Olivet cemetery while sheriff's posses from eight counties scoured the country. They moved to Mill Creek, and once two detectives passed close enough to the hidden Coughlin that their dog came up and smelled his rifle.

The boys stole two horses in front of a saloon in Murray and rode across Salt Lake Valley. Then they were seen near Grantsville. Toward evening they stopped at a mine and got a meal from a miner named Barres, but as soon as they rode away Barres headed for the nearest posse. The boys got past one posse and headed toward Johnson's Pass. Sheriff McKellar of Tooele County led a posse twenty miles to get ahead of the outlaws.

The boys had planned to get up at midnight and head for the Nevada desert, but they overslept and were just getting up when the posse sighted them and fired a volley of shots. Coughlin got to the brush, yet when Sheriff McKellar ordered him to come out with his hands up the order was obeyed. Coughlin said bitterly, "This is the first chance we've had to surrender without being shot down like dogs." He maintained that Sheriff Harrington had fired the first shot.

They were taken back to Randolph, Rich County. There they were tried for the murder of Dawes, and both were convicted of murder in the first degree; however, the jury recommended mercy for Fred George, a young man who had never been in any trouble before.

Coughlin, according to an account in the *Salt Lake Tribune*, was taken out on a flat, tied to a chair, and shot to death by a firing squad concealed in a tent. (Utah permits a man who is to be executed his choice of shooting or hanging). The Catholic priest said, "Keep up your courage, Patsy, it will soon be over."

"You bet your life I will," Patsy Coughlin replied with a smile.

Fred George served fifteen years in the penitentiary, returned to Park City and lived out a quiet and uneventful life.

Park City had quite a respectable and law-abiding population from the first, and though those who made fortunes moved elsewhere to spend it many of the common people made permanent homes there. Lawrence Berry is typical of these. He was born in the camp and has lived there all his life and raised a good Mormon family. He was a blacksmith by trade, as was his father before him. His wife also is a native. Lawrence worked for thirty-four years in the Daly-Judge mine, doing blacksmith work and tending the horses underground. He still belongs to Park City's volunteer Fire Department and is caretaker of the old Park City Hall. He obligingly shows the visitors downstairs to see the old dungeons, three little windowless six by eight cells with narrow iron doors, which were made by his father. On a wall in another room are the wrist and ankle irons fastened to the wall by eye-bolts, which were made by Lawrence Berry himself while he was a blacksmith. And on the floor are the balls and chains with which prisoners were manacled to work on the roads.

We rode up to the old Marsac mill to which, said Mr. Berry, the ore from the Ontario mine was carried by overhead tram, and he told us that more ore is still being taken from the Ontario than from any other mine in the district.

While up there on the ridge, Mr. Berry pointed to a brush-covered flat across the canyon where there are now no houses and said that his wife had been living in a house there when they were married. In eighty years Mr. Berry had seen a lot of changes.

Religious differences constituted quite a thing in Park City. The largest church in town was the Roman Catholic Church of St. Mary of the Assumption. The more numerous Protestants were divided among several sects, the Methodists, Congregationalists, Lutherans, and Episcopalians and warred merrily among themselves; but all presented a united front against the common enemy, the Mormons. Most of the Protestants were united under the emblem of Masonry, but when a Masonic Association was formed June 25, 1878, it was denied a charter by the Grand

Lodge. Nothing daunted, the Parkites formed an informal association which prospered so much that the reasons for denying a charter were invalidated, and the Park City Lodge, known as Uintah Lodge No. 7, was granted a charter in 1880.

Mormons were an outcast and unwanted group. The *Park Record* of July 31, 1886, reported: "For a long time it has been generally understood that several scores of adherents of the Church of Jesus Christ of Latter-day Saints resided in Park City, but many of them took good care to conceal the fact. Recently the Saints who were evidently ashamed of their faith have been properly sized up by the community . . . . The Saints say that God through His mounthpiece is declaring Himself, He must be heard, His enemies put to flight and His Kingdom built in Park City, the only Gentile town in Utah."

There was talk about building a $2500 Mormon church, but the project failed. At the same time a Loyalty League was formed with a branch in Park City. The purpose of the Loyalty League was to eradicate by peaceful means, but lawful force, the doctrines of the Mormons.

On July 29, 1887, the *Record* said: "Last fall a branch of the Mormon church was established here in Park City with Gad Davis and P. W. Timms at the head of the rickety craft. Meetings were held in Erickson's cellar on Park Avenue, and in the rear of Hop Chong's 'washee.' But it no longer exists in Park City."

The Mormons, as usual, won the final victory. During the prohibition days, and after, the Parkites lived pretty much as they pleased. There was little disorder, but there were drinking and gambling, and legalized prostitution, and admittedly even some tea and coffee drinking, and the ever increasing Mormon population of the surrounding towns did not like it. The Park City Mormons had a church now, and being neighborly were inclined to let things ride, but in the early 1950's a group of vigilantes from a nearby 100 per cent Mormon agricultural town called Kamas rode into town and closed out the bars and the lone house of ill fame. No longer does one see long strings of taxicabs from Salt Lake City lined up on Park City streets.

Th original inhabitants would not have submitted so tamely,

but they had been tried in the crucible. Like Bingham and Alta the town was subject to snowslides and fires. In December, 1882, a fire of unknown origin caused $20,000 damage. July 4, 1884, a pyromaniac set fire to the Catholic church to get even with the townspeople whom he imagined had mistreated him. But the big fire of June 29, 1898, caused a million dollars worth of damage. More than two hundred business and dwelling houses were wiped out, and more than five hundred people were left homeless.

Most of the buildings on Main Street were gone and Chinatown was destroyed, as were the residences on Rossie Hill. Many of the buildings on Park Avenue, which included schools and churches, were burned. No lives were lost, but many animals were killed. Many valuable records and documents were destroyed, as was the *Park Record* which had just installed new equipment in a new building.

The *Deseret News* of June 30, 1898, said: "Park City, Utah's proud and prosperous mining camp has practically been wiped out of existence, being visited yesterday by the most disastrous conflagration in the history of Utah. It may be the city will be rebuilt and rise again from the ruins that now cover the canyons where it once stood, but it will be many years before it can fully recover, if recovery is at all possible under the circumstances from the terrible visitation."

The word *visitation* implies that the church organ felt that Park City was being punished for its wickedness, and had little faith that it would ever recover. The proud Parkites announced that they would handle the situation by themselves, but they didn't have to do so. Money and supplies poured in from all over the country. The supplies were carried free of charge over both the Denver & Rio Grande and the Union Pacific railroads. All churches, Catholic, Protestant, and Mormon, united in the common effort. The Catholic church and school had escaped the fire, and the Sisters of the Holy Cross cleared a schoolroom to be used as a supply depot, and the Mormon farmers from the surrounding districts donated free milk and butter so long as the people were destitute.

The *Park Record* set up a tent on a hillside and gathered the news. The paper was printed by a Salt Lake newspaper. Every available man toiled at the rebuilding, while the women cooked and sewed and took care of the homeless.

On July 9th the *Park Record* was moved to say: "This is the hand of charity that the Good Book speaks to us as the greatest of all Christian acts. It is the kind of work that elevates mankind."

Park City was indeed rebuilt, and a new era was begun. Better understanding took the place of traditional enmity, and perhaps the "visitation" was worth while. A not too far removed instance of the new unity was displayed when some women of the town decided to refurbish the run-down Public Library. Businessmen were persuaded to supply paint and other materials, the unions did the labor free of charge, and book stores in Salt Lake, as well as many individuals, donated books. The late Marge McCullough, of Snyderville, was the inspirational force behind the movement.

Park City had its Chinatown, whose people lived in small houses underneath "the Chinese Bridge," but there appears not to have been the hatred and prejudice against the yellow men as was rife in Alta and other towns. The favored residential district was on Rossie Hill at the east side of town, and it was necessary for the people to cross China Bridge to reach their homes. Its history is described by Mary Pappsideris in an article in the *Salt Lake Trbiune,* November 14, 1954.

"A lot of history is wrapped up in some new stairs in Park City which replaced the mining town's old China Bridge, which got its unusual name from the time when the town was a bustling community of 10,000. Old timers recall two China Bridges . . . There is no record of the construction of the first China Bridge, but it was back when the Easterners were after Western wealth and were flocking into the city and building their homes on Rossie Hill . . . .

"Steps provided the first means of access, but they were inadequate. The first China Bridge was big bright red one, big enough for two teams of horses to cross, old timers say. . . . The second China Bridge went up in 1900 and was much smaller than the first . . . . With the passing of the China Bridge in its recent razing some memories of Park City's colorful cosmopolitan past are also dimmed. It was in the late 1800's and early 1900's that Finnish and Swedish people, the Irish and the Cornish, all used China Bridge to get to their homes, while the sizeable Chinese population followed its colorful Oriental customs underneath it.

"Park City's Chinatown provided the domestic help for the large boarding houses. The Chinese were cooks, waiters, porters and janitors. They operated laundries and cafes, and they were some of the shrewdest gamblers in the town's 27 saloons. Early day housewives relied on the Chinese for their fresh vegetables, which the Chinese would peddle from door to door with baskets hung over their shoulders from yokes."

The roster of men who made fortunes in Park City would include nationally famous financiers like Hearst, Haggin, Tevis, and J. J. Daly. It would include Jacob Bamberger, W. W. Armstrong, W. S. McCormick, the Ferry brothers, David Keith, Thomas Kearns, John Judge, Ezra Thompson, and many more who were powers in Utah. Their names are attached to the great buildings and business firms in Salt Lake City. Two of them, Ezra Thompson, who made his fortune hauling ore from Park City, and W. Mont Ferry, served terms as mayors of Salt Lake City.

Best known of all Parkites was Thomas Kearns, a Canadian Irishman who served Utah as United States Senator from 1900 until 1906. His parents moved from Canada to Nebraska when Tom was eight years of age, where he acquired a common school education. He became a miner in the Black Hills, and before he was of age was working as a teamster and miner at Tombstone, Arizona.

At the age of twenty-one he drove a team across the desert to Utah. Failing to get a job in the mines, he worked on construction of the Denver & Rio Grande between Salt Lake and Ogden. He started to Butte, Montana, but destiny led him back to Park City, where he worked in the Ontario for seven years.

Kearns formed his partnership with David Keith in 1889 to drive a tunnel through the Woodside property. He noticed an ore vein bearing toward some undeveloped property and in association with Keith, John Judge, A. B. Emery, and W. V. Rice, got a lease on the Mayflower property which eventually produced

$1,600,000 in ore. They then got possession of the Silver King mine, which paid out more than ten million dollars in dividends, and many more after consolidation of the Silver King Coalition Mines Company.

Kearns, like most of his fellow mining magnates, moved to Salt Lake City and built a mansion said to have cost three-quarters of a million dollars when building material was cheap. After the senator's death the mansion was given to the state of Utah to serve as the governor's mansion, but the upkeep was so great that the state built a smaller mansion for its governors and the Kearns mansion very fittingly became the home of the Utah State Historical Society and is one of the sights of the city.

The Kearns office building is one of the largest in the city, and Kearns became active in banking and railroad circles. When he entered politics, Kearns cast yearning eyes toward the *Salt Lake Tribune*, Utah's largest and most influential newspaper, which for years had made a career of fighting Mormonism. Knowing that the owners would not sell to him, he had the deal handled from San Francisco and the sellers were baffled and surprised when they learned that Tom Kearns was the new owner. The paper is still under control of the Kearns estate. Never a bitter anti-Mormon, Kearns gradually changed the policy of the *Tribune*.

Senator Kearns' charities were many. He donated $10,000 to complete the Cathedral of the Madoline, and he and his wife provided for the erection and maintenance of St. Ann's Orphanage. He was an able if not spectacular senator. He was a member of most of the prominent clubs in Salt Lake, including the aristocratic Alta Club, originally founded by the millionaires from Alta.

A story about Kearns and the Alta Club, for which the authors of this book do not vouch, is that Kearns was asked to donate two-thousand dollars to buy an ornamental chandelier for the club, but he refused with these words: "I wouldn't mind the two thousand dollars, but in just a little while you fellows would be asking for another two thousand to teach somebody how to play the thing."

Senator Kearns was a Catholic and a Republican, and on the

whole he did a great deal toward better relations between the Mormons and the Gentiles of his adopted state and city.

One of Park City's ablest citizens was Robert C. Chambers, superintendent of the Ontario under Hearst's ownership, who contributed greatly to its prosperity by the introduction of improved mining methods. Chambers was the original backer of Keith and Kearns.

Park had its quota of oddballs, such as "Paddy, the Pig," a man with a mountainous appetite who could eat a roast intended for twenty men, and "John the Baptist," a tall and angular miner whose time was occupied with sin, damnation, and salvation. Because of his sincerity, the name given him in derision was finally maintained out of respect.

Of richer plumage was Susanna Emery Holmes, known as Utah's Silver Queen. She was born in Kentucky, raised in California, and married to Albion B. Emery, postmaster of Park City and Speaker of the House in Utah's last territorial legislature. He died in 1894, leaving his widow a fortune. Two years later she married Colonel Edwin F. Holmes, another Park City colossus, and was given the name of Silver Queen because of her costly and elaborate social affairs. She owned the Semloh Hotel, which was Holmes spelled backward, in Salt Lake City. It is now the Congress. The lady traveled all over the world and maintained residences in Paris and London. She became a Princess when she married Russian Prince Nicholas Engalitcheff. Her occasional returns to Salt Lake and Park cities were social triumphs.

The so-called Cornish pump was installed in the Ontario at a cost of a quarter of a million dollars when water became a problem. It could raise 3,606,400 gallons a day to a height of 400 feet, but one day the pump stopped and all efforts to start it were unavailing.

Finally in desperation the owners asked a Scotch engineer from a neighboring mine to come over and see what he could do. He obligingly came to No. 3 shaft, climbed up on the flywheel, struck it a mighty blow with a sledge hammer, and at once the pump started to work.

Thanks and congratulations were not enough for the Scotchman, and he tendered a bill for one thousand dollars. The outraged Ontario owners demanded that he itemize, which he did as follows: "For hitting the wheel with a hammer, 50c; for knowing where to hit the wheel, $999.50."

Historic and once lively Park City, despite the mining that still goes on, looks like a ghost town. The streets are lined with vacant buildings with boarded up windows. In front of one building is a sign: THE PARK RECORD, but one is disillusioned to learn that inside the building is only one lady who serves as business manager and reporter, while the paper itself is printed over in Morgan, in another county.

But appearances can be deceptive. There is a land boom in Park City and lots are selling at fantastic prices. The reason: since one of the largest mining companies decided to build a great new park, people from Salt Lake are building summer homes, and the trek between the two cities is being reversed. No country could be more beautiful than Park City in the summer time and no climate more salubrious. Park City is more accessible than either Alta or Brighton, best known of Utah's winter resorts, and it could easily outstrip them. Ecker Hill has long been famous for skiing, and there are plenty more.

Parkites are confident that their city will yet become another Sun Valley, and its mining is by no means finished.

CHAPTER EIGHT

Tintic

One hundred miles southwest from Salt Lake City, located in Juab County, Utah, and lying on the fringe of what was once called the Great American Desert, are three great north and south mountain ranges called Wasatch, Oquirrh, and Tintic. Running under them was one of the abundant mineral belts of the North American Continent. Tintic was one of the richest of these deposits.

Because of the mountainous terrain, this district was actually one of six towns: Dividend, Mammoth, Silver City, Diamond, Eureka, and Robinson—all loosely joined together and known as "Tintic." Estimates of production, although nothing could be accurately stated, range from four hundred to five hundred million, the lower figure more generally accepted.

A virgin valley of unparalleled beauty, the Tintic rangeland was known in the Sixties for the waist-high, blue-green grass that fattened the vast herds of cattle. Tintic lay like a green oasis on the edge of barren desert, near an area called the Ibapah, "The Deep Down Waters," of the Goshute Indian Tribe.

Tintic's godfather was General Patrick Connor, so-called father of Utah mining. Most of Tintic's early people, and exclusively so for the first thirteen years of the life of this camp, were Irish-Catholic, although the original discovery of the minerals was made by a Mormon party. But these people early sold out and it remained for the Irish to come in and actively do the mining and opening up of the mineral deposits during the days of the first "glory holes."

The district obtained its name from a Goshute Indian chief—a renegade who never made peace with the whites—Chief Tintic. Old Tintic was known for the chant "Amerikats kill Indian—Indian kill Amerikats."

The site of Eureka camp was Tintic's favorite haunt, and from the slopes of Tintic peak he descended with a vengeance upon the early settlers and freighters of the time.

It is a safe guess that Tintic is about as far north as the Spanish miners worked their way. After the first big strikes in Tintic, roving prospectors unearthed abandoned Spanish mines. One of these was found less than ten miles from Eureka, and ore in it assayed over five thousand dollars a ton. Despite the fact that they uncovered rich rock, the Spanish abandoned the mines for the more profitable business of slave-trading. They sold captured Indians in Mexico where a healthy, good looking squaw brought as high as four hundred dollars.

The Spanish vanished from the scene and these finds lay forgotten until the discovery of the Sunbeam Lode.

This valley was wilderness in December of 1869 when a party of Mormons, William Jasper Harris, Joseph Hyde, S. J. Worsley, S. B. Moore, and E. M. Beck, staked out their claim. They were in the picture less than a year, however, when these claims were sold for pittances and the Sunbeam Lode was purchased by an English syndicate whose director was Lord Claude Hamilton. Most financial backing for Western mining enterprises of the era was centered at London and many Tintic mines were controlled from there.

The English owners took the shaft of the Sunbeam down, and it opened into richer ore all the way. For seventy years the Sunbeam mine poured forth silver and gold ores, and no one has any way of knowing the real value of the ore taken from it; so the value can be estimated and given only by comparison. The Eureka-Hill, by 1874, was selling her stock for one hundred dollars a share and the amount of wealth she produced was never given out, but in 1899, after less than twenty years of operation, it was estimated that Eureka Hill had paid over four million dollars in dividends in addition to paying over a million for a mill as well as other expenses. Both Eureka-Hill and the Sunbeam were gold producers as well as rich in silver, lead, and copper.

Both of these mines produced for over seventy years and ore was mined from Eureka Hill having a gross value of at least fifty million dollars. It is assumed that the Sunbeam produced equally.

The excitement stirred by this 1869 discovery in Utah brought a new boomer into life, one that was destined to be unique among mining camps of the west for longevity and sobriety.

Tintic in Utah was destined to become a steady producer of minerals for eighty years—an almost unparalleled record among "boomers," and to own the only saloon-free, prostitute-free mining camp in the West—Knightsville.

In the vanguard of the early pioneers was the West's own Father Lawrence Scanlan. Spreading his blanket with his flock, and sleeping on the floor of hut or cabin, or under the stars, he lived as they lived, asking nothing better. From Camp Floyd, where he labored among the soldiers, Father Scanlan came into the Tintic Mining District to hold services and baptize.

This Catholic priest traveled the largest parish in the United States. Two thousand miles on horseback and on foot, this indefatigable priest made his rounds, traveling to the remote mining camps of his Irish miners until his Church "put a fair mitre upon his head and clothed him with the garments of the high priest."

More early ones came in from the west. "Pioche" and "Buckshot" were typical in every way of "the boys." Most of the men of this early camp were known only by nicknames. In Tintic were such authentic characters as Diamond Denny, Rattlesnake Bill, Donkey Frank, Peg Leg, Fog Horn, Tex, Buckshot, Shorty, Buffalo Dave, Tommy the Hog, and Pioche. Later came the Wild Dutchman, Scoopshovel, The Little Pony, and Whiskey Charley. (Pony and Whiskey Charley were former members of the Butch Cassidy gang, who, like Porter Rockwell and Bill Hickman, retired themselves into the Tintic Valley.)

The Mammoth was the biggest strike in the central area of Tintic district, made by two Texans, the colorful McIntyre brothers, Samuel and William. Medium of height and stockily built, they were tough as the country they drove their cattle herds across. When they trailed their herd of longhorns into Tintic grazing lands, the McIntyres were already a combination of business and power.

The father of the McIntyre brothers had been a Texas land owner and possessor of Negro slaves who had fought under Sam Houston. At the end of this service, soldiers were presented with scrip entitling them to take up land, and William McIntyre, Sr., made shrewd use of all his scrip for this purpose. After using up all his own land rights, he bartered mules and horses to other soldiers of his company in return for their scrip. With this, he obtained extensive tracts of land north of Houston.

It was this Texas acreage that the brothers sold and turned their money into the cattle business. They wintered their herd in Tintic and in the spring sold stock for $24.00 a head that had cost them $3.75 a head. With their first profits, the brothers journeyed to Omaha and purchased another herd driving them back into the valley. They traded one of their herds of long-horned steers for the undeveloped claims of the Mammoth Mine. A good trade, for the Mammoth lay over the mother lode of Tintic.

Tintic's most historic court battle occurred in 1901, when this mine tangled with the powerful Grand Central in a no-quarter struggle. The bone of contention was the Silveropolis and Consort claims . . . with both mines boring into the same vein. This case went to the Supreme Court of the United States in what became known as The Law of the Apex. This was a heavy artillery battle with each company employing batteries of lawyers who kept up the fight until a satisfactory compromise was reached.

John Beck was the owner and locator of the rich Bullion-Beck and Champion mines. This German immigrant came to Utah in 1861. Beck was a "loner" who worked apart from the other miners of the district until he made his discovery in 1870. Known as "The Crazy Dutchman," he made and lost fortune after fortune in Tintic and his two mines, Eureka-Hill, and Mammoth, were producers for seventy years. The shafts for these five mines went down in 1870-71.

"Little Billie" Hatfield, discoverer of the South Swansea claims, was one of the happy-go-luckiest hunters ever to go marching off in search of a claim. So much so, that his trek over the hills has been captured in a Western ballad:

THE SOUTH SWANSEA CLAIM

> They talks of the Swansea claim,
> Of the luck of the silver camp,
> Way back in the early time
> Of the candle and kerosene lamp.
> They tells of Little Billie,
> With his happy-go-lucky ways,
> Who wanted to vote with the rest
> An' have 'is political say.
> Unless 'e owned a claim
> He couldn't vote, he found,
> So he started out one mornin'
> To stake an' own some ground.
> He walked out into the sagebrush,
> An' over the sandy waste,
> With the prairie-dogs yelpin' at 'im
> Fallin' in holes in haste . . . .

In Silver City camp, over the old Swansea claims, pay dirt had been hit in the early Seventies, but the first owners hit Tintic's iron cap and water and the claims had been abandoned as worthless. They suited Billie's lazy purpose and he used two end stakes of a distant claim for a starter. It was as good a place to start from as any, but by one of those strange turns of fortunes made and lost in mining . . .

> "And tons came tumbling out,
> As he worked it to the core,
> With silver and gold and lead
> Of the highest valued ore.
> An' now he's a millionaire,
> Is Billie the happy-go-luck,
> An' his mine is the richest strike
> In Silver camp ever struck."

Other notable producers of Tintic were the Black Dragon, located in 1870, The Ajax, whose drifts were famous for the clinging handfuls of golden nuggets that Tintic miners picked from the walls of the drifts, the Wyoming, which had originally been a "salted" claim sold to bilked Ohio mining scouts for twenty-two thousand dollars, the Centennial Eureka, Tintic Standard, Eureka Standard, Chief Consolidated, Eagle, and Blue Bell, to name but a few. All of these mines have a story behind them, but the legend and history would be book length.

It is to be noted that Tintic District has in her record sixty producing mines and the district has constructed and operated no less than thirty mills and smelters.

Tintic mines have paid for the erection of public schools as well as business sections in cities and the public library of Salt Lake City. The benefactor in this instance was John Q. Packard.

Packard was a generous eccentric, considered a miser by some. An immigrant from Holland, he joined the California gold rush when he was seventeen, became a San Francisco business man, then entered the mining field in 1852. He was advised by his mining scout, V. L. Thomas, to invest in the Tintic District and by this means came into possession of twenty million dollars and the famous Eureka-Hill mine, a great gold and silver producer.

The names of Eureka-Hill and Tintic's colorful Watson Nesbit are synonymous. Nesbit was a hand-picked superintendent and trouble-shooter brought in to hold this hotly contested property. The tall, erect figure of Watson Nesbit was the best known on the boardwalks of Tintic. He wore a full, flowing beard and carried himself with an almost regal grace. Despite a saintly mien, this man was one of the fiercest fighters in the West. Nesbit had been a freighter in "Pikes Peak or Bust" days and fought Indian attacks against his wagon trains as well as his share of personal duels. This man passed through harrowing experiences which he could relate by the hour, and it is doubted by those who know his history that Daniel Boone or Kit Carson themselves had more adventure crowded into one lifetime than did Watson Nesbit of Tintic.

His first defense of the "Hill" was against William Rose when

Rose's Montanent property clashed with Eureka-Hill over a disputed survey. There was a pitched gun battle fought up and down the mountain over this mine, and Watson Nesbit constructed a stone fort on Hill property which stood for years, until the mine constructed its mill upon the site.

Another over-lap of claims occurred when Watson Nesbit fought another battle with imported gunmen from Nevada who represented the interests of English owners who also laid claim to Eureka-Hill. This was a mine worked and operated under siege for years, and Nesbit held this rich real estate for Packard by right of might. The Hill was constantly patrolled until it became generally accepted that the disputed real estate was too hot to handle.

Two well known figures in Tintic were Orrin Porter Rockwell and Bill Hickman, alleged chiefs of the Mormon Danites. Rockwell moved into West Tintic and took up ranching, characteristically getting into a bitter feud over water rights with J. O. Freckleton and five other families. The case was fought in the courts for two years until Judge Emerson, of Provo, decreed the water to Rockwell, who promptly sold the water to the Mammoth mine. It appeared to be a shady piece of business.

Rockwell was a fierce looking man with a long flowing beard and hair so long he frequently wore it in braids. He would never have it cut since Joseph Smith had promised him no bullet could ever hurt him so long as it was uncut. He remained a monogamist, though whiskey finally laid him low. He was as much feared in Tintic as he was in other parts of the country.

The Gentile estimate of him (*Utah Guide Book*) is given in a popular song sung to the tune of "Solomon Levi."

> Have you heard of Porter Rockwell?
> He's the Mormon triggerite.
> They say he hunts for horse thieves
> When the moon is shining bright.
> So if you rustle cattle,
> I'll tell you what to do,
> Get the drop on Porter Rockwell,

Or he'll get the drop on you.
They say that Porter Rockwell
Is a scout for Brigham Young—
He's hunting up the unsuspects
That haven't yet been hung.
So if you steal one Mormon girl
I'll tell you what to do,
Get the drop on Porter Rockwell
Or he'll get the drop on you.

His favorite expletive was "Wheat in the bin." It was supposed to refer to the Gentiles and apostates he had blood atoned for the salvation of their souls.

When he wails through the night
His dread war cry
"Wheat . . . wheat!"
Somewhere a wife with her babes kneels to pray
For she knows she's a widow and orphans are they.

Each spring brought a new influx of settlers into the Tintic District, but two arch-pirates who came with the early ones were LeDuc, the French-Canadian, and his partner, Jack Gillin. This fine pair arrived in 1870.

Le Duc, a slender, good-looking, lithely built man, was, without a doubt, one of the unique characters in early Utah. Le Duc himself told so many stories of his background—to which was added a propensity for disguise—that it is impossible to give an accurate account of where he really came from.

Many incongruities in his character have added spice to the legend of the Frenchman, but that he tried his hand in many endeavors to make the fortune he was determined to have, is well authenticated. As far as is known, Le Duc never attached himself to a completely legitimate enterprise in his life. For him, it would have been out of character.

These two became the champion "high-graders" of Tintic and first saloon-keepers of the district. In the spring of 1870 they came into the camps with a pack train of whiskey and three hundred dollars starting cash. Gillin took over an abandoned claim, "salted" it, and left Tintic with over twenty-two thousand dollars profit; but by a quirk of fate the abandoned shaft he had salted became the Eagle and Blue-Bell Mining Company, the greatest gold-producing mine in Tintic.

Over in Mammoth, his partner Le Duc had hit upon his own get-rich quick scheme. The Frenchman by now had established his second saloon, but in the Mammoth Mine above him he saw more wealth made in a day than he could make in a lifetime tending bar, thriving as business was.

The Mammoth was at this time emptying her first glory holes of gold—gold that even now adorns the Utah State Capitol—and Le Duc suddenly developed an intense interest in an "ore collection." Could his customers perhaps bring him some really good specimens? He would be glad, he informed the Mammoth miners, to trade drinks for high-grade speciments. Rich ore from the Mammoth mine began slipping over Le Duc's bar and the floor in the back storeroom of his saloon began to glitter.

In this way, the Frenchman amassed a fortune, and when Le Duc disappeared, the Mammoth belatedly realized that she had been robbed. Federal authorities were called in and a state-wide search was on. Word went out over the Territory of Utah that the missing saloon keeper was a hunted man.

After selling his stolen ores, Le Duc went to the old Salt Lake House, one of the early hotels of the Utah city. While the search was on for him, he never left his room in the daytime, but at night he went boldly out into the streets. He attended theatres, wandered to the various resorts, took in the early-day versions of the night club, and in general lived it up, thoroughly enjoying his stolen money. Officers finally gave up the search, reasoning that the wily half-breed had slipped through their hands and out of the Territory.

Many years later, the death-bed confession of a Salt Lake City milliner cleared up the mystery. This milliner had, for a very handsome price, provided Le Duc with a wig of long dark curls and a woman's attire. It answered the question of what had become of the free-spending young lady with the long curls who had been such a familiar figure about the gay spots of Salt Lake.

His partner was never apprehended either . . . both got away clean as a mine whistle.

The folklore of this camp is rich in true stories of people good and bad, admirable and pathetic.

There is the story of the Hermitess of the Desert, Ginger, a former saloon girl, disfigured in a saloon fight, who was taken care of by the miners for the rest of her life.

Stories from the "Rainbow Era" during the eighties and nineties are abundant. But one of the most vicious characters ever to cut a swath of destruction through this camp was a man known as Hank Parish. Hank drifted in from the mining camps of Montana and Colorado and was soon known throughout the Tintic district as a dangerous bully. He became quarrelsome and mean when he drank, and upon one such occasion provoked a quarrel with a well liked little cripple known as "Peg Leg." Peg Leg was small but his courage wasn't to be measured by his size when Hank slapped him in the face, and the "bad man" was immediately challenged to a gun duel.

It was more than Parish had gambled for, and Hank knew that this time he had hit the wrong man. The time for the duel was fixed for five o'clock in the afternoon back of the main street saloons. As the little man limped up the street, living up to his agreement to shoot it out, Hank Parish murdered him. A shot in the back from behind a fence was Hank's way of doing it.

> "Oh, whiskey, oh, whiskey
> You've been my downfall
> If the ocean was whiskey,
> I'd drink up it all."

The familiar refrain wobbled its way up Church Street in Tintic for years and as the off-key tremors quivered into the distance residents of the camp knew that Little Billy King, the printer, was on his way home.

For a half-century, Billy never left Tintic for any reason other than to attend an occasional funeral. He preferred his friends there and stayed away from strangers. Every morning for twenty years, Billy walked the six miles around the mountain to the offices of the *Mammoth Record,* seldom wearing a coat summer or winter. Liquor always stood Billy a stout substitute for food, or fuel.

Billy lived in a little one room cabin where the wind and snow blew in through cracks in the walls. Even in winter, Billy made a fire only to cook what little he ate. Snow blowing in through unmended openings drifted into the room, but Billy slept as if he were in a heated room. Billy called his home "Paltry Palace." Quaint, but lovable, he was a genuine character-about-town.

While under the influence, Billy imagined himself in all kinds of heroic roles. His favorite fancy was that he was a great prize-fighter. After a few drinks, the slightly-built little printer would relate stories of the battles he had engaged in. He was known in the camps as "The Belfast Spider."

When Billy had consumed more Valley Tan than he could handle, he would hike up the mountain to a favorite spot on a sunny ledge where he slept away the warm afternoon.

Billy awakened from one such midday nap to see Tom Spaulding running up the hill with a butterfly net in his hand. Tom was keenly interested in entomology and spent his spare time collecting specimens of the many butterflies that frequented the mountain valleys.

Billy watched the newcomer fishing in the sky and decided that this stranger needed help. Making his way down the mountain, he laid a gentle hand upon Tom Spaulding's shoulder.

"You come on down to the saloon with me," Billy said kindly, "and I'll fix you up."

"Oh, I'm all right," Spaulding answered, "I'm just chasing bugs."

"Sure, sure," Billy agreed sympathetically. "But you come with me before they get you. I've had 'em myself . . . only with me it's lizards."

The Overland Pony Express raised the dust twenty miles west of the Tintic Towns where Faust and Fish Springs relay stations were the district stops. Remains of these Pony Express stations can be seen today.

For the first three years of the life of Tintic the mail was brought into the camps by pony express. This pony express is not to be confused with the Overland. It was the same type of service, but an independent branch that operated from the Pelican Point relay station.

First telegraph service was brought to Silver City camp in 1871 with Don C. Johnson as operator. However, it was not until 1878 that Utah Southern Railroad reached into Tintic District with a line to Ironton and Uncle Sam established a post office in November, 1880, with Pat Cusic as postmaster. Salt Lake and Western Railroad then came into Silver City in 1883 and the stagecoach lines that had serviced the district gave way to the railroads. Then, in 1891, Rio Grande Western began construction of "the railroad that couldn't be built" through Little Valley of Homansville. Surveying rugged Pinion Canyon, experts declared, "It is impossible. No one could ever put a railroad through that canyon."

Rio Grande, however, had one brilliant engineer who carefully studied this route. Night and day he pored over his board, drawing and re-drawing plans. "I can build it," he told Rio Grande officials. Unbelieving, they nevertheless gave him the assignment.

The route laid down by the survey looked insane. It wound around mountain sides, first on one side of the canyon then over to the other. Sometimes the direction changed back toward the mouth of the canyon while the route continued to climb up. Seven high trestles were provided reaching hundreds of feet long, and at one point a giant loop was made to pass high up above the lower track. But the engineer who planned this road suffered a nervous breakdown from overwork and it was necessary to send him to a mental hospital. Somewhere along this line, there should be a mounment erected to him.

The sport of these camps was never what you could call a relaxing kind. Diversions of the boom camps were active, busy, and lusty . . . but one of the highlights of any holiday was the rock drilling contests.

Before the days of the mechanical drill, the "buzzies," blasting holes in the mines were drilled by hand. This daily stint developed experts on the double jack. In flashes of silver, the hammers fell on the heads of the drills with an amazing speed, the hammers striking as high as eighty-five to ninety blows a minute.

The highest prize money paid in the West was paid for the rock drilling contests. One champion from Butte, Montana, collected thirteen thousand dollars in prize money—that was when a dollar was a dollar.

The single and double-jackers of the boomers of the basin are memories now—men of yesterday. But no machine could equal their symmetry, nor match their speed. It was only the body weariness of a man that defeated him against the inexhaustible buzzies.

Best known newspapers of Tintic district were the *Mammoth Record, The Tintic Miner,* and *Eureka Report.* Their editors were of the old-time independent breed, some really good newsmen, but all displaying a common characteristic of a huge curiosity about everything in general. Early editors were I. E. Diehl, Charles S. King, and C. E. Rife. Some of the early ads are priceless:

Over in Mammoth camp, F. V. V. Doane, the barber, wrote his own copy:

DANDERINE

Cures that dandruff itching head,
Regenerates life in hair that's dead,
Brings back flowing hair so pert,
That disease plucked out in lingering lert,
All that's necessary, let it soak.
On shining heads it does the work,
Hair's normal beauty it will restore,
The public's endorsement you can't ignore.
COME SEE—F. V. V. Doane, your barber

Nearly every paper carried the ads of "I, SAM."

Sam Locke, the district man of all trades, was a consistent and faithful believer in advertising. Sam was a shoemaker, window shiner, carpenter, paper hanger, wood cutter, plumber, and exceptionally gifted painter who used two paint brushes at the same time! His ads always started with, "I SAM LOCKE . . . ."

This familiar figure on the boardwalks of Tintic was staunchly British. He continually defended Queen Victoria and British foreign policy in this equally staunch Irish-Catholic camp.

Sam was always in a fist fight.

Labor troubles ebbed and flowed from 1880 on, as mines, men, money, hours, and working conditions jockeyed for place between worker and owner. The bitterest strike in Tintic history occurred in 1892. The cause of this trouble was an old bone of contention, the company owned enterprises, particularly the boarding houses.

At this time, the miners' wages were $1.70 a day and board. For this, they worked twelve hours a day. The mercantiles, stores, meat markets, and homes, were all company owned, and the men lived, bought, and traded at these establishments which were owned by the mine they worked for.

Then, the boarding houses of the district raised their rates to $1.25 a day over the prevailing dollar average, and the miners gathered in angry groups while meetings were held in the Union Hall. Space does not allow for a detailed account of this bitter tug of war that settled scores for all the miners of Utah but this issue was fought to a standstill in the Tintic district. There were shootings, hundreds of fistfights, riots and parades. This strike was never settled until the Utah Legislature passed the Boarding House Bill making it a misdemeanor for any company to compel employees to board or buy at one particular place. Working conditions were not what they are today by any means, nor were safety regulations, although in all fairness to the mines, reasonable precautions were always taken.

Mine disasters pointed up the superstitions that existed among the miners . . . a matter of little known knowledge among readers of wesern lore. But there were superstitions among the miners, as common as among the sailors of the sea. Saxon or Celt, these beliefs about the mines had come with them from the old world. One was the "Tommy Knockers."

The Cornishmen said that the wail of the dead could be heard from those who had been killed in the mines. These experienced miners, for generations accustomed to the dangerous work below, feared nothing about a mine except these spirits. It is told in one of their ballads:

THE TOMMY KNOCKERS

'Av you 'eard of the Tommy Knockers
In the deep dark mines of the West
Which the Cornish miners 'ear?
Ah, tis no laughin' jest,
For I'm a Cornish miner,
An' I'll tell you of it today,
Of the 'knock-knock-knock' of the tiny pick,
As we work in the rock an' clay.
We go down in the skips with our buckets,
With 'earts which nothing fazes,
Each man with a candle to light the way,
Through the tunnels, winzes an' raises,
An' the stale air smells of powder,
An' the mine is full of sound,
But 'tis only the noise of a Tommy Knocker,
Which makes our 'earts rebound.
"Pick . . . pick . . . pick"
Some one be'ind us knocked,
('Tis souls of dead miners)
For they're locked in the earthen wall,
Those that found death down there.
An' 'tis the 'knock-knock-knock' of their pick,
W'ich makes on end stand our 'air.
So we leave the 'aunted place,
For we won't work where they be.
An' w'e'ere we 'ear them knockin'
We sure will always flee.

For it means w'o ever 'ears it
Will be the next in line,
For the pick, pick, pick of the Knockers
Is a last an' awful sign.

There were those among the Cornishmen who claimed to have heard the warning of the phantom pick in certain parts of a mine. Once this warning had been given, nothing could induce a Cornish miner to work these drifts. They would refuse, saying they had been warned by the dead of danger in the area.

A typical success story, but with a benign overcast that leaves yet a mystery played in the shadowed depths of a mine two thousand feet below, is that of Utah's well-known Mormon, Jesse Knight.

This man was unusual among mining magnates, in that his fortune was dedicated to a church . . . and that was before he either found the mine or made the fortune.

Jesse Knight became known as the man who saved the credit of the Mormon Church . . . almost single-handedly built her university, and stood good the payment of her million dollar debts.

Jesse, his widowed mother, and two brothers, crossed the American plains in 1850 to the marching hymn of the Mormon Church, "Come, Come, Ye Saints"; and whether or not one is a Mormon, this is one of the most moving and stirring, if slightly militant, hymns ever written.

Jesse Knight was five years old when the company reached the Great Salt Lake. Four days after their arrival, the mother had, with the assistance of her small sons, begun the construction of an adobe cabin. Here she opened a school and supported her children by teaching, doing needlework, and washing. Her life was a continuous fight for existence. From the time the boy arrived in Deseret, Jesse Knight knew nothing but hunger, hardship and struggle. He herded cows barefoot over the rock and stubble of fields, gathered pigweed and sego roots to add to the family's meager food supply, and was dressed incongruously in homespun, in sacks, and in madeovers of any description.

At sixteen Jesse was doing a man's job in a logging camp where he worked for a man who treated him well and fairly. One of the reasons Jesse Knight was a good employer himself was because of the kind of treatment he received from this man who remembered his own hardships . . . the western frontier dealt out hardship enough for all.

After his marriage to Amanda McEwan, the Knights had five children and it was during a time of serious illness that one of them died and Jesse Knight was re-converted to the Mormon Church. After the healing of his remaining four sick children, which was attributed to "the laying on of hands" of the Mormon elders, Jesse Knight pledged his future, and his fortune to the Mormon Church.

Many men were passing through the town the Knight family lived in telling of the rich deposits of ore being uncovered in the western Oquirrh Range of the land of old Chief Tintic, and Jesse Knight began making prospecting trips into the range.

It was here, in Tintic Valley in 1896, as he stood on the slope of Mount Godiva, that Jesse Knight heard a voice say, "This country is here for the Mormons." He instantly had the overwhelming feeling that the message pertained to mining, and to the particular spot on which he stood. From that day, Jesse Knight confined his search for minerals to the Godiva Mountain area.

Thus began the unusual story, in the annals of western history of million dollar mines operated under benign influences.

One morning Jesse Knight turned to his son and made one of his pronouncements: "Will, I want to tell you something. We are going to have money . . . all the money we want, as soon as we are in a position to handle it properly. We will also someday save the credit of the Church."

Young Will Knight looked at his father in stunned disbelief. At the time, the Knight family had no money and were, as a matter of fact, heavily in debt; they had mortgaged their ranch as security for the money to develop Jesse's first mine, the Humbug.

Space does not permit a detailed account of Jesse Knight's

106

ability to point the way to ore body after ore body where none seemingly existed, but the millions that piled up in the banks attested to his success. And it was as he had predicted, when the properties and credit of the Church of Jesus Christ of Latter Day Saints were in jeopardy, Jesse Knight's wealth from the Tintic mines averted bankruptcy.

Knightsville was the seventh town of Tintic. Worthy and noteworthy among any saga of the boomers of the basin, from the standpoint of an almost unbelievable characteristic in mining towns . . . this camp was free of gambling, drinking, Sunday work days, and prostitution. Knightsville, owned lock, stock and barrel by "Uncle" Jesse, never had a saloon!

From the time of the first shipment of ores from the Tintic district, it was common knowledge in this wealthy mining country that she was being exploited by the outside smelter interest. Up to the time that Uncle Jesse waded into this free-for-all between Tintic and the smelters, in 1907, the district had constructed thirty mills and smelters in an effort to hit back at this as well as out of range freight rates. Tintic was still licking her wounds from numerous beatings by these outside powers when Jesse Knight decided to take them on.

First, he organized Tintic Smelting Company with a capital stock of one half million. From that time on the story is one of a very successful smelter . . . the most efficient operation in all Tintic history. But there is also an undercurrent of deliberate sabotage until the day Jesse's smelter was wrecked and put out of operation . . . no one ever knew how, for sure, but the job was done.

For example, builders neglected to erect the mill so the waste could run down by gravity, saving operating expense. Power companies refused to sell him electricity, coal companies wouldn't sell him coal, railroads wouldn't haul his coal from his own mine, water was refused him. The list of obstacles placed in his path is long. Despite every handicap hurled in his way, the Mormon giant built his smelter.

In the long run, Jesse won the battle, because for all Tintic district he forced a reasonable compromise from the smelters who handled the ores of the Oquirrh. Jesse Knight was a fine and honest steward of great wealth, a top source of his church's economy, and a stout fellow for all Tintic in any emergency.

The deaths of Tony West and Matteo Messa about the turn of the century when the Rainbow Era came to a close, marked the end of a way of life in this boomer on the edge of the desert.

Matteo Messa was one of the most incredibly kind and vital figures in the Tintic story; yet so typical of the "old timers" was he that a recount of his experiences gives the essence of the life.

Blessed with an instinct for handling animals, Matteo Messa became a freighter and while driving freight and supply wagons for the military, followed Johnston's army into Utah. He was born in Mexico and his memory went back to boyhood days upon the sea . . . from the rolling waters to the illimitible hills of his native land where he searched for the veins of silver. He was the story teller of the towns and enthralled the land-bound miners with tales of seafaring days and of pulse-quickening times on the decks of the whalers.

Matty was one of the few more interested in what lay above the ground that in what was beneath it. In the surging tides of battle he took little part, respecting all men, but none of them too much.

If Matteo died poor, it was by choice. Like many who came to Utah with the military, Matty had gone prospecting for gold. When ore was discovered in the Ophir area, he went to that camp where he made a rich strike. Matteo Messa made a fortune in old Ophir camp which, over the years, he gave away. Matty's bankroll, his food, his cabin, were shared with any man down on his luck. His soft Portuguese voice forever whispered encouragement to the discouraged.

Tony West, another of the early pioneers, was a Civil War veteran who had been a freighter in Montana and Nevada before he came in on the Tintic boomer. Tony was over eighty years old at the turn of the century and the boys in town had been concerned over his living so far from camp.

"Now what if you get sick out there all alone and need help, Tony?" they would ask. "How would anybody know?"

"I feel fine."

"Just the same, you better come into town," they would urge. "You could get sick and die out there all alone."

"Mebee I will," would be the undisturbed reply. "Man's gotta die sometime."

"Wonder what it'll be like up yonder, do you think, Tony?" the old man was asked upon one occasion. "Streets all paved with gold 'n such?"

"Don't rekon I'd be much at home in a place like that," replied Tintic's old timer, "druther look fer my own God and my own gold, streets full of gold don't interest me much. I'll jes' do my dyin' and trust that good Almighty to give me a place sumers in His mountains. Guess a big man like Him kin find a place fer old Tony."

They were like that, so many of them. Simple, trusting, accepting life in a way that voided frustrating complications.

CHAPTER NINE

Mercur

Sheep bells tinkle over what was once Mercur. This boomer, whose first claim was located April 20, 1870, is one of today's ghosts; a parched and thirsty one, located in Manning Canyon of the Oquirrh Mountain range in Utah, in Tooele County, 28 miles west of American Fork.

The first location, a placer claim, was located by L. Greeley. After this strike, The Sparrow Hawk, Last Chance, and Marion claims were surveyed for patent in 1872. Silver ore claims assaying as high as $4,000 and $5,000 a ton were sold to an English syndicate, but Mercur only carried "pockety" claims and this company lost its shirt in a shirttail camp. The story of Mercur is that of much more being expended than extended. The English company spent seven hundred thousand on a mill and development work—they made only one hundred thousand.

After the Sparrow Hawk was discovered, a rich strike was made on Carrie Steele. But Carrie was only a "pocket" also—rich enough, for the men who owned it made $83,000 in three months. This brought on the swarm of prospectors and the town of Lewiston was built on what is the present site of Mercur. No steady producers were ever located, however, and Lewiston, which had become a town of 1,500 people by 1880 gradually dwindled down to one house and one inhabitant. Again, in Lewiston it is estimated that $350,000 was taken out, but many times that amount had been spent.

Mercur was named by a Bavarian, Arie Pinedo, in 1879. Pinedo, who found the Mercur lode, believed he had discovered cinnabar and named his claim after its product—mercury. As Mercury in German is "der Merkur," the name of the town grew from that.

Mercur's gold discovery was made in 1883. About 1890, the cry for more gold and less silver was going up in the West, and a group of promoters consisting of John Dern, E. H. Airis, G. S. Peyton, and Hal W. Brown organized the Mercur Gold Mining and Milling Company. The first plant was built at Manning, which is located three miles south of Mercur in Manning Canyon, because water was available in this area.

These men adopted the McArthur-Forrest cyanide process for the treatment of the gold ores, a process that saved Manning. When this treatment of the ores proved workable, Captain J. L. De La Mar in 1885 bought the Golden Gate group located near the Mercur Mine. After two years of methods improvement, Golden Gate became the major factor in Mercur activities employing most of the Mercur miners. In 1889 De La Mar joined with Mercur interests and formed Consolidated Mercur Gold Mines Company and Consolidated was the prime factor in the life of this camp until 1917.

Mercur owned an interesting railroad line, the Salt Lake & Mercur Railroad. Originally the line brought ore from the Mercur area three miles south to Manning Mill. The tracks were then extended on down the canyon to Fairfield to connect with Union Pacific. This provided an all-rail route from Salt Lake City via Lehi and Fairfield. James W. Neill gave an account of a ride on the Salt Lake and Mercur:

"This railroad is a wonder to the traveler: the trip over it is well worth the taking even if the mining camp at its western end were no attraction. . . . it is twelve miles long and in four miles of it you can't find a straight rail. It crosses a divide 1,800 feet above the Fairfield station, reaching this point by a series of curves, loops, twists and turns which fairly make one dizzy, and discounts any of the scenery on the famed Marshal Pass on the D. & R. G. Railway or the Hagerman Pass of the Colorado Midland. The single car is taken over by a diminutive engine of the Shay type, and at every turn, the passenger holds his breath for fear this little

111

machine will actually jump over what, to all appearances, is the end of the track. . . ."

Mercur "boomed" and "busted" in three different periods of history which could be roughly separated into 1870-1893, or the Lewiston period, 1890-1917, when the town of Mercur proper flourished; and 1933, when W. F. Snyder and Sons took over the Consolidated Mercur properties. It has been a boomer with a highly uncertain record of activity, but maybe some new discovery will make it good for a fourth try.

Residents of Mercur who moved on to prominence in the state and nation were D. C. Jackling and George H. Dern. Jackling was the builder of Golden Gate Mill and the man who founded the open cut mining method which revolutionized mining.

George H. Dern was general manager and superintendent of the Consolidated Company at twenty-nine years of age. He later gained national prominence as governor of the state of Utah from 1924 to 1930, and as Secretary of War under Franklin D. Roosevelt. His last comments of life in the old town are poignant:

". . . and if we wanted to roam the hills, we either did our roaming on our own power or rode horseback. So long as I live I shall cherish the memory of dear old Topsy, my saddle horse, known to everybody in town.

"Not only were we in horse and buggy days, but we were also in that primitive age when there were no movies. Can you imagine that? How did we ever stand it?

"We stood it fine. I venture to say that every old Mercurite today will say with fervent sincerity, 'Those were the happiest days.' At this time, Mercur was a one-mine Camp, and we were all working for, or dependent upon, the same company, and were one big, happy family.

"It was an ideal community life. Nobody high-hatted anybody else. Everybody knew everybody else, and everybody was interested in everybody else."

The nostalgia expressed by Governor Dern is shared by many others for the first week of every September the old timers go back for the Mercur Pioneer Reunion. For a long time these were gala occasions with excursions, picnics, and all sorts of games of skill, and oratory. But as usually happens the ranks of those who remembered the old camp grew ever thinner. The games and the oratory no longer had the same robust appeal. But the old tales can still be told.

Mercur, they say, was such an exuberant town because of the fine quality of its sidehill whiskey and because water was too expensive to drink. The only spring was owned by a man named Nicholsen, who dispensed it by the cup and bucketful.

Just around the mountain was the rival camp of Ophir, which the Mercurites claimed got its name because disgusted prospectors would take one look and exclaim, "Oh, fer Gawd's sake!" But when water was struck in Ophir in 1895 that could be piped to Mercur the rival camp went up in esteem for it broke the water merchant's monopoly.

A favorite tale told at the reunions was of the fist fight between Soda Water Fred and Horse Jaw Kid for the affection of Katie, the pretty waitress. Jack Schaefer, proprietor of the Mercur Hotel, acted as promoter and the fight was held in a dance hall, the winner to take the girl and the receipts. Schaefer was referee and his partner took in the money. Horse Jaw claimed a foul which Schaefer, wanting the bout to last longer, wouldn't allow.

Staggering to the center of the ring Horse Jaw shouted. "Milner took the money at the gate, Schaefer refereed the fight, and Soda Water owes Schaefer twenty dollars, so how in hell can I win?"

He couldn't. In an interview later Schaefer said, "Katie was in cahoots with me on the deal. The gate was $20.15 and Soda Water Fred and Horse Jaw lost out on the deal, girl and all." Katie married a wealthy Easterner and became known in society from coast to coast.

In its prime Mercur could swagger with the best of them.

CHAPTER TEN

Frisco

The most dead and deserted looking of all Utah boom towns is Frisco, in the middle of the desert. To find anything drearier one would need to drive acrosss the desert in a southerly direction to a place known as the Mountain Meadows where one can almost feel the presence of the ill-fated Fancher party sitting around their ghostly campfires, wondering if they might not have been wiser to have fought to the death rather than surrender to an apparently kindly disposed enemy who shot them down like animals after they had given up their weapons.

There is nothing left of Frisco except a few old foundations of buildings, and old dumps of the Horn Silver mine a mile distant. In its day, like several other noted mines, such as the Emma and the Ontario, the Horn Silver claimed to be the richest silver mine in the world.

Frisco was one of an allied triumvirate of wealthy camps which sprang into existence in the 1870's: Pioche, Nevada, and Frisco and Silver Reef in Utah. Pioche was the older of the three, and it was miners from there who flocked into the other two camps when their booms started. The camps had many things in common, including their source of supplies. They were plagued by the same outlaws, and they all knew the same man who did most to clean them up, a man of mystery named Pearson whose first name was either unknown or has been forgotten. He was at various times marshal of two of the towns, and was not unknown in the other, and was far more ruthlessly efficient than any of the far better known marshals whom books and television shows have made household names. Where he came from and where he went no man seems to know.

Frisco's history properly begins more than twenty years and a little less than a hundred miles from where and when Frisco came into existence. It might be said to have begun when Brigham Young sent Isaac Grundy into Iron County to start a foundry in 1852. This venture was not too successful, but in 1858 at a point midway between the towns of Beaver and Milford, a Mormon named James A. Rollins came upon an old Spanish mine containing almost pure lead ore, and it provided much needed lead for the early Mormon settlements. At first it was called the Rollins mine, a name later changed to the Lincoln mine.

Beaver was at that time the metropolis of the entire region, and it had a small mining boom of its own, but it had a larger connection with the later one in Frisco, principally because much of the outlaw element used the peaceful Mormon town as a base for supplies until the Mormon peace officers got too rough. It was in Beaver that John D. Lee, chief executioner at the Mountain Meadows Massacre, was tried and convicted.

Beaver, however, soon gave way in importance to the struggling little frontier town of Milford, which became the shipping point for Frisco, forty-eight miles to the west, when silver was discovered in the Horn Silver mine. Two of the great titans of American finance, Jay Cooke and Jay Gould, played an important part in extending the Utah Southern Railroad from Milford to Frisco.

Jay Cooke, the New York banker, though in financial difficulties, had bought the Horn Silver mine. Cooke was the man mostly responsible for financing the Union during the Civil War, and "solid as Cooke's bank" was the ultimate in financial stability. But Cooke had got into trouble trying to finance the Great Northern Railroad. He called on his friend Jay Gould for assistance, and Gould was instrumental in getting the railroad built, of which the Mormon church owned one-fourth interest and the Union Pacific the rest.

Cooke had heard of the marvelous mining development in Frisco through an associate named Lycurgus Edgerton. The two started for Utah, but Edgerton died of a heart attack on the way. Cooke went on and bought the Horn Silver property for five million dollars. From a hole 900 feet long, 400 feet wide, and 900 feet deep the Horn Silver produced $54,000,000.00 in ten years.

In those days freighting was big business. Always eager to find a market for their produce, the Mormons could welcome the opening of a new mining camp despite their disapproval of its morals. There was no tougher town than Pioche in all the West, though it failed to get the publicity enjoyed by tamer towns such as Dodge City and Tombstone; but its population had to eat, and the Mormon farmers from as far away as Sanpete Valley had potatoes, onions, carrots, and other vegetables, as well as hay and grain, that they had to sell. Their freight wagons began to roll over the sagebrush flats and the juniper and cedar covered plateaus.

For a time York, and then Juab, in Juab County was the railhead, and heavy goods as well as food was hauled away from these places by horse, mule, and ox teams. Black Rock, in Millard County, was the last jumping off place. From there it was a long weary road to Pioche, and the country was infested by outlaws as well as the hazards of nature.

Rustling was a recognized occupation, and the state of Nevada was a sanctuary for the badmen who preyed upon the supposedly mild Mormons, who were not always as mild as they were thought to be. At Beaver thirty-eight men were convicted of grand larceny.

Because the three camps of Pioche, Frisco, and Silver Reef were so closely allied, it is necessary that their mutual problems be discussed here. The chief authority for this section is a lecture by Dr. William R. Palmer, known as the dean of Southern Utah historians, delivered to the Utah State Historical Society May 9, 1958, and printed in the *Utah State Historical Quarterly* for October, 1958. What follows is a digest of that speech with no attempt to copy it verbatum.

Before the other two camps became populated, Pioche was the primary market for the Mormon farmers. Mr. Palmer was a youthful clerk in a Cedar City store, and so was in a position to know what was going on.

It was a relatively easy matter for the Mormons to haul their freight to Pioche, but getting home with the much needed money was a different proposition. They resorted to various stratagems in hiding their money, the favorite method being to bore secret holes in their wagons. But this was not always successful—nor did the bandits escape unscathed.

At first the Mormons were welcomed by the miners, but the time came when the Pioche merchants began to squeeze the peddlers. Since the goods could not be of uniform quality, they picked out the best, forcing the Mormons to peddle the remainder from door to door. Not liking this, the merchants hired "goon" squads to harry and beat up the peddlers. Since it was impossible for the Mormons to haul their stuff back home, and they needed the money for tithing and missionary work, they took what they could get and ran the risk of being robbed of that on their return journey. Many a Mormon farmer found himself looking down a gun barrel when he rounded a hill.

One such was a Millard County man who was held up by two robbers. Finding no money after a search of his person, one of them held a gun on him while the other wrapped a whiplash around his thumbs, about six inches apart, then inserted the whip-stock in the loop and began to twist. The Mormon refused to talk, but while the torture was going on the other man found the money where it had been hidden in the folds of the wagon cover. The Mormon drove his team into Frisco, where his wounds were dressed; but then he had to go to Salt Lake, where both thumbs were amputated at the second joint.

Two other robbers did not do so well, and it can only be hoped that they were the same ones. A Mormon named Athe Meeks, of Parowan, had been to Pioche and disposed of his load. On a previous trip he had taken his little eight-year-old daughter, Sadie, to stay with an aunt who lived in Pioche. Returning with only the running gears of his wagon, he had placed their bedding on the back hounds, and the little girl was perched there with a rope across the top of the bolster for her to hold onto. Meeks sat on a horse blanket on the front bolster with his feet on the tongue hounds.

Six or eight miles out of the little Mormon settlement of Panaca, two bandits with drawn guns rode out in front and stopped his two span of mules, ordering Meeks to throw up his hands. Instead, Meeks dropped down between the wheelers and pulled a gun from his boot top. The men were trying to shoot him, but the lead mules were turning around and they couldn't get a bead on him. Meeks shot the front outlaw, a man named Al Miller, dead. The other outlaw, known as Little Frank, was riding alongside the wheel mule trying to get a shot at Meeks, who grabbed the horses's reins and gave a jerk. The horse reared, Little Frank's shot went wild, and Meeks shot him in the chest. Little Frank dropped his gun and spurred away, but Meeks wounded the running horse.

Meantime, the mules had turned around and were running back down the road with Sadie clinging desperately to her rope. When the mules reached Panaca, they slowed to a trot and men on the street stopped them. Sadie told them she thought her father had been killed. A posse was quickly formed, but up the road a mile or so they met an exhausted Meeks who was running as he had never run before.

Al Miller's body was still in the road, and Peter Fife took the trail of the other man. A couple of miles out in the cedars Fife found both Little Frank and his horse dead.

Meeks drove home, and though he knew the Nevada outlaws had sworn vengeance against him, he made many more trips to Pioche, though it is improbable that he ever took a child with him again. Always when he crossed the Nevada line and passed through Hell's Gate, he carried a rifle across his knees and pistols in his boot tops. But the word had gone out that he was a dangerous man to molest, and he had no further trouble.

Athe Meeks was a nephew of Priddy Meeks, well known doctor and philanthropist, but according to Mrs. Peter Nielsen, of Springville, Utah, a distant cousin, was utterly unlike the kindly, benevolent Priddy. He was, says Mrs. Nielsen, a remarkably large and handsome man who never stood any nonsense from anyone.

Once he was assigned to guard an outlaw named Backman in a covered wagon. When the man started to climb out, Athe Meeks ordered him back, and when he refused Meeks calmly shot him dead.

Athe Meeks, one of the men who gave the lie to the belief that Mormons wouldn't fight, lived out his life in Parowan, and the little girl who took the wild ride in Panaca married a Parowan man, and for many years these were the dominating figures in the community.

Another notorious outlaw named Nate Hansen was shot dead by a deputy sheriff as he was trying to drive a bunch of stolen horses across the state line. He got within a mile of the line, but no farther.

A Utah deputy named David Bulloch one day came upon the tracks of a band of shod horses, and supposing rightly that they were stolen from the freighters, trailed them into Pioche. He found the horses and was told that a dark-complexioned man from Utah and a well known Nevada outlaw had brought them in. Bulloch guessed who the dark-complexioned man was and went into a saloon looking for him, and found his man standing at the bar. He said, "Come on, Bob, I've come for you, and we're going back to Cedar City right now."

Four men at a gambling table drew their guns and formed a half circle around Bulloch. One of them said, "You don't have to go, if you don't want to, Bob."

Bulloch retorted, "You're dog-gone right, Bob, you're going to go, and I don't want any trouble about it either."

Bob knew Bulloch of old and said he had worked for Bulloch's father and didn't want anything to happen to him, so he put out his hands to be handcuffed, and the gamblers resumed their game. Bob went back to Cedar City, was convicted of grand larceny, and served out his sentence.

Dr. Palmer comments: "A remarkable thing about that arrest was that a Nevada sheriff was in the saloon, and didn't lift a finger to help Sheriff Bulloch because Bulloch was a Mormon from Utah."

Freighting persisted well into the present century, even after

119

automobiles came into use. Nat Gardner, of Cedar City, was hauling a load of grain to DeLamar, but sold out when he reached Caliente. Two men watched him receive his money and put it in his pocket. The wind was blowing hard; so to keep the wagon cover from being blown away Gardner folded it in quarters and lay down under it for warmth and drove his team with the lines passed through a crack between the two sections of the wagon-box.

Near Panaca a car circled him and halted on his right, stopping his team. One of the men he had noticed got out of the car and ordered Gardner to stand up and thrown his coat on the ground, then empty his pockets and throw the contents on the coat.

Gardner, an ex-police officer, obeyed, but scattered everything as much as possible. When the bandit reached to pick up the valuables Gardner grabbed his own rifle and ordered the bandit to thrown up his hands.

Gardner had both men covered, and made the second man get out of the car and kick the gun under the wagon. Then he said to the man who had drawn on him, "Take off your overcoat and throw it down; put your coat on top of it; take that sweater and your hat off and thrown them down."

"Good hell, man," the outlaw pleaded, "have mercy. You wouldn't turn a man out on a cold day like this in his shirt sleeves, would you?"

"Do what I say, and do it quick," Gardner commanded. "You didn't think of that when you were stripping me." The man stripped, and Gardner made him turn his pockets inside out. He told them they could pick up their things at the marshal's office in Panaca the next day, but the things were never called for. Nor did the Nevada officers make much effort to apprehend the men.

Most colorful of all the outlaws, as well as one of the meanest, who somehow has escaped the attention of Western writers, was old Ben Tasker, who maintained a place at Desert Springs just inside the Utah line, handy to the communications lines between Pioche, Frisco, and Silver Reef.

Tasker had been educated for the ministry and could "quote Bible by the yard." He lived there with a Negro woman known

120

A section of the Bingham Canyon copper mine, largest open-pit copper mine in the world. *Courtesy Willard Luce.*

Traffic in Bingham, Utah, the one street town. A short dead end street comes in from the right; Main Street is steep, narrow, and crooked. *Courtesy Willard Luce.*

The Catholic graveyard is located on the hill across Bonanza Flats from Silver Reef, Utah. *Courtesy Willard Luce.*

One of the more pretentious graves in the Catholic Cemetery at Silver

The old Wells Fargo express building is still standing and in good repair at Silver Reef, Utah. *Courtesy Willard Luce.*

Grave of Michael Carbis is overgrown with Trees of Heaven. Carbis was killed by a Mexican worker

This general merchandise store at Frisco, Utah, was named after the town's most famous mine, The Horn Silver. Iron shutters were common features of such establishments in the stormy mining era of the Great Basin. *Courtesy Nell Murbarger.*

Historic court house at Belmont, Nye County, Nevada.

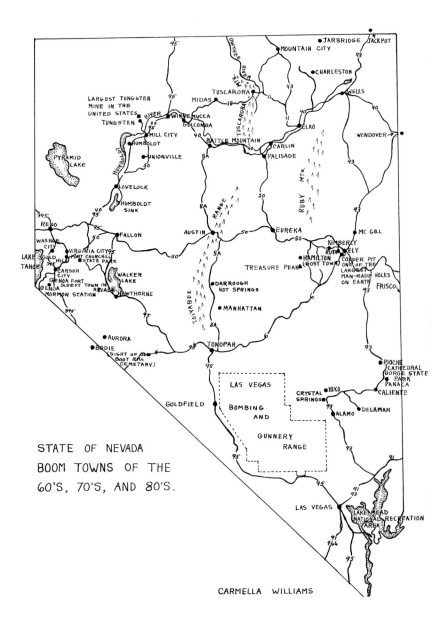

STATE OF NEVADA
BOOM TOWNS OF THE
60'S, 70'S, AND 80'S.

CARMELLA WILLIAMS

124

Freighting to DeLamar about 1895.

Ruins of Wells Fargo building at Treasure City, Nevada, 9,000 feet above sea level. Hamilton, three miles distant, via dim trail at right was 1,500 feet lower. *Courtesy Nell Murbarger.*

125

J. B. Withington Hotel at Hamilton, Nevada, erected in 1869 of sandstone and lumber ox-freighted from Oregon, was the most elaborate and costly structure of its kind in Nevada. For years after the town became a ghost, the building remained a showplace, collapsing only a few years ago. *Courtesy Nell Murbarger.*

This "tipsy" saloon is one of the two remaining buildings in one-time tough Charleston, Nevada. Site of the old town of the 1890's is now headquarters for a cattle ranch, and the two old buildings are used for storage purposes. *Courtesy Nell Murbarger.*

Diamond Field.

Bottle House, Rhyolite.

Early view of Tonopah.

All aboard for Silver Mountain.

as Nigger Lize, and his place was a hideout for the outlaws who plied their trade back and forth across the state line.

Tasker had two or three cellars dug into the hill in which he kept hindquarters of beef which he boldly peddled to the merchants of Pioche. The hides and heads he destroyed, and fed the front quarters to his pigs. The cattle, of course, were all stolen.

For years Tasker kept a German butcher named Engleking working for him but would not settle up with him. When Engleking insisted on leaving, Tasker gave him a few dollars and promised to settle up with him in Pioche. Engleking set out on foot for Pioche but never got there.

A few weeks later a freighter camped at Desert Springs went out in the cedars and came upon what looked to be a recently dug grave. Keeping his mouth shut, he waited until he saw one of the Iron County cowboy deputy sheriffs. When the grave was investigated, Engleking's body was found with a bullet through the head.

Tasker was arrested for murder and taken to Beaver to stand trial, but he bribed the guards and made his escape. Hurrying back to Desert Springs, he collected his money and guns, two horses and a pack outfit, and moved on to Mexico.

A few years later Anthony W. Ivins, later second highest authority in the Mormon church, who was a frontiersman and cattleman himself, and knew Ben Tasker, met him face to face when Ivins was head of the Latter-day Saint church in Mexico. Tasker was dressed in priestly garb and was pastor of the town's Protestant church.

The Mormon farmers and freighters felt competent to deal with Tasker and his outlaws, but the greedy merchants of Pioche were something else again. The price of grain was dropped to two cents a pound, about one-third what it should have been. Seeing his people being unmercifully robbed, Brigham Young personally took a hand in the matter.

"Don't go to them," he told the people. "Stay home, and they will come to you." His judgment was vindicated when the Pioche merchants, suddenly bereft of produce, came to Cedar City with

their hats in their hands begging the Mormons to resume freighting.

Down in St. George, in Utah's Dixie, where he spent his
winters, Brigham Young said, "This is a two-edged sword the
mining camps are swinging against us. They are as dependent
upon us as we are upon them. We will make the sword cut the
other way until they recognize that their game can be played by
our side, too."

When the Pioche merchants sought peace, Brigham appointed
an agent to deal with them and contract at Mormon prices, paying
for the goods, and the freight bill, as well, in advance, before the
wagons rolled.

The Mormon leader dealt with the crisis while trade was
stopped by establishing United Orders, in a number of towns, and
"Co-op" stores which issued script that served as currency. Dr.
Palmer, who was clerking in a Co-op store in Cedar City at the
time, said: "I weighed this produce at the granary and gave the
person a due bill for it. A notebook was tacked on the grain bin
in which I entered the receipts. Then tearing off the lower half
of the sheet on this I wrote, 'Good for 75 cents, or $1.35, or $4.20
(as it might be) payable in merchandise at the Cedar Co-op
store.'

"The due bill was good anywhere, and was used to pay the
salaries of schoolteachers, the children turning them over as part
of their tuition. The store due bills circulated around like cash
among the home people, and the Co-op store did a sort of produce
banking business."

In addition to this, Tithing Office due bills, called T.O. script,
was issued at St. George and was redeemable at any tithing office
in the church. There were many other forms of script issued by
private companies such as the Beaver Woolen Mills. One of the
most popular, says Palmer, was called K.K.K., Kane Kounty Kur-
rency, issued by the Bowman Mercantile Company of Kanab,
which issued small "bearer" checks in denominations of $1.00,
$2.00, $3.00, and $5.00, which were widely used to make change
for larger bills.

Once again Brigham Young and the Mormons proved that they

ere able to hold their own under any and all circumstances.

The opening of the much nearer Frisco camp and the building
f the railroad were welcomed by the freighters. Not only did
1ese developments provide a new and nearer market, but they
hortened the haul to Pioche and eliminated some of the outlaw
azards.

In 1875 two Pioche prospectors, James Ryan and Samuel
Iawkes, wandering through the San Francisco Mountains, ac-
identally discovered the Horn Silver mine on the hill a mile west
f where Frisco was to be built. Thus, said Murray Shick in the
alt Lake Mining Review in 1936, was an important link forged
etween strangely divergent men. ". . . No one, Jay Cooke least
f all, could picture him in connection with a pair of sun-browned
rospectors he had never seen piloting a burro train through sage-
lad mountains twenty-five hundred miles away. . . . Water rather
han minerals induced them to spread their blankets at a water
ole in the San Francisco mountains called Squaw Springs. Loath
o leave the water they scrutinized the neighborhood carefully.

" 'This ledge looks kind of good,' said one as he drove his pick
nto a limestone outcrop. It was good. Beneath the weathered
urface galena ore glistened in the sun. . . . They agreed it was a
onanza and scratched that name on a location notice."

True to prospector nature, Ryan and Hawkes sank a twenty-
ive foot shaft in solid ore, then went looking for a buyer. They
old the claim for $25,000 to Matt Cullen, Dennis Ryan, and
\. G. Campbell, and disappeared from the scene.

Because the ore bore a strong resemblance in color and texture
o the horn of an animal, and was so rich that it could be whittled
nd the slivers curled up like the horn of a mountain sheep, they
hanged the name to the Horn Silver, sank the shaft to a depth
f 280 feet and took out 25,000 tons worth $100 a ton. In 1879
hey sold out to Jay Cooke for five million dollars.

By this time Frisco was booming. Miners arrived from Nevada,
Colorado, Arizona, and the booming districts in the neighborhood
f Salt Lake City, and with them came the gunmen, gamblers and
lance hall girls. Frisco became as wild and tumultuous a town
s any in the Great Basin.

Unable to cope with the situation, the citizens brought in the indomitable Marshal Pearson from Pioche to clean up the town.

The *Utah State Guide Book* gives this account: "With the simple philosophy that dead men gave no trouble he put on a law enforcement campaign; there were no fines to be paid, no jail sentences to be served, and burial expenses were not excessive. Pearson gave a man a choice—shoot it out or leave town. Many tried to shoot it out, but Pearson had strong nerves and a quick trigger finger. He was known to have killed as many as six men in one night, and it finally became necessary to hire a 'body mover' to clean up after him. The wagon made the rounds every morning and hauled away one or two corpses; they were buried without questions or funeral announcements. Frisco acquired the reputation as the wildest camp in Utah. Each of the twenty-one saloons had its stories of killings. In one place two men were killed over fifty cents in a faro game. . . . But Jay Cooke was not concerned with the morals of the town."

Working conditions appear not to have been much better. The heat was sometimes 108 degrees in the mine and as many as forty miners a month went to the hospital with "miner's con," developed from the dust of the ore. Only DeLamar, a mining town over the border in Nevada, ever matched it as a widowmaker. Unfortunately, in both places young Mormon farmers who decided to try mining to eke out their incomes were the chief victims. Used to working in the fresh air, they were not able to withstand the poisonous dust that the miners were used to, and there were weeping and wailing in many a Mormon hamlet in Southern Utah.

Seldom had greed been more ruthlessly displayed. Production increased at a tremendous rate between 1880 and 1885, without proper safeguards. The Horn Silver was being gutted. Then one day as the night shift came off work and the day men were lined up waiting to go down, they were stopped by the mine officials who told them there had been a trembling in the shaft. A few minutes later the whole mine caved in with a crash that broke windows in Milford, fifty miles away. The dust rose in a blackening cloud. Hundreds of men could have been killed, but fortun-

tely not a life was lost. It was the practical death of the Horn
Silver.

A new shaft 910 feet deep was sunk at a cost of twenty-six
dollars a foot, but in the meantime the miners moved out, taking
their houses with them. Residential Grasshopper Street became a
pile of rubble, and Frisco itself a ghost town.

From time to time efforts were made to reopen the mine, and
in 1928 a new company was shipping 10,000 tons of ore a year,
but the old glory was gone. The railroad was torn out, and the
country is not much different from what it was when Ryan and
Hawkes arrived there in 1875. A few other mines were located
nearby, but the only ones who profited from them were the
brokers on the Salt Lake Stock Exchange.

The district did enjoy a sort of revival between 1905 and 1910
when Samuel Newhouse, the Salt Lake and Bingham capitalist,
reopened the old Cactus mine which had been filed on back in
1870, built a model town around it called Newhouse, and took
from it $3,500,000. It bore little resemblance to the old boom
towns, and had none of the lawlessness which made Frisco, just a
few miles away, notorious.

Frisco's greatest handicap was lack of water. During its heyday
all water was hauled a distance of seven miles. The price was four
cents a gallon. Needless to say nobody had running water in their
houses.

Today as one drives northwestward toward Garrison, a one-time
outlaw hangout on the Utah side of the Utah-Nevada line, where
the rustlers once held and fattened their stock, but which now is
a peaceful little farming community, one may occasionally see
wind or gas powered pumps over wells from which stockmen
water their stock, and in Wah Wah and other desolate, lonesome
valleys one may occasionally see a band of mustangs which indicate that the primitive conditions are still there.

Only once did Frisco make the headlines in this century. In
1922 the epic motion picture, *The Covered Wagon*, was made at
Garrison, which had been settled back in 1850. The director was
James Cruze, and the leading lady was Betty Compson. Both
were natives of Utah, but Miss Compson had the distinction of

having been born in Frisco. For sentimental reasons Miss Comp son decided to get married in the old ghost town, and newspaper all over the country ran the story. It was a gala occasion. Holloywood lived up to its reputation, the lack of water was n great handicap.

CHAPTER ELEVEN

Silver Reef— Where Silver Couldn't Be

Silver Reef was the smallest of the triumvirate of Pioche, Frisco, and Silver Reef, and it was unique in many ways. It was a place of contradictions. First, though allied with the other towns of the Great Basin, it was not geographically in it though the rim of the basin was no more than twenty-five miles distant and could easily be seen from it. Its drainage is into the Colorado river.

Second, it was a great silver producing camp from a geological structure where geologists and mining men agreed silver couldn't possibly exist.

Third, it was the one camp where those thoroughly incompatible interests, Mormons and Gentiles, got along harmoniously. They worked together, danced together, and sang together.

In 1877 the beloved Catholic Bishop Scanlon came to Silver Reef but had no place to hold services. The story is related by Mark Pendleton in his papers now on file in the archives of the Utah State Historical Society. "In 1879 . . . an invitation was extended Father, afterwards Bishop, Scanlon, by the Mormon authorities at St. George to hold services in their Tabernacle. A choir was needed, but as the Tabernacle choir did not know Latin it was thought that the singing of the Kyrie Eleison and Gloria and Credo could not be carried out. The leader of the choir asked for Catholic music and being given Peter's Mass, in two weeks his choir knew the Mass and could sing it in Latin. . . . High Mass was sung in the tabernacle, the Mormon choir executing it with great credit to themselves, rendering the Gloria and Hosanna in clear, sweet tones."

The Catholic Sisters at Silver Reef taught a school and many Mormon children attended it. The miners were welcomed at Mormon socials and dances at Leeds and Harrisburg.

Trade was fair and mutually profitable. The crusade against Mormon polygamists was at its height, but they were free to go and come in Gentile Silver Reef. When the U.S. Deputy Marshals, who were called "Cohab chasers," came into the country, they always put up at Silver Reef on their way to St. George, which was full of "Co-habs," but they never caught anybody; the reason was that the telegrapher at Silver Reef would wire his counterpart at St. George, whose office was in a furniture store, for "two chairs," the agreed upon signal that two officers were in the country. The polyg hunters never found anyone in St. George except sober monogamists, but they were usually conducted out of town to the tune of derisive songs.

It was not easy to convict a polygamist, for only the wives and children could give the damaging testimony, and they were adept at dodging perjury. Once in Kanab a little nine-year-old girl was put on the stand to testify against her father. When asked if she had a half brother, she replied very earnestly that all her brothers were *whole*. The Gentiles of Silver Reef remained strictly neutral.

Silver Reef is only some twenty miles north of St. George, the Mormon capitol of Dixie. It is in a chopped up, irregular basin surrounded by sandstone reefs of brilliant coloring from white to vermillion. A great pine-covered mountain looms above it, and once it was the scene of violent volcanic eruptions. In no other similar formation in the world have precious metals ever been found, except copper in one comparable place in Russia.

This was a fact readily understood by the miners of Pioche, who laughed heartily at the gullibility of the Mormons who were hunting for silver in sandstone.

The history of three towns within five miles of each other are tied in with the district: the little Mormon towns of Leeds and Harrisburg, and Silver Reef itself. Of the three, only Leeds remains, a quiet little town on Highway 91. Above Leeds was Harrisburg, an agricultural community at the foot of Pine Valley

Mountain. A network of streams bearing such names as Quail Creek run through canyons bearing the names of Water Canyon, Dick's Canyon, and Harrisburg Canyon, join with Cottonwood Creek, finally emptying into the Virgin River. Harrisburg was built at this junction, the first home being built by Moses Harris.

By another of those queer coincidences Dick's Canyon was named after an Indian who was the real discoverer of ore at Pioche.

By May of 1864 there were sixteen families and 128 people in Harrisburg. Orchards and vineyards were planted, and Quail Creek diverted from its channel two miles above Silver Reef for irrigation purposes. In those days freight wagons from St. Louis to Los Angeles, by way of Las Vegas, passed this way and Harrisburg became a favorite stopping place for the freighters, some of whom established homes there.

Leeds and Harrisburg were much the same, typical Mormon farming communities, but Harrisburg received its death blow when its water was diverted to what seemed better land to the pioneer settlers, and only a few houses remained. The kind of houses they were, however, is told by Marietta M. Mariger in her book, *Saga of Three Towns,* which describes her mother's house.

"As one entered the front gate, a row of great smooth flag stones beckoned one on into the house. But one had to stop and look at the two neat plots of lawn that were on either side of the path, each with an immense mulberry tree in one corner. Arrived at the front door, one entered a large rock room carpeted with a Brussels or 'States' carpet, (as my grandmother called it) and furnished as comfortably with rockers, sofa, center table, a hanging book case, what-nots, bric-a-brac, etc., as any modern home. Another great stone room opened from this, the two being the front of the house. Either room had a door leading to the back opening onto a 3/4 enclosed screen porch, on one side of which was a bedroom, on the other the kitchen. This house was so immaculate the fairies themselves must have been busy little people while the family slept.

"At the back door, one went down a flight of about five steps, across a clean hard yard, into a grape arbor, or 'bowery.' Here was a table, a sunken water box half filled with water where floated pans of milk, each snugly covered with a fitted cloth cover, and the whole box was also covered from falling dirt, but had little ventilator openings. The milk and butter were always cold and tempting."

Mrs. Mariger describes the neat fields, orchards, vineyards, and gardens, all in all a typical Mormon home in Southern Utah.

Anyone familiar with Mormon history will recognize many of the names mentioned in the history of Leeds. It must have been a gathering place for prominent Mormon families. The name best known, perhaps, was that of Priddy Meeks, a self-educated doctor who had practiced his profession in the East and was a beloved figure in Southern Utah settlements. Although he settled down in the communal town of Orderville, he was considered one of the more prosperous and helpful men in the southern part of the territory. Another resident was Hosea Stout, who had been a policeman and bodyguard to Joseph Smith back in the stormy days of Nauvoo.

Leeds had some distinguished visitors, but none more colorful, or more unwelcome, than Sam Brannan, the gay cavilier who in 1847 tried to get Brigham Young to go on to California. Apparently Brannan decided to give it another try, for in 1876 or 1877 he appeared in Leeds for a time, clerking in William Barbee's store, supposedly to be near Brigham Young, who was wintering in St. George. He made no more impression on Brigham than he had the first time. An old lady who remembered Brannan when she was a child is quoted in *Saga of Three Towns* as saying that her father would not permit her to remain in a room where Brannan was, nor to eat at a table where he was eating. People spoke contemptuously of him, as they did in California after his fortune was gone and his grandiose schemes had collapsed. But Leeds was considerable of a place and even boasted an Opera House at which traveling troupes from Salt Lake performed.

One of the amusing stories of Leeds had to do with General Patrick Connor's bell. The bell came into Utah with Johnston's army and was used at Camp Floyd. When General Connor established headquarters at Fort Douglas, he took the bell with him, attached to a cannon carriage. It was used to call assemblies.

Since relations between the Mormons and the soldiers were not of the best, the soldiers taunted the Mormons with being stupid and incompetent. To this the Mormons retorted that they could steal their bell and cannon right from under their noses. When they were not stolen, the soldiers taunted them some more; so the Mormon boys decided to do something about it and one rainy night some of them got into the fort, attached tow ropes to the cannon, and left one of their number concealed there. After the sentry passed the man signaled his fellows to pull, and getting astride the cannon he rode it outside the fort, holding onto the bell clapper.

When rewards were offered for recovery, the boys became aware of the seriousness of their prank and hid the stolen articles in a barn and covered them with hay. One Seth Pixton, up from Leeds, heard about the bell and remembered that a bell was needed for a new church in his home town. He was told, "If you'll take the damned bell to Dixie it is yours." He hid the bell in a sack of grain, and for years it did duty in Leeds. Later, the Saints in Leeds decided to get a new bell, and the old one was taken to Cove Fort, where it still reposes in a museum. The cannon was dumped in an old well and buried.

Silver Reef was geologic enigma, and dozens of scientific papers have been written as to how silver came to be there, and why it was divided into two main ore bodies. It is still largely speculation. Several stories have been told as to how it came to be discovered, the most widely circulated being the story of Metaliferous Murphy. If that story is true, then Silver Reef was discovered in Pioche, but the preponderance of evidence seems to be against it, and the first discovery was made by a man from Harrisburg.

Metaliferous Murphy was an assayer in Pioche who had the habit of looking on the brighter side of things, so much so that the miners began to lose faith in the accuracy of his assays and thought they would show him up once and for all by giving him rock to assay which they knew was worthless, confident that he would, as usual, report high values.

The Mormon farmers from Leeds and Harrisburg were hauling produce to Pioche at this time, and among them was a Saint named Nephi Moroni Jennings, who at home made grindstones out of the sandstone near his home. The best version of the story has it that Jennings took one of the grindstones on top of his load of produce and sold it to a saloonkeeper in Pioche who set it up in his place of business as a convenience to his customers who needed to sharpen their knives before they started to carve up one another.

In one of these brawls the grindstone was broken so the miners smashed it up in small pieces and joyously took the fragments to Metaliferous Murphy. Up until then some of them retained a spark of confidence in the assayer, but when he reported that the grindstone samples carried silver value worth $200.00 to the ton, they were so infuriated that they were of a mind to lynch Murphy, and he had to flee for his life. One story goes that Metaliferous traced down the origin of the grindstone, and another claims someone else did it, thus bringing Silver Reef into existence. Neither story has any foundation in fact. It is reasonably certain that the incident happened but had nothing to do with the founding of Silver Reef.

An even more romantic story has it that a Pioche prospector lolling in the shade of the Mormon temple in St. George, which was built of sandstone hauled from the reefs above Leeds, was astonished to see the walls glistening with silver. To find where the stone came from was just a step. He also learned that the temple, the first built by the Saints in Utah, was probably the most costly building in the nation. Later, some Mormons pointed out that it was a fulfillment of prophesy, for they had been promised that if they came to the mountains they should build temples of silver and gold and precious stones.

Still another story has it that William Tecumseh Barbee was in Pioche when the grindstone was broken up, picked up a piece, had it assayed and traced it back to the volcanic region from which it came, which was the future site of Silver Reef. This story is more credible in that the mine he developed was long known as Barbee's Folly, and Barbee had the best right to be called the father of the camp.

It appears, however, that in 1866 a prospector and assayer named John Kemple from Montana came to Harrisburg and on the northwest side of White Reef found silver float that assayed $17,000 a ton. He dug several holes in an attempt to find where it came from but found only small amounts of silver in the soapstone formation. He filled up the holes and journeyed on, but returned to Harrisburg in 1874 and organized a company. Some men from Leeds also began to prospect and they, too, found good silver on the northwest side of White Reef, though little of commercial importance had been uncovered.

It was inevitable that some of the ore samples should find their way to Salt Lake City, where they attracted the attention of those pioneer opportunists, the Walker brothers.

Already interested in the Emma mine at Alta, the Walkers thought the new field worth looking into, and they sent William T. Barbee, Thomas McNalley, and Edward Maynard down to have a look. The men were well equipped with a large supply of food, an assay outfit, and blacksmith equipment.

This was in 1875, and before the year was over Barbee had struck ore on the White Reef. He went to Salt Lake to report, and on his return as he was walking along Buckeye Reef he noticed where the wheels of some woodhauler's wagon had skidded, exposing rock underneath which proved to be a deposit of rich silver chloride and horn silver. He located his claim, calling it the Tecumseh, and later renamed it The Buckeye Reef Tecumseh Hill.

Barbee shipped ten tons of ore to Salt Lake from which he received $7,000. He made other shipments, but because it was cheaper to ship to Pioche began sending the ore there. Thus started what is known as the Pioche Stampede. For a time Pioche was nearly deserted as its miners made the 125 mile trek over the mountains to Silver Reef and brought prosperity to the Mormon settlers in Dixie who at the time were having a hard struggle to exist. Apostle Erastus Snow, in charge of the Dixie colonization, at a Sunday service in the St. George Tabernacle thanked God for sending Brother Barbee to open up the mines and alleviate the hard times which the Saints were suffering, and asked God to bless his efforts—the only time the church was ever known to bless a mining camp.

A sandy flat at the east end of the hill was called Bonanza Flat, and here Barbee laid out a town which he called Bonanza City. Before Barbee could cash in on it, a little merchant from Pioche named Hyrum Jacobs brought his entire stock of goods over in a wagon and, not liking Barbee's prices, went up on the higher ground, set up his store, and called it Silver Reef. Around the store the mushrooming town of Silver Reef grew.

The Pioche Stampede brought in the same kind of tough people there had been in Pioche. Silver Reef was little different from other booming mine camps, except that there was less violence. There was a double murder when a U.S. Deputy and another man shot it out—some say over a woman—and died almost in each other's arms. One of the three lynchings of Utah occured there, but in general violent death took a holiday.

There is no account that mysterious Marshal Pearson ever held office in Silver Reef, yet he was there, and it is possible that his mere presence contributed to the town's peculiar fondness for law and order. The toughs would not have been anxious for him to clean up as he had done in Pioche and Frisco.

Many rich mines were developed, and a number of mills built; most famous and long lasting of the latter was the Stormont. The twenty-nine big mines were gradually assimulated into four major groups, though ownership was shifting constantly. These companies were the Leeds, the Barbee & Walker Company, the Christy Company, and the Stormont Company.

It is never possible to tell exactly how much any mining town has produced, but the best criterion in Silver Reef is the Wells Fargo receipts which prove that Silver Reef produced more than twelve million dollars in silver. The old Wells Fargo building, now renovated, is one of the few that remain in Silver Reef today.

The ore bodies, it turned out, didn't go very deep and were soon mostly exhausted, though there has been intermittent mining going on there.

A writer (Walker O. Laughlin, in *Salt Lake Tribune*, July 6, 1909) describes the country as William T. Barbee must have first seen it: "From miles and miles this country presents the appearance of the infernal regions or the scene of some stupendous conflagration. Everywhere there is a chimney pot of nature. From small vents six inches square to the extinct crater of a volcano a mile wide, whose crest soars toward the clouds. It appears as if nature had taken the silicious stone, thrown it into a great crucible, and when the mass became liquid this crucible was lifted by a giant hand and its contents scattered. . . . It gave Barbee the creeps, it was uncanny. It was an awful picture. The words of his partner rang in his ears. 'You're daft, Barbee.'"

It is still quite a place as one of the authors of this book discovered a few years ago when he tried to drive up the canyon unguided and got lost.

Not only did Barbee discover silver, but also he uncovered a petrified forest, and in the leaves and knotholes he found black silver sulpherets that assayed as high as 1,000 ounces to the ton. Barbee, or possibly someone else, found a petrified frog that had turned to silver.

There is a story that another frog was found alive in sandstone where it had been interred for no one knows how many million or thousand years. When liberated, the legend goes, the frog gave a cry like a small child, looked an unfamiliar world over, decided that it wasn't worth while, and died.

A dead miner started Silver Reef's second stampede, which changed it from a ghost town to a mass of rubble in a matter of days. Someone decided to tear down the deceased miner's house and haul it away for lumber. Under the floor the astonished house-wrecker came upon several thousand dollars in gold and silver. The word was soon out, and the deserted houses of Silver Reef disappeared like magic as they were torn down and hauled away for lumber, but every nook and cranny was inspected carefully with the hope that some other miner might have forgotten to take his money with him.

While no cash treasures were reported, Silver Reef in its passing again proved an asset to the Mormon farmers who were always in need of building material.

It is said that William T. Barbee died poor. In his lifetime Barbee staked twenty-two claims on Tecumseh Ridge, even though it was called Barbee's Folly, but between 1877 and 1903 more than nine million ounces of silver, worth an average of $1.15 an ounce, were taken from the reef.

There were three cemeteries in the old town. One was a Chinese burying ground, for the town had a population of 250 Chinamen, many of whom died, and in accordance with Chinese custom, food was placed on the graves—and gratefully consumed by the Indians in the vicinity during the night. After the demise of the town, one Sam Gee returned from San Francisco, disinterred the bodies, and shipped them back to the land of their ancestors.

The Catholic cemetery was said to have been the best kept. For a time it was watched over by a woman from Leeds, said to have been Ann Bassett before her marriage to a man in Leeds. Ann Bassett and her sister Josie were raised in the outlaw valley of Brown's Hole and were picturesque figures in their own right, though from all accounts were ladies of high charcater. Ann died a few years ago well up in her seventies, but her elder sister Josie is said to have remarked that she had warned Ann that cigarettes would be the death of her if she didn't give them up. Josie still lives alone in Uintah Basin and does her own branding and butchering.

To return from the digression, a man from Leeds, thinking that the wrought iron fence around the cemetery was doing nobody any particular good now that there were no more people living there, decided that he could put the fence to better use. Ann thought differently and assured the gentleman that she would fill him so full of lead if he didn't cease and desist that it would require a four-horse team to haul him away. The fence may be somewhat dilapidated, but it is still there. Nobody ever took liberties with the Bassett girls.

The proudest building in Silver Reef was the two story Harrison Hotel, across the street from the Wells Fargo building, but it has long been gone. Oddly enough, there is still mining in Silver Reef, but it is not silver. Uranium is the mineral they are finding now, but few people are optimistic enough to believe that the old camp will ever regain its former glory.

The people of southern Utah no longer need the "blessing" of a mining camp. It is a land of ultra-modern motels, for it is the heart of some of the best scenery in the West: Zion's Canyon is only a few miles away, and Grand Canyon, Bryce, Cedar Breaks, and the Wayne Wonderland are within easy driving distance. Besides, it is on the main highway, 91, to Las Vegas, the playground of America's idle rich.

CHAPTER TWELVE

Pioche

In a sense Pioche was the parent of the two sister camps of Frisco and Silver Reef, though there was little mutual affection ever manifested. Pioche was discovered first, and its stampeding miners gave the two other camps life.

The people on both sides of the state line were dependent on each other, but the purintanical Mormons and the don't-give-a-hoot miners were strange bedfellows. Brigham Young had taught his people that mining and miners were evil; Nevada chafed under the memory that Young had once laid claim to all of Nevada as part of his empire of Deseret, and for a time Nevada had been part of Utah territory. In retaliation, U.S. Senator Bill Stewart had introduced a bill in Congress which would have dismembered Utah by giving the panhandle of Idaho to Washington and compensating for it by dividing Utah up among the states and territories of Idaho, Wyoming, and Nevada. In no other way, Stewart maintained, could the Mormon question be solved. It naturally did not appeal to the Mormons, who still were determined to establish Zion in the midst of the Rocky Mountains. By the plan, Southern Utah would have become part of Nevada.

The Mormon opinion of Senator Stewart was less flattering than that of a correspondent of the *Boston Globe* which was quoted in the *Rhyolite Daily Bulletin* of December 21, 1907, many years later: Ex-Senator Stewart was taking a vacation from the Bullfrog Mining camps and while walking down F Street in the crowded shopping district was approached by the manager of a large department setore. "Excuse me," said the toy man, "I don't want to offend you but if you'll come to the store and play Santa Claus until Christmas Eve, I'll pay you fifty dollars a week."

"The white bearded senator who had just made himself another fortune answered, 'My friend, I've been playing Santa Claus for three quarters of a century—it always cost me money. Sorry I can't accept your offer, but I'm glad an old man like me is worth fifty dollars a week.'

Before Pioche's time, some mining had been done in the south tip of Nevada, and over the Utah line. El Dorado and a few other camps had produced quite a lot of silver. Before Lincoln County was even organized, efforts were being made to have the county seat located at Crystal Springs. The modern traveler, familiar with Las Vegas or Pioche, would wonder why Crystal Springs, now a mere cattle ranch in the desert, would ever have been considered. But before the county could be set up, ore had been discovered at Hiko, a few miles away, and the seat of Lincoln County was set up there in 1867.

By 1871 Pioche was in full bloom as Hiko withered, and the county seat was moved there. Hiko was an outlaw headquarters, anyway, where herds of stolen livestock could be safely hidden. That was changed somewhat when a group of irrate Mormon ranchers pursued a bunch of horse thieves into Pahranagat Valley and were joined by a number of harassed ranchers of the valley. One of the thieves was caught and a rope fitted around his neck. They were about to swing the culprit into his appointed destiny from the rafters of a barn when a voice from the darkness commanded them to let the man go. Not knowing how many others might be outside, the order was complied with, and the rustlers rode back to the safety of Hiko.

Enraged by this insolence, the settlers organized a vigilante band calling itself the Committee of 601 and proceeded to clean up. Best known of its victims was L. B. Vail, purported horse trader, suspected cow thief, and known gunfighter. Vail was known to have left Pioche with a young cattle buyer named Robert Knox, but Knox was never heard from again. A search revealed a shallow grave containing Knox's murdered body, and Vail was arrested and placed in the Hiko jail. The fact that Vail was suspected of having killed a couple of his associates, and had bragged of having slept on their graves, did not help his cause. But fearful that he would be liberated or acquitted if given a trial in the courthouse, the proceedings were held in a saloon, while the gallows and the prisoner's coffin were being noisily built just outside.

After the "judge" announced that it was a trial and not a neck-tie party, witnesses were heard whenever they could shout loud enough to be heard above the hammering on the gallows and the coffin. A very few minutes sufficed to hear the testimony, after which the jury retired to a rear room to wait until the hammering ceased; whereupon they marched back and rendered their verdict of guilty. Since gallows and coffin were ready, there was no sense in delaying the proceedings, and the jury and executioners, their duty done, lined up at the bar for a drink.

There are many instances of Indians showing white men where they could find silver or gold, but almost invariably these white men were Mormons. The famous Panacker mine was one. Panaca is the Indian word for silver. The Mormons had a settled policy of treating the Indians fairly and justly, and they had men like Jacob Hamlin, Ira Hatch, and Thales Haskell who devoted their lives to missionary work among them. It was Indians who led Ira Hatch and others to the Panacker.

Among the Mormons at Leeds was a former Pony Express rider named Daniel C. Still. One time he and a partner had a bunch of sheep out near where Pioche was to be located, and they befriended a sick Indian called Dick. In gratitude he led them to a ledge showing silver and lead ore, saying, "Here white man's rock I have found. You helped me. You have."

This ledge eventually became the great Raymond & Ely mine, the richest in the district, but Dan Still was not to enjoy the fruit of it. Unwisely, he and his partner told of their find and were offered money for it, which they declined. One morning they became sick after drinking their coffee, and Dan's partner died in agony. Dan survived, but realizing that the coffee had been poisoned decided that it wasn't worth risking his life for silver.

He returned to Utah to live out a calm, useful, and uneventual life. Pioche was not a land for peaceful men.

On a billboard just outside Pioche a few years ago was a big sign stating that sixty-seven men were buried there before one died a natural death. Pioche seems justified in its claim that it was tougher than Bodie, Dodge City, or Tombstone.

Sheriff Andy Fife had two gunfighting deputies named McKee and Kelley who were known to have killed their man, but Pioche found it necessary to hire the indomitable gunman marshal, Pearson, whose motto was "Get out of town or shoot it out." How many of those sixty-seven or more men he killed is not recorded, but the way he pacified Pioche was the reason he was invited to take his talents over to Frisco a little later.

Pearson was not a peace officer at Silver Reef, but Marietta M. Mariger, an authority on that region, states that he once arrested two horse thieves in St. George and started back to Pioche with them, but shot and buried them a little way out of St. George. Years later curious teachers and students from Dixie College opened the graves and found the two skeletons.

There is a story that Pearson owned a ranch in the Paranagat Valley and employed Indians. When one displeased him, Pearson would rope the Indian and drag him. But no one cared much about what happened to an Indian, which was one of the reasons the Indian Queho turned renegade and terrorized Southern Utah and Nevada for many years. Many attempts were made to capture Queho, but he knew every inch of the country and it was full of hiding places. He was never caught. When his body was finally found he was equipped with the latest modern weapons.

Pearson was unquestionably the most feared peace officer of his day, and Queho the most deadly outlaw. It is anyone's guess which would have survived had they ever met.

Pioche took its name from a French mining man named F. L. A. Pioche, who had a big hand in the development of the wealthy Meadow Valley mine. For a time the camp was called Pioche's, but the apostrophe s was soon dropped.

The big names in the district were William H. Raymond and John Ely. Raymond is said to have been a small man physically, shrewd in all the devious ways of a mining camp. Ely was every inch the picture of a prosperous mining magnate, who was naturally the public relations man of the firm.

Raymond and Ely were involved in Pioche's most famous feud with Tom and Frank Newlands. The Newlands brothers owned the Washington & Creole mine around the shoulder of the mountain from the Raymond & Ely, and received permission to drive a tunnel through the latter property to facilitate the development of their own mine. This act of neighborliness Raymond & Ely had cause to regret when the Newlands opened up a rich ore body on the way and paused to mine it out without an accounting.

Ordered to move out, the Newlands men barricaded themselves and the war was on. In an underground fight, December 28, 1878, Thomas Ryan, a Raymond & Ely employee, was killed, and on the same day another of their employees, Charles Swanson, was shot on his way to work. Since it was dark, it was claimed that Swanson had been mistaken as an intruder and was killed by a guard.

Gunmen were employed on both sides at twenty dollars per day and upward. Raymond & Ely's crew was headed by Morgan Courtney, one of the West's most feared gunmen. Courtney had a reputation long before he came to Pioche and apparently had a quick temper. In a list of murders compiled by Thompson and West in their *History of Nevada* is a simple mention that one Sullivan was killed by Morgan Courtney for using abusive language.

In addition to his regular pay, Courtney was offered a bonus of $15,000 if he would move the Newlands men out. This was accomplished by bribing a teamster taking supplies to the Newlands camp to include a keg of whiskey. It had not been ordered, but the surly teamster refused to take it back, and it is improbable that the Newlands gunmen were very insistent. When the Newlands men were thoroughly drunk, Courtney and his men moved in and the battle was brief and one-sided. When the smoke cleared Courtney was in possession, and the Newlands brothers were out.

How much of the ore Newlands had not had time to ship out came into Courtney's possession is not known, but he is said to have spent considerably more than the $15,000 bonus he received, and for some time the strutting Morgan Courtney was king of Pioche.

But while Courtney was enjoying his fame as "chief" of the town, a quiet young man named George McIntyre came in from Elko with a reputation of his own. Because McIntyre had taken care of himself against several brawny woodchoppers in a barroom brawl, the Central Pacific railroad had hired him as watchman over a lot of freight intended for Pioche, Eureka, and White Pine.

As soon as McIntyre got the job, the woodchoppers announced their intention to "get him." Soon a mob of them showed up at Elko, drunk and ugly, and moved to the freight yards demanding that young McIntyre show himself. McIntyre waited for an hour, letting them shout themselves hoarse, then stepped out in view with a six-shooter in each hand and opened fire before the mob could get their guns in action, killing three of them and wounding several more.

After that McIntyre was let alone until he arrived in Pioche and met the great Morgan Courtney in the street. Courtney warned him that Pioche wasn't big enough for the two of them. McIntyre replied that he liked Pioche and that Courtney was at liberty to leave. Courtney blustered and challenged McIntyre to a shoot-out the next time they were both on the street.

That afternoon Courtney strolled down the walk, his hand ready for a quick draw. McIntyre, with a strong belief in the law of self preservation, was concealed. When Courtney came along McIntyre calmly let him have six slugs in the body, and Morgan Courtney died with his gun still in the holster.

McIntyre was arrested and as promptly acquitted, the court taking the popular view that he was not called upon to commit suicide as he would surely have done had he tried to out-draw one of the slickest gunmen the West ever knew. McIntyre had not sought the quarrel, and Pioche was glad to be free of the trouble-making chief of the gunmen. McIntyre remained peacefully in Pioche for a while then dropped quietly out of history.

For the most part the mining companies depended on hired

gunmen to protect their property, leaving ordinary law enforcement to the regular officers, who were not always equal to the occasion. *Pioneer Nevada,* a book of Nevada folklore published by Harolds Club of Reno, relates the exploits of Bandit Jack Harris, who had a penchant for robbing Wells Fargo stages. He had a way of appearing so suddenly that gunplay was seldom necessary. The stage drivers were sure that Harris was the robber but could get no evidence.

Finally the Wells Fargo agent decided that it would be cheaper to pay Harris a weekly salary and, to insure good behavior, made him agree to be on the company's porch every time the stage came in. Harris agreed readily. Being a man of his word, he was always on hand to greet the stage. Yet the robberies continued at frequent intervals.

Not until later did the agent realize that though Jack was always on hand to keep his appointment, not enough track was kept of his movements at other times. Jack Harris would hold up the stage a few miles out of town, then, mounted on a good fast horse, would beat the stage back to Pioche and be on the platform to meet it.

The same source, *Pioneer Nevada,* divulges another hazard faced by the men of Pioche. 1876 was leap year, and civilization in the form of more and more women was moving in. On July 8, 1876, the *Pioche Record* said: "An association is being formed in Pioche amongst the unprotected male sex, the object being to protect themselves from the encroachment of the female sex, which of late has become so dangerous that the poor male is getting to be an object of pity. Many have been caught up lately and married before they know it! Females are arriving from all directions by stages, private conveyances, etc. . . . men are getting so timid they hardly dare to venture on the streets for a short talk for fear they will be married before they can return. The association proposes to ameliorate this condition of affairs."

In succeeding issues the *Record* told of other meetings of the Single Men's Protective Association. An assessment of $5.00 was levied to procure a secret meeting place. All members also pledged themselves to resist feminine wiles throughout the whole of 1876.

"The membership was engaged in a lengthy and spirited debate on this very question as to how much assistance the men could be expected to give each other, when there was a loud clamor, and the doors were forced open by a large number of females. . . . A general stampede followed, with members jumping out of windows, and hiding under tables. The *Record* advised its readers to watch the wedding columns for news of any men who might have failed to escape."

Other news of the Association followed in the weeks to come, chiefly dealing with the election of a new sergeant-at-arms, (because of the notorious failure of the previous officer when the meeting was invaded).

Pioneer Nevada editorializes, "This sort of spirit, and the making of original fun, still continues today in many of the smaller mining and ranching communities of Nevada . . . where the ready-made amusements of television and other scientific recreations of the modern age are not yet found."

Pioche rather liked to burlesque its formal functions. The *Pioche Record* of July 7, 1875, describes the Fourth of July celebration. The program was under the auspices of The Mystic Crew of Cosmus. The Presidio Band furnished the music, and Tom Campbell gave a flowery oration. At that time the reverend Henry Ward Beecher personified the blue-noses of the country, and in no place were blue laws more hated than in Pioche. At the program Reverend Beecher was impersonated by Ed Thompson, and Mrs. Beecher by Billy Gleam. Had the Beechers been there their low opinion of Westerners would have sunk lower still.

Another hilarious time was had when someone stole the key to the jail and no one could get in or out until a new one could be made.

Pioche didn't believe in asking or granting favors. When a customer demanded more ice from a bartender named Anthony, he obligingly crammed a whole scoopful down the customer's throat.

The *Pioche Record* and its editor, P. Holland, was not above crossing swords with even New York newspapers: "There i published in New York, that harbor for fungus politicians, decayec brains and vapid wit called the New York Day Book. Whereve: tides rise and fall we can expect a great deal of foul substance stranded on the beach."

In passsing it took a sideswipe, July 22, 1875, at George A Smith, a high Mormon official, for condemning John D. Lee, o: Mountain Meadows infamy, while praying for Colonel Dame Lee's superior, whom the law never caught up with. Poking a little gentle fun at the spirit of the press, the *Record* said, "Speak ing of whiskey reminds us of a Colorado man's indigation abou a boom town of that state. 'Would you believe it, they started a newspaper, and there wasn't a saloon in the place.'"

Pioche had no complaint on that score, for its three principa streets of Main, Meadow Valley, and Lacour were well suppliec with saloons. Pioche lies in a bowl-shaped basin with the lowe rim cut out. The rim at the top is a jumble of mine dumps frown ing down upon the town.

Names of mines one comes upon frequently in the old files of the *Record are* Raymond & Ely, Raymond & Ely West, Meadow Valley, Newark, Pioche, Alps, Silver Peak, American Flag, Pioche West Extension, Washington & Creole, Kentuck, Spring Mount and others. They all had their day and are forgotten, where once they were names to stir the blood. The Bristol properties are the big modern producers.

In the Seventies the entire country was dotted with more or less rich camps, and they were kept in touch with each other by a sometimes overlooked industry, the stagecoach business. Gilmer & Salisbury stages ran about everywhere, but Pioche's main com munication for a while was Hugh White's Hamilton & Pioche stage line. Later, the Eureka & Palisades railroad connected the district with the outside world, and it was the link which probably led the old timers to include most of eastern Nevada in the Reese River district.

John H. Ely had been with Ira Hatch, David Sanderson, and others at the discovery of the Panacker, and he and his partner, Raymond, organized one of Pioche's two largest mines. The

154

Meadow Valley Mining Company was the other. The Frenchman, Pioche, was heavily interested in the Meadow Valley property and sent Charles E. Hoffman in to organize it. Subsequent development was largely due to these two companies.

Water to run the mills was a big problem at first. There was plenty of it at the little Mormon settlement of Panaca on Meadow Valley Wash, but the people there preferred to grow crops. The miners built their own town called Bullionville a couple of miles from Panaca, and a narrow-gauge railroad connected it with Pioche.

For some years after its beginning Pioche thought of itself as another Virginia City, and though it never quite achieved its goal it was a rich camp which at one time boasted a population of ten thousand, and its total production compared favorably with that of any other camp in the great basin. The Raymond & Ely alone produced $40,000,000 from 1870 to 1873.

There was always some danger from Indians, and Pioche was involved in the Indian scare of 1875, along with Hamilton and Cherry Creek. Pioche appears to have got a maximum of scare and a minimum of danger.

The *Pioche Record* of September 7, 1875, reported hostile Indians at Spring Valley, and volunteers were called for. The result led W. W. Bishop to remark: "We are not a fighting community from the fact that the committee couldn't find arms. At the present time the Indians could swoop down and gobble up the whole town unless we could stand them off with a few six-shooters and clubs. So after all the reputation Pioche has earned for itself in the past exists only in name. There was a time when there was no lack of arms, but they have been taken out by every prospecting party and never returned."

Volunteers were never very dependable since there was seldom any proper authority, and they did pretty much as they pleased. Mormon discipline was always rather a striking contrast to the free and easy ways of the boom towns. In 1862 President Lincoln needed volunteers to protect the telegraph lines. Though Brigham Young hadn't any legal authority for six years, Mr. Lincoln asked him, rather than the governor of the territory, to raise a company of cavalry for that purpose, and Brigham obliged with a company of seventy-five men which did an effective job.

The *Elko Independent* described another kind of volunteer. "Mr. Chapman, of California, passed through here on his way to the Indian trouble at Hamilton. He had 16 Henry rifles and 6,000 rounds of ammunition. He probably stopped to buy another thousand rounds." The paper implied plainly that the rounds were not ammunition.

The country was plagued about as much by lawsuits as by Indians. Sammy Davis, in *History of Nevada*, tells of a lawyer named Barnes who drifted into town on a mule and before twenty-four hours had elapsed had convinced the management of the Hermes mine that Raymond & Ely were taking ore from within the boundaries of the Hermes. He showed how easy it would be for them to start a suit. He then called on Raymond & Ely and told them the Hermes was planning to start a blackmail suit, but that he could show them how to beat it. Before the week was over, he was in the employ of both companies. He suggested the same list of jurymen for both sides and manipulated the drawing through the County Clerk so that both sides thought they had the jury. It was easier for lawyers to find causes for litigation than it was for prospectors to find ore.

When the crash of '73 came and the mines were in trouble, there were so many Apex suits that many of them closed down in disgust.

"The Story of Pioche" by Miner Mike, in the November 25, 1946 *Utah Farmer*, continues: "A mine operator thought more of a good gunman than he did of his miners. Old payroll records of the Meadow Valley Mining Company . . . showed at the top of the payroll sheets: guards $20.00 per day; superintendent, $5.00 per day, and miners $3.00 per day. Guards were the toast of the bars and they boasted that they would not eat breakfast before they took a shot at some claim jumper.

"It is a curious fact that the rich, booming community of Pioche, nearly broke the county of Lincoln . . . a number of times because the numerous bristling gun battles involved too many court battles and murder trials. (Most of the murder trials were cleared up as self defense.)

"Order was finally brought about by Jake Johnson, a deputy sheriff who set up what became known far and wide as Johnson's Law. Johnson was one of those big, square built men who carried a Sunday punch in either his right or his left. Those who knew Johnson said that he would seek out the trouble-makers, strip them of their guns and then take them on in rough and tumble.

"Those who were not convinced with his first treatment were then taken to the county line, given another working over and sent on their way.

"Such was the life in early day Pioche, and it took Jake Johnson to smooth out the troubled waters. He became a legend throughout southeast Nevada, and he had a hand in helping Snyder with his early day struggles to rebuild the camp."

Legend, Johnson undoubtedly was, and part of the legend is that Johnson, a young Mormon from Spanish Fork, Utah, went to the camp, got involved in a shooting scrape, and fled Pioche for some years to avoid standing trial. Later he returned to find that no charges had even been filed against him, and eventually became sheriff for many years. Johnson appears to have used some of the methods employed by Marshal Pearson in an earlier and cruder day but was never as lethal as Pearson.

In its palmy days Pioche decided to build a fine, handsome courthouse. That was back in the days before Clark County. in which Las Vegas is located, was cut off from Lincoln County. Even today Pioche brags wryly of its "million dollar courthouse" which still proudly overlooks the town, though a new and modern courthouse has taken its place. Citizens argue that it should either be renovated as a museum or torn down before it kills somebody, but they refused to allow the old building to be hauled away to Las Vegas as a tourist attraction. Its real cost, admittedly, was but a fraction of a million dollars and the rest was sheer, unmitigated graft.

Pioche loves its old courthouse not for its beauty, nor as a monument to folly, but because it recalls the good old days when money was plentiful and nobody cared a whoop about how it was spent. The old jail is built into the hillside and is reached from the top floor of the courthouse, and beyond a doubt it once harbored some of the toughest badmen who ever inhabited the West.

William Brooks, who was for many years sheriff of Washington County, Utah, and later postmaster at St. George, worked in Pioche between 1091 and 1904, and states that at the time a 25c piece was the smallest coin used in making change. You paid 25c, 50c, 75c or $1.00. The customer got the benefit if the price was over that amount. If the price was 60c the customer paid four-bits. If it was 65c he paid six-bits. Pioche never did things in a small way.

In the early days, as has been related, Pioche and neighboring camps, such as DeLamar, were entirely dependent on the Mormon freighters for farm produce, and they didn't do much to protect the Mormons from the ravages of the border outlaws, such as Ben Tasker and Nate Hansen, who could operate in Utah in comparative safety, and spend their money in Pioche freely.

Those freighters, who wouldn't use profanity, had other troubles. Billy Brooks tells of one with an overloaded team hauling kerosene in cases of two five gallon cans who got stuck going up a long, sandy slope. After long unavailing effort, he pried the top off a packing case and with a stick dipped in the black grease oozing out of the hubs wrote on the smooth pine board all the cuss words he knew, along with his opinion of the team, the road, the country, and anybody who might read it, thus avoiding the use of profanity but relieving his feelings.

Howard Cox, of Manti, Utah, says an old time teamster who used to haul gasoline to DeLamar in 100 gallon drums used to lighten the load by driving a spike or other sharp tool up through the bottom of the wagon-box and into the drum, but full price would be collected when they reached DeLamar.

Cox says he has been told that in the early days some of the freighters, along with their produce, also hauled rot-gut whiskey from the two distilleries in Manti, and from a larger one on Whiskey Creek in Millard County, and it was customary for them to raise a hoop of the barrel, bore a small hole, and draw out several

158

gallons of whiskey before plugging the hole and replacing the hoop—then collecting for a full barrel.

Some of the Mormon boys were sometimes inclined to get a little wild. Mr. Cox spent some time at a camp called Fay inside the Utah border and relates that while walking past a saloon one evening on the north side of a gulch he heard a commotion inside and looking through the saloon window saw the owner with a gun in his right hand while slapping the scared and tear-stained face of a young Mormon kid from Toquerville with his left. The kid had used his first wages to buy a Browning automatic pistol and, feeling very tough, had told Herman McLaughlin, the barkeeper, "This is a stick-up," which quickly changed to cries of, "Don't shoot, Herman, don't shoot."

Herman threw the new Browning out the open door, with the young Mormon close behind it. The boy picked up the gun and ran across the gulch to a public privy, where he fired the whole box of cartridges into the pit, which ended the episode.

The new and modern buildings of Pioche deny that it is a ghost town, or likely ever to be one, though its population is only about a tenth of what it once was. In 1946 former President Herbert Hoover, a mining engineer of renown, visited the district and pointed out that it had the possibility of becoming the greatest producer of lead and zinc since the development of the Burma mines around 1900.

Much of the development along these lines was conducted by a Utah mining man named Edward H. Snyder, and for many years now Pioche has contributed greatly to the wealth of Nevada and Utah.

Like most of the boomers, Pioche is today a quiet, law-abiding town. A few miles distant is the old Mormon settlement of Panaca, and you can drive over a paved road to Caliente, a town that sprang into life when Senator William A. Clark, of Montana, built the Salt Lake, Los Angeles & San Pedro railroad. *Caliente,* in Spanish, means *hot,* and Caliente has the weather to prove it.

Farther on, the highway passes within a few miles of DeLamar, the old widow-maker, now a ghost town. It was a producer of silicosis, and it wasn't until it passed into the hands of the Bamberger interests of Salt Lake City, a few years before Simon Bamberger became the first and only Jewish governor of Utah, that a wetting down process made the mines safe to work in.

On down the road, through as weird a wasteland as there is in the West, one comes to the oasis of Crystal Springs, and a short distance to the right are the ruins of old Hiko, and a few prosperous ranches which give no intimation that Hiko was once an outlaw hangout. If one keeps going past Crystal Springs to Alamo one would find himself near the edge of the Gunnery Range of Yucca Flats—and no way to go but back.

CHAPTER THIRTEEN

White Pine County

The optimistic traveler through the endless miles of sagebrush will feel hope in his bosom when his road map tells him a county named White Pine lies ahead, and he will likely dream of green, stately forests as he heads for the county with the promising name. But he will be disillusioned when he learns that he will need jeeps or horses to get him where the timber grows. No matter which way he comes into Ely, the county seat, doubts will assail him, and he will wonder if it wasn't named after a single tree, probably imported.

If he comes in from the east over Highway 6 he will cross a hundred mile desert between Delta, Utah, and Ely. If from the west over Highway 50, he will find little but desert between Fallon in the western part of the state and Ely. If he drives south from Wendover down Steptoe Valley, it will be the same; or if he comes from California by way of Tonopah the last 168 miles of his journey across the drab landscape will be broken only by a few miles of juniper-clad hills at the last end of the trip. He will think that the name White Pine is a misnomer, and that Nevada is still just Nevada. To find pine trees he would have to go a long way back. The coolest place he could find would be Lehman's Cave at the base of lofty Mt. Wheeler, and it would be well worth his time. If he wants to see timber in Nevada, he should watch the Bonanza television show.

White Pine County lies between the two largest counties in the state, Elko and Nye, and is bounded on the west by a long sliver of land called Eureka County. Utah is on the other side. Except for

Elko County, however, it is probably the largest stock raising county in the state. And it is today producing more ore than any other section, but its wealth is copper rather than silver and gold. The great open pit mine just outside Ely vies with Bingham, Utah, as the nation's greatest producer of copper. The four towns in the center of the county, Ely, Ruth, Kimberly, and McGill, all owe their existence to copper.

Ely has had a couple of bad fires in the past two years but without visible hurt, and the town competes lustily with Elko to catch the tourist trade from Utah. Utahns are told that if they want to meet their friends they should come to one of these two towns, and you can always find plenty of automobiles with Utah license plates in either city—and not all of them are driven by Gentiles. Plenty of Mormons find the blue laws of their own state irksome at times and like to enjoy the freedom which Nevada offers. Yet Ely has a considerable Mormon population, and one will not find any sign of the old gun-toting West there. But one can buy drinks at a bar and gamble at the numerous casinos if one is so disposed. And Ely is a racing center where devotees of the sport of kings can at times find action.

In the old days the redlight district embraced nearly an entire block where the girls sat at their windows and called to the passersby, but it is so no more—which is not to say that a few girls cannot still be found.

As a Western town of the old era, Ely is pretty tame. The working men belong to the union and work in the copper mines and the smelters, and the old time prospectors no longer tie up at the hitching posts. Yet White Pine has had a few stampedes that ranked with the best of them.

In the eastern part of the county were such boom towns as Steptoe City, Schellbourne, Taylor and Ward, each of which made a big dash in the roaring Seventies. But the big one, the king-pin of them all, was Hamilton, a few miles west of Ely and a few miles south of present Highway 50.

No matter what the prospects were in Reese River, Pioche, or elsewhere, every word of a new strike caused a stampede. Naturally there were many fly-by-night towns, each of which hoped to become another Virginia City, but only a few lived up to the initial promise. They blossomed and bloomed and died when the ore gave out, but all of them started out with the requisite number of saloons and a newspaper, but the only papers to make a lasting impression in that part of the state were the *Pioche Record,* the *Reese River Reveille,* published at Austin, and the *Eureka Sentinel.* Most of the history of eastern Nevada can be found in those three lively newspapers.

New counties were constantly being created, and county seats jumped from place to place like a spider on a hot skillet. For instance, the town of Current is mentioned as having been a county seat, but of what county is not clear. It is at present within the bounds of Nye County, of which Tonopah, a hundred miles away, is now the seat. It is located between the Pancake and Grant ranges, and is much nearer to Ely than it is to Tonopah, and about the same distance from Eureka, and is close to Duckwater, which once had a minor rush; but the impermanence of most of these camps made counties and their leading towns at any given date largely a guessing matter.

At any rate life was much the same in all of them, and one disillusioned stranger wrote: "There is a population of one to the house. Oh, Lord forgive me, deliver me from these towns." Another expressed his disgust in these words: "No life, no energy, no money. Beans straight, and squaws their diet. How in the hell they can enjoy such a life, God only knows!"

But enjoy it they did, and no matter how a town was booming, news of a new strike could well nigh depopulate it. Austin was rolling along beautifully in 1867 when news came of strikes in the White Pine district and the stampede was on. Cherry Creek and Schell Creek were objects of attention, and they and others had their booms, but the discoveries at Hamilton made them all look small.

Previous to 1868 when the town of Hamilton was laid out by W. H. Hamilton, Henry Kelly, and E. Tobin on the north slope of Treasure Hill, there were a few prospectors in the district who lived in dugouts, if they lived in anything, and the place was inelegantly called Cave City.

But an unbelievably rich silver deposit was discovered on Trea
sure Hill, and people flocked in by the thousands. By the end o
1869 there were ten thousand inhabitants. Because of the scar
city of wood and brick for building material, most of them livec
in tents. Yet before the year was out speculators from New Yorl
to San Francisco were bidding fantastic prices for Hamilton rea
estate. This was it! This was the big one!

The *Sacramento Union* in February, 1869, said, ". . . The Pacifi
Railroad Company has disposed of 10,000 passenger tickets from
Chicago to White Pine for the month of March alone, and refuse
to sell any more on account of inability to transport a larger num
ber."

Albert S. Evans wrote in the *Overland Monthly*, "Long lines o
mules and oxen, drawing heavy wagons laden with supplies o
every kind were to be seen. Bullwhackers with whips a dozer
feet in length . . . 'honest' miners with salted claims, ready tc
sell to the newly arrived greenhorns; footpackers without a cent
who had packed their blankets and luggage all the way from Elkc
. . . sleeping in snowdrifts if they slept at all; painted Jezebel
from every mining camp from Idaho to Sonora; Shoshone Indians
Chinamen and 'capitalists' crowded the streets of Hamilton. Al
was bustle and hurry, noise and excitement and confusion. The
stores were crowded with men in huge overcoats, the pockets of
which were filled with specimens, small silver bars, rolls of locations and assay certificates . . . "

It was not long until Hamilton was claiming a population of
between thirty and forty thousand people, but there was a galaxy
of surrounding towns which were included in the claim. These
were Treasure City, Eberhardt, Shermantown, Swansea, Menken,
White Pine City, Monte Cristo, Mammoth, Greenville, and Babylon.

"Those who revelled in this Miracle of Mammon," says Nel
Murbarger in her *Ghosts of the Glory Trail*, "would have deemed
it rank heresy to suggest that their mountaintop money-box ever
would be emptied; or that there would come a day when I would
walk through the mine-torn streets of Hamilton and Treasure
City, Shermantown, Seansea and Eberhardt, and in all that high

land would not hear one sound louder than the restless rustle of a lizard's feet, no call more seductive than the thin sighing of a lonely wind."

There is no ghostlier ghost town in all the West than Hamilton —yet it possessed the richest glory hole of them all.

The nearest railroad point was Elko, far to the north, and the tenderfeet poured in by the hundreds. Stagecoaches did a thriving business. Describing one, the *Reese River Reveille* of February 18, 1869, said, "It was fuller than a stuffed toad. . . . It looked like an irregular pyramid of men, women, cats, dogs, Chinamen, gimcracks, trunks, bandboxes, parcels, blankets, bottles of whiskey, sacks of flour, fresh beef, a plow, bars of steel and iron—all held together somehow, and drawn by four horses."

Prices were fantastic. Lumber of poor quality was selling at three to four hundred dollars per thousand feet, when it could be obtained. Packing crates and whiskey barrels were used as building material. Store buildings rented at $500 per month, and hay sold for $250 a ton, barley at 35c a pound, and everything else in proportion. Business lots sold at from five to six thousand dollars a lot.

Property jumping was more common than claim jumping, and from it grew Hamilton's Law of Enclosure, which implied that if a man stuck stakes in the ground at the corners of his property and fenced it with anything from a rawhide rope to a piece of twine it was his by constructive possession. A number of men who questioned the legality were buried in Boot Hill, and the slayers acquitted for having killed men trespassing on their property.

A *Reno Crescent* reporter in February, 1869, expressed a measure of resentment over Hamilton's high life: "A couple of gamblers were shooting at each other all around the streets over a woman. I regret to say neither of them were injured, but a faithful horse was shot, and the clothes of several people were shot through . . . .The people are talking of forming a Vigilance Committee."

A reporter for the *New York Herald* saw things more favorably. "You can see in some of the saloons as handsome a display of cut glass as in any place of a similar nature in San Francisco. And, strange as it may seem, there are some paintings—of nude women, of course—that would not disgrace a well-selected picture gallery. The first class restaurants are good, and serve up a meal in a style similar to Delmonico's of New York, or Martin's of San Francisco." One may well imagine that expense accounts were not unknown even in those days.

Hamilton had its solid citizens and was quickly made county seat of White Pine County. It had a newspaper, *The Daily Inland Empire,* which was one of the best in the state. The Hamilton Opera House opened with Olivia Rand as the first offering. The St. Luke's Episcopal church and the Withington Hotel were regarded as two of the finest structures of their kind in the West. One of the first official acts was to set up a school district and elect a board of trustees, and there was a lyceum with a debating club and reading room.

An interesting feature of the district was that it got its beef from trail herds that were driven all the way up from Texas, and it is probable that the thirsty and dried-out cowpokes contributed their mite toward enlivening the life of the various towns.

Hamilton proper had about 15,000 people. Shermantown and Eberhardt claimed about 7,000 each, and Treasure City, 9,000 feet above sea level, had six thousand people. A number of others camps rose and died without attracting too much attention. One dying camp gave the editor of the *Inland Empire* a ready-made headline: "Babylon has fallen!" It told the whole story.

Treasure City was snowbound most of the winter and only saddle horses could get through. There were two rival express companies, Wells Fargo and Pacific Union, and their riders would always make it through with the mail from Hamilton, three miles distant. Since life became a little tedious at Treasure City during such times, all the males of the town were on hand each day to bet on which rider would arrive first. The riders entered into the spirit of the thing and spared no effort to win the race. A free drink was undoubtedly the reward of the winner.

Hamilton was soon connected with Pioche by the Hamilton & Pioche stage line, and there were various other lines going hither and yon, for all a man needed to set up in the stage business was a rig of some kind and four horses or mules. The prospectors were a restless breed and did a lot of travelling in their own little world. Most of the miners worked for wages, and they moved from camp to camp, not necessarily expecting better wages or working conditions, but they liked to be on the move. The wiser ones tried to go into business, and at that a man's future might depend upon his finding the right boom town.

Treasure City at one time had more business houses than Hamilton, but Hamilton grabbed off the county seat and a $55,000 courthouse was erected. Eastern capitalists flocked into the city to get their slice of the wealth, and put up at the elaborate and ornate J. P. Withington Hotel. No picks and shovels for them but prospectuses and gilt-edged stocks which could be lifted as easily as a glass of whiskey.

Pure silver seemed to sprout from the grass roots, and the name Hidden Treasure was almost a misnomer since it was there for all to see. But the real bonanza was the Eberhardt, where silver was taken from an open pit glory hole, said to have been the richest in the world. $3,200,000 was mined from an excavation seventy feet long, forty feet wide, and twenty-eight feet deep, an average of $1,000 a ton for 3,200 tons of ore. One boulder weighed six tons and ran eight to ten dollars to the pound.

Owner Eberhardt apparently attempted to run his town without permitting any form of vice, as the Mormon, Jesse Knight, succeeded in doing a few years later; but in neither instance was it far to other towns which looked with a more lenient eye upon the well-known frailties of mankind.

In passing, may it be noted that in all these supposedly tough towns there was no more opposition to churches than there was to saloons, and there is scarcely a town that can't recall with affection some kind-hearted and respected minister of the Gospel.

Treasure Hill was 9,000 feet high, and if the ore had gone all the way to the bottom there would have been more silver than there was in all the rest of the world. Many confidently expected that it would do just that. It was no wonder the eyes of the world were on Hamilton. Mining engineers came from everywhere and rubbed their eyes with astonishment.

Rossiter W. Raymond, Special Commissioner of Mining Statistics for the U. S. Treasury Department, wrote of the Eberhardt in 1869: "Descending the mine on a rope, we found ourselves among men engaged in breaking down silver by the ton. The light of our candles disclosed great black sparkling masses of silver ore on every side. The walls were silver, the roof over our heads silver, the very dust which filled our lungs and covered our boots and clothing was a gray coating of fine silver."

The next year found Mr. Raymond equally enthusiastic. He found the silver so pure that a nail could be driven into it.

One spectacular story tells of a couple of miners who built their winter cabin out of rocks, and in the spring milled $75,000 out of the walls. The people of Hamilton could not be blamed for believing that Treasure Hill was solid silver.

With ore of such richness, hauling it to Elko across a 140 mile desert would have presented little of a problem except for the danger of robbery, but scarcely a week passed that some bullion-laden stage was not held up and robbed. The county had a large outlaw population and killings were frequent.

But nature had played one of her most fantastic tricks on Hamilton by putting the ore in the top of the mountain instead of the bottom, and when the crust had been penetrated, the silver was gone. Hamilton's career lasted little more than ten years. It was incorporated in 1869 and disincorporated in 1885. Its water system had cost $380,000, but it wasn't good enough to prevent the fires which destroyed both Hamilton and Treasure City one or more times.

The Crime of '73, and the problem of vanishing ore, had the boom town rocking on its heels. An alarmed opportunist named Alexander Cohn, who operated a cigar store, decided to burn his place of business and collect the insurance, and thoughtfully closed the city's main water valve before applying the torch. One-third of the city went up in smoke causing a loss of more than six hundred thousand dollars. Mr. Cohn got seven years in the state penitentiary.

The next year Treasure City was destroyed by fire, and by 1880 its population had dropped from 6,000 to less than one hundred. Shermantown shrunk from 7,000 to a single family.

Hamilton fought bravely to retain the county seat, but when a fire destroyed its fine courthouse in 1885 the county seat was moved to the more substantial and steadier growing town of Ely. Out of gratitude, perhaps, Ely still keeps the old Hamilton bell.

Soon all that remained of any importance at Hamilton was its postoffice, Jim Riley postmaster, at an annual salary of $3,200, which he kept going by personally buying enough stamps to do the requisite amount of business, and trading the stamps for commodities, until the government became curious and arrested him. Postmaster Riley was taken to San Francisco to stand trial, and the government put him up at the Palace until he was acquitted on a technicality. "Taken all together," Postmaster Riley declared, "it was a damned interesting experience." The whole Treasure Hill episode might be described with those same words.

13,000 claims were filed on during the first two years of the camp, but the first real claim, as so often happened, came about from information by an Indian, in this case one Napias Jim. Napias, in Shoshoni, means money, and never was an Indian better named, though Napias Jim handled very little of it. What he did get for his knowledge was a kettleful of beans.

Napias Jim came to the cabin of two prospectors named A. J. Leathers and Thomas J. Murphy in the winter of 1867-68, and finding the owners absent helped himself to the beans on the stove. Being intrinsically an honest Indian, Napias Jim later sought out Leathers, and, as payment for the beans offered a chunk of silver ore. All that Leathers asked was that Napias Jim show him and his partners, Murphy and Marchand, where the ore came from. On January 4, 1868, Napias Jim took the men up the east side of Treasure Hill, nearly to its 10,000 foot summit, and showed them what was to become the Treasure Hill mine.

There were good Indians and bad Indians in the country, and the murder of wandering prospectors brought on a mild Indian war which threw Governor "Broadhorns" Bradley into something of a tizzy and made copy for the newspapers of the country, but there was more sound than fury. The volunteers marched, the Indians disappeared, and peace settled over the land. Had such old warriors as Winnemucca, Tintic, or Pocatello still been around they would probably have given the Reese River, White Pine, and Pioche settlers a far rougher time.

When the silver lid of Treasure Hill had been lifted, mining developments shifted to the eastern side of White Pine County, and with it went the population that had made Hamilton the standout of its day, and Ely became the new metropolis.

It presently became apparent that the real wealth of the country was copper. The Nevada Consolidated Mining Company became the biggest producer. Ely's future was assured when the railroad reached there September 29, 1906, the last spike being driven by Mark Requa, son of old Isaac Requa, who had used his Comstock wealth to build the Eureka & Palisades railroad, which had been turned over to son Mark.

Searching for new mines near Ely, Mark Requa bought a copper property near Ruth for $150,000, and began promoting the railroad. On "the Day," as Ely calls it, special trains were made up at Reno, Salt Lake, and Ogden and a mammoth celebration was had. The town was gaily decorated for the occasion, and the festivities began with the arrival of the first train, the one from Salt Lake. It may have been the West's biggest barbecue. Tons of beef and huge kettles of beans and scores of washboilers full of coffee had been prepared.

At 2:30 p.m. the Reno and Ogden trains arrived, and Mark Requa drove home the copper spike from Ruth. The celebration continued for three days. Held's band from Salt Lake played in the Northern Hotel, and people danced in the streets. There were baseball games and every form of fun and frolic that could be thought of including, appropriately, double-jack drilling contests. After that Ely settled down to the life of a modern and sedate— for Nevada, that is—city.

At one time the towns of Ruth and Kimberly would permit neither saloons nor brothels, so a place called Riepetown, which called itself "a blow-off town," came into existence four miles southwest of Ely to supply the needs of the unholy. Ely itself soon took care of that, and Riepetown faded into wherever it is bad ghost towns go.

A great deal of capital from Utah and other places came into the Ely district, and the old gold and silver camps are rapidly being forgotten. White Pine County has a large stock-growing industry to draw from, and recently Ely has dared to challenge her northern neighbor, Elko, for the title of amusement center of Eastern Nevada. Special excursions are being run from Salt Lake City and other Utah towns. This also brings them into competition with Las Vegas in a way. If a native of Ely were to be asked what Ely has that Las Vegas hasn't, he would probably proudly reply, "White Pine County is what Las Vegas ain't got." To him, that is answer enough.

CHAPTER FOURTEEN

Austin and Eureka

Situated in the central part of Nevada on Highway 50 are two of the oldest and most durable towns of the great basin, Austin and Eureka. Though their boom days are gone both still hang onto those prize plumes of the pioneer era, the county seat.

Austin is the county seat of Lander County, though Battle Mountain, a more accessible town in the north end of the county, has tried vainly for many years to wrest the prize away from it. Eureka, seat of the county by the same name, has had little serious competition.

Both towns are in what is called the Reese River section, though Austin has the best claim on the river. It also boasts a newspaper, *The Reese River Reveille*, which has perhaps given more Nevada history to the world than any other of the state's many excellent pioneer newspapers, with the exception of the *Virginia City Enterprise*, on which Mark Twain cut his journalistic teeth, and which was once published by Lucius Beebe, the New York *bon vivant* who has made a new career of restoring Virginia City to its primitive grandeur and to becoming one of the leading authorities on the state.

In almost every section of the great basin, we encounter the Mormon influence in one way or another. Reese River is no exception. In 1854 Brigham Young sent out a party to aid the Saints in Carson Valley, and on their way they camped on Reese River and named it after their leader.

The Reese River district embraces the Toiyabe Range in the southern part of Lander County, and Austin is the center of the district. The altitude of Austin is 6,800 feet. Nearby Telegraph Peak rises to a height of 9,000 feet. Austin is on the slope of Mt. Prometheus, which is 8,236 feet high, and this is the mountain most of the mineral came from; but in those days it was called Lander Hill and is still called that by the natives. The name was later changed to Mt. Prometheus by some government agent who thought Lander Hill far too plebian for a government map.

Though Austin was to become the metropolis, a group of rich camps grew up close around, some of them antedating Austin. A few of them close around were Amador, Geneva, and Yankee Blade. Farther south were such history-making camps as Belmont, Berlin, Ione, Grantsville, and Manhattan, as much to be associated with the still-to-be-born Tonopah district as with Austin. A burgeoning town called Jacobsville became the first seat of Lander County. Amador, seven miles from Austin, also fought hard for the county seat. With towns springing up like mushrooms, to wither in the afternoons, and county lines constantly changing, it becomes a weary and unnecessary task to keep track of them.

Unlike the others there is still an air of permanence about Austin. The Methodist and Catholic churches are still in good condition. The famous old International Hotel, which was moved there from Virginia City, is not as imposing as it once was because the ornate front was moved to Las Vegas long ago, but it is still in good repair. Another empty hotel up the street has an outside stairway from the sidewalk, and once the owner used a block and tackle to raise it at night. One would not be wise to climb its rotten steps, but there is no reason for it to be torn down for a more modern structure. You will find friendly people sitting on benches in front of some of the going concerns, and they will tell you they have never lost faith in their town.

A mile west are the ruins of Stokes Castle, a three story structure built in 1897 by mining magnate Anson Phelps Stokes, but by way of contrast there are modern brick homes on the lower slopes of Mt. Prometheus.

Highway 50 enters the town through the middle of the old cemetery, following the route of the old Overland stage. As in most old mining camp cemeteries, one is struck by the prevalence of Irish names on the tombstones. America has never justly acknowledged its great debt to the Irish. "Pat," said someone at the funeral of an Irishman, "was only a mucker, but he was a *good* mucker."

As the stage lines spread out like spider webs, stations with such names as Darrough's Hot Spring, Tate, and San Antone sprang up to become as familiar to Austinites as Brooklyn to a New Yorker. The Toiyabe and Toquima ranges were household words, as were the names of the valleys and the canyons.

Everyone knew of Ophir Canyon, where the famous Murphy lode was discovered, giving birth to a town called Toiyabe City, and Pony Canyon where Vanderbosch, Buel, and others spent the winter in sight of the soon to be famous Pony Ledge. Everybody owned a ledge of one kind or another. One noted one was the Post-hole ledge where a miner struck chloride while digging a post-hole. He bounded away to sell his claim for sixty-thousand dollars—a good investment, since the ore proved to be chloride of lead rather than silver. Everybody leaped first, and looked later.

The Reese River district was discovered by William M. Talcott on May 2, 1862, and the rush resulted in the town of Austin. On December 19, 1862 the county of Lander was carved out of Humboldt and Churchill counties, and Austin was named county seat September 1, 1863, making it one of the most venerable of present day county seats.

The White Pine rush greatly reduced the population of Austin between 1872 and 1877. During that time the Manhattan Silver Mining Company acquired title to most of Lander Hill and continued its operations until 1887. But as early as 1867 there were eleven mills and more than six thousand miners in the camp.

Buel and Dorsey were pioneers in the milling, and in the middle of 1863 had erected a five stamp mill known as the California. Others built a little later were the Rhode Island, Union, Pioneer, and Clifton. The ten stamp Oregon mill was doing business in 1864.

Lumber had to be imported from California at a cost of $250 to $500 per thousand feet, and it was hard to interest capital.

In 1864 Vanderbosch erected a roasting furnace, which was a big event in the history of Reese River, as it proved that the ore could be treated successfully even if the bricks of the furnace had to be covered with blankets in the winter time to keep the heat in them. The yields ranged from $150 to $175 a ton. But the miners were broke—and nobody had thought to bring in such unimportant things as food and clothing. However, in 1864 about two million dollars from San Francisco was invested, and things began to look up.

Of the winter of 1862-63 Browne says, "Everybody was wonderfully rich—in feet. Tents and wigwams soon began to sprinkle the hillsides. Then came great wagons loaded with lumber, and whiskey, food and raiment which brought fabulous prices . . . . About five thousand people gathered in and around Austin during the spring and summer of 1863. They came from California, from Washoe, from Idaho, from Salt Lake and from every point of the compass. Speculation soon reached a pitch of extragavance. Lander Hill, Central Hill, and Mount Prometheus soon became riddled with claims, looking like naked giants lying on their backs, sprinkled with small-pox. Every man who had a pick and shovel dug a hole two or three feet in the ground and called it 'The Grand Magniff,' or, 'The Great Stupendous Ledge,' and thereupon took to speculation. It was all feet and little or no mining."

Austin lost its first major battle when it failed to persuade the Central Pacific to built its line through the town that would have been a natural to handle the vast amounts of freight and passenger traffic. It was in the center of the state, and had long been known by overland travelers, and many optimists believed its mineral wealth would outdo the Comstock. It also had that Nevada novelty, a river—a river in which enthusiastic promoters had once sold stock for a project to make it navigable, quite forgetting that except in flood time Reese River was seldom more than a few inches deep. But the people of Nevada then as now would take a chance on anything.

The stubborn Central Pacific laid its tracks down the Humboldt, and Austin had to do its freighting from Battle Mountain, ninety-two miles to the north, which wanted the county seat as well as the railroad.

Battle Mountain was a boom town in its own right, its mining district having been organized in 1866. The Little Giant mine was located in 1867 and became its most important early producer. By 1872 Battle Mountain had thirty-two mines, a mill, and two smelters, with numerous satellite mining towns it could draw upon. Besides, it was on the Humboldt river, with many agricultural possibilities which made it no mean rival.

Battle Mountain had Austin by the throat, and it cost Austinites $1.25 per hundred to haul its freight to and from the railroad. The only solution was to tap the main line with a branch railroad, and to do so it would have the support of the state. It ran into trouble immediately with railroad-hating Governor "Broadhorns" Bradley.

In 1874 M. J. Farrell put life in the scheme with plans for a narrow-gauge road between Austin and Battle Mountain. Lander County agreed to put up $200,000, with the proviso that the road must be completed within five years. Governor Bradley vetoed the aid measure, but Farrell persuaded the legislature to override the veto. More capital was needed, and when Eastern capital couldn't be interested the narrow-gauge dream became known as Farrell's Folly.

In 1878 the Central Pacific evinced some interest, but nothing more substantial until the wealthy Phelps-Stokes interests took over the project August 30, 1879. Work started at once, but only five months remained in which to claim the original $200,000 subsidy. It was a Hollywood type deadline, with the surprise ending, and Hollywood doesn't overlook such opportunities. Within recent years movie and television viewers have been permitted to see the old plot, with variations, a number of times.

The contractor, General Ledlie, approached the task with great drive and vim, employing as many men on the project as could find room to swing a maul. Though the ground was frozen and the nights bitter cold, there was no letting up in the work as the crews worked by torch and bonfire light. With seventeen days to go, the track end was still twenty-five miles from anxious Austin.

On February 9, the crews were two miles from Austin's city

limits. The deadline came at midnight. The tracks had to be inside the city limits by that hour to claim the subsidy. Austin, however, was equal to the emergency. The Common Council met and unanimously passed a resolution extending the limits of the city out past the railroad tracks. "When the railroad comes, the city will need more land in which to expand," the Council argued with irrefutable logic, and Austin had its railroad, even though it is not on the main line. And it still, after nearly a hundred years, has the county seat, and many of the remnants of its former glory.

At the beginning there were two towns, Austin and Clifton, but citizens combined to grade a road from the lower to the upper town, and then there was only Austin.

By April, 1863, the new city had a hotel, newspaper, and post-office. A Pony Express was started by G. L. Turner to the various mines, and Wells Fargo & Company soon established an express office. Austin was a central point for the Overland stage line east and west, and special lines were started wherever needed. Austin was always transportation and communication conscious.

The passenger traffic between Austin and Virginia City in 1865 was estimated at 6,000 fares at forty dollars a fare. The freight carried over this road cost $1,381,000 besides what came from Salt Lake City. Lumber from the Sierra sawmills cost upward of $250.00 per thousand, and that sawed from native pinion pine was worth $125.00 per thousand. Bricks manufactured at Reese River sold for from $12.00 to $18.00 per thousand.

That one year alone Wells Fargo carried treasure valued at six million dollars. There were three banking houses and professional men enough to supply every normal need. Austin was a fast-growing metropolis, and what it might have become had the Nevada Central Railway been built a few years earlier is anybody's guess. Though it still has to watch its courthouse with an eagle eye against its old antagonist, Battle Mountain, it can take satisfaction that it has outlived many of the other boomers who have been ghosts these many years.

Austin was ever a place able to meet emergencies in a typically Western manner. Being a wild and woolly town, it was not easy to raise money to build a Methodist church. Yet, any kind of stock could be sold; so the proponents of the church simply incorporated the Methodist Mining Company and listed its stock for sale. They realized a profit of a quarter of a million dollars, and with it built the finest church in Nevada.

It was Austin which originated the $175,000 sack of flour whose story had been told many times. The proceeds went to charity, specifically the Sanitary Fund of 1864 for the relief of war suffering, though at the beginning its purpose was not so high-minded and started out as an election bet.

As in other places in Nevada, opinion on the Civil War then raging was divided, although as a rule the Southerners were in a minority. They made up in noise and vehemence what they lacked in numbers. Among the supporters of the Southern cause was an Austin merchant from Missouri named R. C. Gridley. The campaign for mayor between Democrats and Republicans was a hot one, and Gridley made a campaign bet with H. S. Herrick on the outcome. If Gridley lost the bet, he was to carry a sack of flour on his back from lower town Clifton to upper town Austin, accompanied by a brass band playing "John Browne's Body," while if Herrick lost he was to do the same thing, with the impartial band playing "Dixie."

The Republicans won, and the morning after election Herrick appeared in front of Gridley's store with the brass band and Gridley shouldered a fifty pound sack of flour and began his march, which soon turned into a parade as practically the entire population of Austin joined in. A crepe-draped broom, the symbol of democracy, was held aloft, and the flour sack was covered with Union flags.

When the march was completed, the sack of flour was auctioned off, and it was announced the proceeds would go to the Sanitary Fund. The bidding was spirited, and each time it was sold it was donated back to the fund by the successful bidder and auctioned off again. Six thousand dollars was raised before the day was done.

So enthused was Mr. Gridley that he took the sack of flour to Virginia City for another auction, and $25,000 more was raised. It then went to San Francisco and other Pacific coast cities, and

total of $175,000 was raised in Nevada and California, before
he sack was sent east to be auctioned over and over again, and
hough the total amount raised was never disclosed it was a great
um and proved to be one of the largest fund raising campaigns
or charity in the entire nation, and redounded to Austin's ever-
asting glory. In the process Mr. Gridley changed from a staunch
secessionist to an ardent Unionist, and later became head of one
of Austin's largest banks. Who can say that gambling is always
harmful?

Austin had its tragic figures and its glamorous ones. With all
kinds of people gathering there, it could not have been otherwise. Perhaps Jacob Breyfogle was the most tragic of all. In
1864 he left Austin, a young, energetic prospector with a strong
belief that he was going to strike it rich, and apparently he did.
After a long absence he staggered back into town, a wild-eyed,
feverish, delirious bearded figure with his arms full of a reddish
ore as rich as any ever found in the great basin. But he couldn't
remember where he had found it, nor in forty years of frantic,
pathetic search was he ever to find it again.

So began the legend of the Lost Breyfogle mine, and for nearly
a hundred years prospectors, geologists, and plain tenderfeet have
searched in vain for the ledge from which these samples came.
Many times men have thought they found it, but no ore anywhere
ever was like the samples Breyfogle brought back with him. Few
think it will ever be found, for Breyfogle had tangled with the
cruelest enemy of all, the desert in the summer time. In his delirium he never could remember where he had been. An Indian
admitted tracking him for many miles to murder him for his
shoes, but never quite got up the courage. Other Indians are
supposed to have found him dying from thirst and nursed him
back to moderate health.

No life was ever more completely wasted than Breyfogle's, as
he wandered the cruel desert year after weary year, until Indians
finally put an end to his sorrowful life somewhere in the vicinity
of Las Vegas.

By happy contrast was Austin's great opera star, Emma Nevada,
whose artistic triumphs equaled the best that America could pro-

duce. Born Emma Wixom at Alpha Diggin's, California, February 7, 1859, she was brought to Austin when five years of age by her doctor father, and her mother, who was a dealer in a pioneer gambling establishment.

The first account of her singing was in the parade of the famous Gridley sack of flour in which her girlish voice joined the marching chorus of "John Brown's Body." Her father was one of the auctioneers. She sang at the dedication of the Methodist church. Her mother died when Emma was thirteen, and her father placed her in Mills Seminary.

In 1877 Emma went to Europe to study music, having done post graduate work in languages at Mills. She studied in Vienna under Mme. Marchesi, and her voice attracted favorable attention. Her father joined her and became her manager on the concert stage of Europe and America. She was a tremendous success everywhere she sang. Queen Victoria is said to have presented her with a diamond necklace worth $100,000, and she sang at the coronation of King Edward the Seventh.

Emma Nevada remained loyal to the state from which she had taken her name and was called its ambassador of good will. Personally popular everywhere, she received her most heart-warming reception when she returned to Austin after her great triumphs abroad. The town never had a citizen of whom it was more justly proud. Emma Nevada died in Liverpool, June 26, 1940, at the age of eighty-one, a universally beloved lady of song.

Eureka County was carved out of Lander County, March 1, 1873, because its mineral resources justified a separate existence within the Reese River district. The town of Eureka was founded in 1869 by W. W. McCoy and Alonzo Monroe, and it was made county seat.

Like most Nevada counties, Eureka County is a pronounced north and southness, understandable since that is the way the mountains and valleys run. It was easier to go up and down a valley than to cross a mountain range. If the rich mines were in the south and the railroad in the north, you needed a county to connect them, so some of them, like Eureka, look like an upright slab. If Lander County had its Big Smoky Valley, Eureka had the Little Smoky.

The chief mineral district was on Mt. Tenabo, 30 miles south of historic Gravelly Ford, and was the anchor post of one of Nevada's richest mineral belts. All the ore from surrounding districts was brought to Eureka for reduction in its sixteen furnaces. The yield of the district for 1871 was ten million dollars, and the total for the next seven years was twenty million.

Like so many other boom towns, Eureka bore the tribulation of fire and flood. It had three major fires and in 1874 suffered from a cloudburst which cost seventeen lives. Each time the town was rebuilt.

The altitude of Eureka is 6,500 feet, and the highest mountain in the region, Mt. Prospect, towers 9,604 feet in the air. The district of Ruby Hill is two miles west, so close that the names have often been used interchangeably. Secret Canyon lies to the south, Spring Valley to the southwest, and the Pinto or Silverado to the southeast. All contributed to the district.

Eureka was a focal point on the Hamilton & Pioche, and Belmont & Eureka, stage lines, and the postoffice, established in 1870, did a big business. The eighty-four mile long Eureka & Palisades Railway was completed in 1875, giving the district access to the transcontinental line.

Since Nevada's transcontinental lines still parallel each other across the state, in general following the old emigrant trail along the Humboldt, it was necessary to build short north and south lines, many of them narrow gauge, and the history of Nevada's railroads would fill a book—in fact has done so in an excellent volume by Lucius Beebe and Charles Clegg. The Eureka & Palisades was undoubtedly one of the more important.

Ruby Hill on the northerly spur of Prospect Peak, and Adams Hill north of the town, have contributed a great deal to the prosperity of the Eureka district. The mines of Eureka were the first important lead-silver mines in the nation. In the earliest days of the camp the high lead content kept it from being important until better methods of smelting were introduced.

Major McCoy and his associates operated rather unsuccessfully at the outset, but in the fall of 1869 Colonel G. C. Robbins built a small furnace and demonstrated that Eureka ore could be successfully treated. In 1870 Albert Arentz introduced a syphon system which revolutionized the method of discharging bullion. The McCoy furnace was leased to Colonel David E. Buel, and he and his associates bonded several mines and founded the Bateman-Buel enterprises which became prominent not only in the eastern Nevada mines but also in the Bingham and Mercur districts of Utah.

The Eureka Consolidated Mining Company was organized, and in 1874 the Richmond Consolidated became the second largest producer in the district.

The first Apex case, forerunner of the numerous Apex suits which vexed the West and the whole mining industry, was brought in 1877 between the Eureka and Richmond companies, and resulted in a final victory for the Eureka Consolidated in 1881.

Water was encountered in the Eureka Con shaft at 765 feet in 1881 that drowned out the shaft the next year, and continuous pumping was necessary thereafter. As the bonanza bodies became exhausted, the mining passed into the hands of leasors, who made the most production from 1885 to 1890.

In 1890 the Richmond smelter was shut down, and the Eureka smelter was abandoned in 1891. The camp entered into a long period of inactivity. In 1905 a revival of interest in mining occured as a result of the merging of the old Eureka and Richmond companies into the Richmond-Eureka Mining Company.

A more recent revival culminated in the formation of the Eureka S. & M. Mining Company. It is hardly probable that present day operations will ever surpass the halcyon days between 1869 and 1883 when the production was approximately $40,000,000 in silver, $20,000,000 in gold, and 225,000 tons of lead.

An incident is related in *Pioneer Nevada* which proves that frontier justice was not always infallible, but could, in at least one instance in Eureka, be rectified. In the winter of 1888 an Eureka merchant named Phil Paroni was suspected of a rape that had had the town seething. He was found innocent in two trials and a grand jury investigation. Nevertheless, a mob was formed which seized Mr. Paroni at his home, took him to the lime kiln, stripped him to the waist, and covered him with hot tar and shreds of paper. Some wanted to set fire to the tar and burn him alive, but others prevailed and his hands were tied behind him and he was sent down the railroad tracks with orders never to return.

Cut and bleeding and half frozen, Paroni covered twelve miles to a section house at Diamond Station where the section boss, Barney McCook, took him in, cleaned him up, and gave him clothing. Mr. Paroni returned to Eureka. Although he recognized some of the mob, he could not prove anything. The citizens realized that he was innocent and tried to make up for the blotch on the town. Mr. Paroni became a leading and respected citizen and served as county commissioner.

The incident was reminiscent of the blind stupidity of a mob which had wanted to hang James Reid, of the Donner party in 1846, at Gravelly Ford, in the same county, but had compromised on banishment, which had seemed as certain death as what had been done to Phil Paroni. Reid, like Paroni, lived to become an honored and respected citizen.

Central Nevada was never without its shares of Indian and outlaw troubles. From the days when Joe Walker had clashed with the Piutes back in the early thirties, up to the Modoc war at the turn of the century, the resentful and beleagured redmen were seldom averse to sticking an arrow or a bullet into any lone white man they chanced to encounter, and if they chanced to kill more than one the whites promptly declared that an Indian war was on and volunteers were called for. Reese River and White Pine shared such a war, but in terms of casualties it was scarcely worth writing a history about.

The worst depredations occurred during the Pony Express days, and though most of the pony boys escaped, thanks to the swiftness of their ponies, a number of stations were burned and the attendants killed.

It cannot be said that the Indians were altogether, or even mostly, to blame. Nick Wilson, an express rider who had many narrow escapes, tells of an instance in his book, *The White Indian*

Boy, in which a passenger on the Overland Stage got out and calmly shot a harmless old Indian who was trying to shoot a squirrel for his dinner. The man from the civilized East said smugly that he had promised his friends that he would shoot an Indian.

The Indians responded to good treatment, as the Mormons proved over and over again. The late Louis Lemaire of Battle Mountain stated that his father used to contract hay to the soldiers during the early days, hired Indians to put up the hay, treated them fairly, and never had any trouble with them at all.

Present day tourists of Nevada are frequently waited on by courteous Indian gas station attendants or waitresses who are descended from those once feared and dreaded Piute warriors.

Eureka did, however, once have some trouble which some have called the Charcoal, or the Fish Creek, war, but it was not against Indians.

The smelters at Eureka were dependent on Italian workers, known as the Carbonari, for the charcoal required to operate. This the immigrants burned in their own kilns and sold by the bushel, and it was a major business. The insatiable furnaces soon depleted all the scrub timber close to the towns and the camps had to move farther back, adding to the transportation costs. While the Carbonari was planning to ask for an increase in price, the smelters lowered it from 30¢ to 27½¢ per bushel.

The Charcoal Burners' Union numbered several thousand men, and they marched on Eureka to voice a protest, gathering strength as they went. Their pleas unheeded, they went on a rampage and literally took over the town in definance of police authority. There was considerable rioting, and no arrests. The riots began August 11, 1879, and for six days Eureka knew a reign of terror. Meantime, the Carbonari were in control of the charcoal pits, and smelter operations came to a dead halt.

Frantic wires were sent to the governor urging him to send troops to "quell the insurrection," and steps were taken by Major Butler, while the stalemate continued and the Carbonari stood firm in their demands.

Then Deputy Sheriff J. B. Simpson rode out thirty miles with a posse to a camp of charcoal burners on Fish Creek. The affair was brief and sudden, and not too much has been written about it, not even whether these were the same Carbonari who had been in Eureka or not; but when the smoke cleared five of the charcoal burners lay dead and six more were wounded. Not a posseman received a scratch. The unbiased investigator will have to make up his own mind whether it was a case of resisting arrest, or a rather coldly planned massacre. At any rate it broke the strike and the Carbonari went back to work.

There was long a rivalry between Austin and Eureka, though the former city had its hands full with Battle Mountain. Each city boasted one of the best newspapers in the state, the *Reese River Reville* at Austin, and the *Sentinel* at Eureka; yet they joined forces when anything threatened the welfare of the entire district.

Like the rest of Nevada both sides had their supporters during the Civil War, but in most places they were level-headed enough to keep local war from breaking out, and hostilities were usually limited to fist fights. Both sides could join in celebrating the Fourth of July. Often one side or the other would predominate in some camp, and the weaker in numbers would sing small.

Pioneer Nevada relates one incident which occurred in a small town between Austin and Eureka where all were Southern supporters and they had announced that no display of the Stars and Stripes would be tolerated on the Fourth of July. They received a surprise when a lone wagon bound for California containing a man and his family drove through town with the Stars and Stripes flying, with the man of the family on the seat with his rifle across his lap, and his wife and daughters singing, "Rally 'Round the Flag." They had been warned of the danger, but patriotism would not be denied, and as the family left town they shouted back a triumphant, "Hurrah for Abe Lincoln!"

Austin and Eureka are typical of the endurance and never-say-die spirit of the pioneer towns of the Great Basin. They had outlaw troubles, Indian troubles, and financial troubles; but they are tolerant towns today, and they only get a little mad when tourists are foolish enough to think that they are ghost towns.

CHAPTER FIFTEEN

The Humboldt Country

None of the weary travelers to California who tried to follow the twisting course of the Humboldt had any idea in those first few years that on either side of them millions, perhaps billions of dollars worth of mineral lay buried. All it meant to them in their long journey was grass and water; yet the ore was there, soon to be claimed by a breed of men no less venturesome than they.

Gold was to found even at Gravelly Ford (Beowawe) where James Reed killed Snyder in the first known instance of white man killing white man in the great basin, and where lynching was almost introduced by the feuding Donner party. Beowawe is now just a few miles off Highway 50. There used to be a descriptive marker on the highway put up by Harolds Club, pointing the way to the historic spot and giving an account of the Reed-Snyder affair, but as in so many other places vandals have torn it down.

Drive that country today and one is in mineral country all the way, but one would be little more aware of it than were those early day emigrants, for the mining country is back in the hills, and the towns are mostly ghosts; but all of them have a history which writers such as Nell Murbarger and Don Ashbaugh have given to the world.

Chief towns along this river are Wells, Elko, Carlin, Battle Mountain, and Winnemucca. All have been important towns and still are. All of them retain most of the old Western flavor. Some of the ghost or near ghost towns back in the mountains, such as Unionville and Tuscarora, had histories comparable to those of the towns along the Humboldt which are still growing. Even a more modern ghost town called Tungsten can be seen on a mountainside near old Mill City, a few miles below Winnemucca, for tungsten, once a rare metal, has lost its economic demand.

The railroad and the highway have kept the other towns prosperous, and tourism is a big business. Modern hotels and motels bear no resemblance to the old time stage stations which were once so welcome. Few travelers between Winnemucca and Lovelock can imagine the horrors of the Carson Sinks, or the road that was once called, "Forty miles of hell!"

Wells, the first town on the way west after leaving Utah, and just past noted Pilot Peak, was the point where the early day emigrants thought they had it made—when they could forget about the High Sierras which still lay ahead. Humboldt Wells, as the region was then called, was a fine place to stop and rest, and it still is.

Wells is a smaller edition of Elko, fifty miles on, which is the county seat of Elko County, in the northeast corner of Nevada, which now claims to be not only the largest county in the state, but also boasts that it has more range cattle than any other county in the nation. It is cow country today, and is proud of the fact that Bing Crosby once owned a ranch there. The amazing Humboldt which from the highway doesn't appear to have enough water to quench the thirst of a pack train of burros, still manages to provide enough irrigation water for hay to feed the thousands of livestock.

It was along that river that a few Frenchmen, more optimistic than practical, once tried to build a canal deep enough to float barges loaded with ore down the river. Remains of the old canal can still be seen in places, and it reached nearly to Winnemucca, and the only thing that was ever wrong with it was that there wasn't enough water, and somtimes what there was would have had to run uphill.

Elko, a booming town of seven thousand, in the old days was a transportation center for the Pioche and White Pine districts, as well of those to the north as far as the Idaho state line. Today, it is wide open gambling town with three big casinos, which though perhaps not so large as some in Reno or Las Vegas are yet large enough to accommodate any stranger looking for action. Like its rival, Ely, in White Pine, it constantly runs excursions to Salt Lake City and other Utah points, and one can't walk a block without seeing a Utah license. It has a fine library, churches, a branch of the University of Nevada, and the State Industrial School. It is the home town of the present governor of Nevada.

Elko and Eureka counties was once the field of operations for Nevada's most famous woman cattle rustler, Susie Raper, who, if not so famous as Belle Starr or Cattle Kate, Elkoites will tell you, was a darned sight prettier. So cute was Susie, in fact, that no jury would ever convict her; yet she had the nerve to stand off a sheriff's posse with a comb in lieu of a gun, and she escaped the law so long as she retained her good looks. Then it was the less gallant Southwest which finally put her behind bars.

It is a little hard to believe that Elko and Wells are in earnest when they advertise the wonderful hunting and fishing which can be had back in their mountains, yet they are not exaggerating. They have fine mountain lakes and creeks, and deer and other game; indeed the country is becoming widely known for its dude ranches.

The little town of Palisades where the Eureka & Palisades railroad took off from the Central Pacific, was once something of a rip-snorter. One of its favorite amusements was to stage fake Indian attacks and stage holdups for the edification of the pilgrims on the way to the boom towns. Sometimes these boomeranged, but in the words of the old timers, "What the hell!"

Carlin, a few miles down river from Elko, was an important mining and railroad center, and it had one boom that was unique in Nevada history when coal was discovered there.

Beyond Carlin lies Battle Mountain, itself once an important mining as well as transportation center. The town takes its name from a battle in a nearby canyon where a bunch of hostile Indians were trapped and wiped out. Once stage lines ran out across the desert to reach the boom towns practically to the Idaho border.

When the first automobiles began to be used they were welcomed by the stage drivers though they didn't always make much better time than a fast team. The first auto stage driver out of

Battle Mountain was Charles H. Snow, an adventurer who had followed mining from Canada to South America. When the cars broke down on the desert, the drivers had to stop and fix them on the spot. Mr. Snow was particularly adept and resouceful at this business. Tires, too, were a problem. Mr. Snow's friend, the late Louis Lemaire, said that Charley used to wrap his tires in rawhide to make them last longer, a trick that served its purpose, but when he drove into Battle Mountain everyone on the street took to cover as the gravel from between the tires and the rawhide squirted out like buckshot.

Once Mr. Snow burned out a bearing in the desert, and the babbit he was using to repair it exploded in his face, putting out both eyes. It put an end to that part of his career. Undaunted, Mr. Snow, who now lives in Napa, California, trained himself to use a typewriter and became one of the better known Western novelists with more than three hundred books to his credit, and at eighty-four years of age was still turning them out. Mr. Snow has an encyclopedic memory and an amazing sense of direction, and can still ride across Nevada and identify practically every curve in the road.

In the early days both Battle Mountain and Palisades were favorite hangouts for con men and card sharpers who laid in wait for the tenderfeet getting off the main line. The stay of the sharpers was usually shortened by request, but new ones coming in presented a perpetual problem.

Golconda was once an important mining and smelting town, and was headquarters for the Frenchmen's Canal. One of the best of the modern day mines, the Getchell property, is located nearby, but one looks in vain for signs of the old high life.

Winnemucca, seat of Humboldt County, and a mining and transportation headquarters, is still a very much alive little city, though it has citizens who never heard of its once great mine, Pride of the Mountains. A paved highway takes off to Oregon, and that road tapped mining towns all along the way and was once, when it was a dirt road, of course, much used by the early emigrants. Instead of the crack of six-shooters one now hears the rattle of the slot machines and the softer thud of the dice.

On down the road toward Lovelock and Fernley is the site of old Mill City, which never seemed to quite live up to its early promise, and the Humboldt House, long a popular way station.

Off to the left of the highway, in Buena Vista Canyon, forty miles from Lovelock, is old Unionville, a ghost town which was once a real boomer. It yet has a few old timers in residence, with whom Nell Murbarger visited a few years ago. We have Mrs. Murbarger's permission to draw on these sources.

Unionville came into existence in 1861, and was for a time believed to be as rich as the Comstock. Even Samuel L. Clemens came over for a look. So beautiful was the canyon that the town was first called Buena Vista (beautiful view). The Civil War was beginning and feeling was naturally divided. Upper Town, inhabited by Union sympathizers, was called Unionville, while Lower Town was called Dixie. A no-man's land between was called Centerville, but a horse drawn stage made hourly trips from town to town. Nevertheless, the people got along well enough. A schoolhouse was built and it served alike as a meeting place for the Union League, and the Knights of the Golden Circle and the Sons of Liberty who were strong Southern supporters. It also served the Masonic Lodge, the Odd Fellows, and the Sons of Temperance, and was an armory for the Unionville post of Buena Vista Guards.

Unionville had only one church, and its pastor, Reverend L. Ewing, was a reformed California gambler. When Rev. Ewing was called to another post, the building was moved to Mill City where it became a Men's Clubhouse and saloon. The financial backer of the church was J. C. Fall, leading merchant and owner of the Arizona mine, which turned out to be the one big producer of the district.

In 1863 Unionville had a population that caused it to be designated seat of Humboldt County, at the time the largest county in the state, but the seat of government eventually wound up in Winnemucca.

"Flanking the single narrow street that twisted for four miles through the canyon, were eighteen stores, including general merchandise, meat markets, pharmacies, and jewelry stores. There

ere also nine saloons and a brewery, two hotels, two express
ffices, four livery stables, a dentist, and a newspaper," Nell
Turbarger wrote in *Ghosts of the Glory Trail.*

This last, *The Humboldt Register,* edited by W. J. Forbes, was
ne of the more flamboyant in Nevada, and Forbes was said to
dip his barbs in vitriolic wit and perfume them with satire," be-
ore Mark Twain popularized that style of writing.

Unionville was hard to get at, and prices were high. Wells
Fargo carried mail to and from Virginia City for 25¢ per pound.
There was also a tri-weekly pony express to Idaho City, Idaho.

Building costs were high, and editor Forbes commented on
he quality of the lumber that was brought in, which would apply
o most Nevada lumber as well: "Half of it is just what it is
racked up to be—the other half is knot."

Despite the high prices, and the inability of the citizens to
istinguish the firewood, mostly sagebrush, from the hay, Union-
ille lived high on the hog, and enjoyed itself to the utmost. It
ad no jail in the early days, and the sheriff did well guarding the
risoners for $12.00 per day each. If lawbreakers became too
bstreperous, it was a simple matter to take them up the canyon
nd hang them.

When the Central Pacific was built down the Humboldt, Union-
ille's days were numbered. It fought valiantly to keep Winnemucca from getting the county seat, but lost out in 1873. W. J.
Forbes, foreseeing the death of the camp, had moved on, later
tarting an unsuccessful paper in Battle Mountain called *Measure
or Measure.* He once wrote: "Out of every twenty men nineteen
atronize the saloon for every one who reads a newspaper. I am
oing to follow the crowd." Old and broken down, the dynamic
ld journalist supposedly died by his own hand.

J. C. Fall, who had spent three million dollars in Unionville,
most of it profits from the Arizona mine, finally announced that
e could no longer operate because of the government's policy on
ullion. That was the death knell of colorful Unionville, and by
880 only a few hardy survivors who loved the canyon were left.
omehow, in retrospect, the old town seems more glamorous than
he up-to-the-minute towns of today.

Elko County has a host of ghost towns north of the railroad, each with its history of hardships, riches, glory, decline and fall. Some of these nearly forgotten towns were Aura, Charleston, Cornucopia, Columbia, Deep Creek, Gold Creek, Jarbidge, Midas, and Tuscarora—of which Tuscarora occupied a position to Elko much like that of Unionville to Winnemucca.

Tuscarora lies forty miles northwest of Elko. The Beard brothers, John and Steve, are credited with the first find of ore on the slope of Mt. Blitzen, but they preferred to enjoy the world rather than set it on fire. There were gold and fish in the creeks, and the Beards divided their time about equally between the two. Then in 1871 W. O. Weed discovered a great silver lode, and Tuscarora sprang into existence overnight. Stores and hotels quickly followed the saloons. With a population of five thousand, Tuscarora became the largest town in Elko County. Its great mines were Dexter, the Navajo, Nevada Queen, Grand Prize, and North Belle Isle.

Completion of the Central Pacific had released hundreds of Chinese laborers who stampeded to Tuscarora, giving it the largest Chinese population of any town in the state. Soon two thousand of them were gathered in Tuscarora's Little Shanghai, and race trouble soon developed. Joss houses, opium dens, and lotteries flourished, and it was said that every third Chinese was a gambler.

The Chinese were adept at defending their property, but one lone white man succeeded in making off with $5,000 by stuffing five pounds of sulphur and pepper down a stove-pipe and covering it with a bucket. Then, while the strangling Chinamen were rushing out the front door, the robber broke down the flimsy back one and got away with the stakes that had been left on the tables In a few weeks he had lost it all back to these same clever Chinese

Between 1872 and 1876 six large mills were in operation, giving Tuscarora its greatest prosperity. Much of the fuel was sagebrush but water and the government's crusade against silver did irreparable damage to the district. A fire in the Dexter that destroyed the pumps, flooding the mine, delivered the final blow, though the Dexter continued to operate until 1898, and in its career produced nearly $40,000,000 in ore, largely silver.

Midas, originally Gold Circle, was another rollicking town with five thousand or more people, and lived up to its name to the tune of nearly two million dollars.

Charleston, once called Mardis after one of Nevada's most colorful characters, "Allegheny" Mardis, was a tough town, close enough to the Idaho line for its outlaws to hide themselves in the badlands along the Owyhee River.

Nell Murbarger says in *Ghosts of the Glory Trail*, "Among Elko county pioneers, a favorite story concerns an early day sheriff whose tour of duty called him to the north part of the county. Returning to Elko after one such trip he remarked that he had enjoyed a most gratifying experience.

" 'Got your man, eh?' inquired a bystander.

" 'Hell, no! . . . I didn't *get* anybody . . . but I rode plumb through Charleston without getting shot at.' "

The fate of Allegheny Mardis was tragic. He had the habit of confiding his love of nature to his burro, Sampson, and preached fiery denunciations of sin from the Old Testament to the same patient audience. But one day as he was preparing to take the long trip to Elko, he was asked by a Chinaman to take along $250.00 in gold to pay a debt. Next day his abandoned team and wagon were found, and close to it his bullet-riddled body. Nearby were the bare-footed footprints of a man—and only Chinamen went barefooted. This particular Chinaman had six toes on his left foot. There followed a great yanking off of cotton slippers until six toes on a left foot were revealed.

The Vigilantes allowed the Oriental two days to prove an alibi, but when it was found unsatisfactory he was declared guilty, and the entire population of Charleston came out to watch, or participate, in the hanging. Popular George Washington (Allegheny) Mardis was avenged in one of the last lynchings to take place in the county.

One of the last boom towns in the area was Jarbidge, almost astride the Nevada-Idaho line. It created great excitement for a while, but nothing much ever came of it. The boom towns died with the last century. Well, not quite.

Just inside the Nevada line, forty miles south of Twin Falls, Idaho, is a little gambling boomer appropriately called Jack-pot.

Like Utah, Idaho prohibits gambling. Once upon a time Mormons and Gentiles struggled for political control, but the Mormons predominate in south Idaho and its customs are much the same as in Utah. In the old polygamy days a U.S. Deputy Marshal named Fred T. Dubois earned a reputation as a cohab-chaser that placed him in the United States Senate, but now Idaho Mormons and Gentiles alike turn a stony gaze on freedom-loving Nevada. Still, many of them like to gamble now and then, and Jack-pot has sprung up to satisfy that desire—or perhaps merely to torment the worthy people who look askance at Nevada.

Many boom towns of the Great Basin can be erased from history like the markings of a pencil on slate, but others left monuments that will endure for a long, long time.

CHAPTER SIXTEEN

The Washoe

Exciting times all round the town,
Glory, Glory to Washoe,
Stocks are up and stocks are down,
Glory, Glory to Washoe.
Washoe! Washoe!
Bound for the land of Washoe,
And I owned three feet
In the "Old Dead Beat,"
And I'm bound for the land of Washoe.

This was the song sung in the 1870's about the mighty Comstock in the days when the Washoe was bonanza country, and before the treasure seekers moved up the canyon from Mormon Station.

Mormon Station on the site of the present village of Genoa was a hotel and store housed in a two story log building. In 1850 a few persons had settled in the Carson Valley for trading purposes with migrating gold seekers, some of whom wintered in that region. During these years several Mormons entered the valley—John Reese first among them, who brought in thirteen wagons of provisions.

When Reese first came into the valley alone, his nearest neighbor was James Fennimore, who lived in Gold Canyon twenty-five miles distant. "Old Finney's" home was a dugout whose front door consisted of rags and strips of canvas, the man being shiftless and a dram drinker. Reese in his *Mormon Station Manuscript*

195

states that Finney had a flume in the canyon for gold washing and that Comstock, who came to Carson Valley in 1865, bought him out.

Among other earlier settlers were three persons named Lee, Condie, and Gibson. By act of Utah Legislature approved January 17, 1854, the limits of Carson County were defined and the governor was authorized to appoint a probate judge whose duty it should be to organize the county by dividing it into precincts, holding an election, filling various offices, and locating the county seat. The choice fell on Orson Hyde, who with Judge Stiles, U.S. Marshal, and an escort of thirty-five men reached John Reese's settlement in June of 1855. Other parties of Mormons arrived this and the following year . . . meanwhile, miners, farmers, and herdsmen from the Atlantic states had settled in the valley and elsewhere on the eastern side of the Sierra Nevada in such numbers as to alarm the Mormons who now desired them to leave the territory. This they refused to do.

This rich land of the western valleys in Nevada could be had for the taking, and some took too much. Men "squatted" on all the land they could farm, but when a man laid claim to more ground than he could handle, his "surplus" was sometimes confiscated by another man—if he was big enough to hold it.

Colonel Reese had, in 1851, purchased Genoa from its previous owners and laid claim to all the land for miles around. But one, Warren Wasson from California, decided that Reese had much land he and his Mormon colony couldn't handle; and to their chagrin Wasson calmly took over a section which he proceeded to fence.

While hauling his fence lumber one day, Wasson found himself confronted by John Trumbo, a son-in-law of Reese, and his sixteen-year-old son. They were armed and attempted to run Wasson off the land.

Wasson, a fighter, later destined to become one of Nevada's heroes during the Indian trouble, knew his rights and paid no attention to the gun-flourishing Trumbos. Finally, Trumbo raised his gun and fired several shots at Wasson. All missed the mark, but Wasson, tired of playing target, drew his sixgun and returned the fire, wounding Trumbo in the thigh. The injured man fell to the ground and Wasson immediately gave him first aid. While his attention was devoted to the injured man, Trumbo's son ran over to Wasson, thrust an ancient revolver in his face, and pulled the trigger.

The muzzle of the gun was loaded with light birdshot which missed Wasson's eyes but left his face discolored for life. Although Wasson had five shots left, he would not fire back at the boy. Instead, he picked up the boy's father, carried him to a wagon, and took him home.

The Gentiles, or non-Mormons, then fortified themselves and assumed an aggressive attitude, and for two weeks the opposing forces were encamped almost within sight of each other but without coming to blows. News of the disturbance reached the mining camps on the other side of the mountains, and numbers prepared to go in aid of their comrades. The aggressors now feared that they would be themselves expelled from the country and proposed a truce under which all should be allowed to remain on their lands.

Public sentiment was all for Wasson, and this incident did much to stop "land hogging" in Genoa. Such adjustments to land titles were important, for Genoa was the first settlement in Nevada to become important.

The Mormon settlers had, in 1855, established another stockaded trading post and opened a lead mine nearby, and in September of this same year a Mormon apostle, Orson Hyde, organized the county government. During the early spring of the next year between sixty and seventy Mormon families from Salt Lake City swelled the ranks of the saints in the Carson Valley while non-Mormons continued in from the California side.

The business-like Mormons elected county officers and set the wheels of government into motion. Within a year after Orson Hyde's arrival, Mormon Station was surveyed and the town renamed Genoa. The first settlers cut trees, grew produce, and sold both lumber and the products of their farms.

Although the Carson Valley was itself at peace, clouds of trouble hovered over the home base of the Saints back in Salt

Lake City; so Orson Hyde returned to the Utah capitol late in 1856. Eight months later, the Mormons were recalled home by their leaders; President Buchanan had sent troops to Salt Lake City.

This exodus depopulated Carson County. Land, buildings, sawmills, and established business ventures changed hands for a fraction of what they were worth, raising the wrath of Orson Hyde.

Seven years later, Orson Hyde addressed a letter to the people of Carson and Washoe Valleys. In this famous epistle, he set down a claim for twenty thousand dollars for his sawmill and land in Washoe. The letter was generously interspersed with scriptural quotations. Elder Hyde charged that "During the time he had been away, he had received as rent one span of small, indifferent mules, an old worn-out harnesss, two yokes of oxen and an old wagon."

Should his demand for the twenty thousand dollars remain outstanding, he threatened, Carson and Washoe valleys "shall be visited with thunder and earthquake and with floods, with pestilence and with famine until your names are not known amongst men."

The Gentiles remained undisturbed and in possession, and there is no record that the account was ever settled. Despite Hyde's curse, Washoe remained richly productive.

Residents of Genoa and Carson City, in 1857, led by Isaac Roop of Susanville—which was in California, but was then believed to be in Utah Territory—convened at Genoa, adopted a constitution for what they called the Territory of Nevada, and asked Congress to recognize their independence. The plea was ignored. After the Mormons and the Federal government called a truce in 1858, an effort was made to re-establish Utah Territorial government, but in the absence of Mormon settlers, Utah officials found themselves ignored.

It was spring of 1850 when a wagon train led by John Orr reached the alkali flat near Spafford Hall's Station on the Carson River. Behind the Orr train lay the worst part of the journey, The

River of Death, the Humboldt, and Forty-Mile Desert, another graveyard.

Ahead stood Sun Mountain, Mount Davidson, a barren finger pointing upward 8,000 feet above the rim of the sea, 5,000 above the floor of the desert, a landmark that could be seen through the metallic heat. At its foot flowed the Carson River, and alongside ran the emigrant route.

While John Orr went to Spafford Hall's Station, William Prouse, one of the young Mormons in the party, took a tin milkpan and went down the gulch. He picked up a handful of dry pebbles and panned out a few flecks of yellow. The sight of it started no fever among the Saints. "Throw it away," they called out impatiently, "and come on."

Had an experienced quartz-miner made this find, nothing would have kept him from following the canyon. But Prouse lacked imagination, knew no geology, and threw away the specks of gold. John Orr, and Nicholas Kelly, another member of the party, did name the stream Gold Creek, however, and the canyon through which it flowed, Gold Canyon.

The Orr party continued on to California, where the news was given to California miners. In 1850 a number of these men came over to placer mine in Gold Canyon. Each year more came, and they worked the canyons leading to Sun Mountain.

But this stream of California-bound emigrants flowed past early Mormon Station and Gold Canyon like a stream to the sea. By August the total of emigrants who swept past had reached 60,000 and still kept coming.

Among the teamsters who drove the oxen over the alkali were Sandy Bowers, a good-natured, canny Scot, and James Fennimore, a young Virginian, equally illiterate, "feather-brained," and on the move. It is said Fennimore had killed a man in California and to escape had fled to Utah and changed his name to Finney. The name was corrupted to "Virginny" and the "old" was added by his intimates. Although still a youth, he was hailed up and down the diggings as "Old Virginny."

During this same period, Eilley Orrum Cowan came out to Carson Valley with her second husband, Alexander Cowan. They acquired a land claim in Washoe Valley. Eilley later divorced Cowan and came to Johntown, a camp that had sprung into being four miles from Spafford Hall's Station. Here, in a log cabin, she took in boarders. In the course of time, she numbered among her boarders such Johntowners as "Sandy" Bowers, "Old Pancake" Comstock, "Old Virginny," Pat McLaughlin, Pete O'Riley, Joe Plato, and others. The nucleus of the discoverers of the Comstock were gathered at the boarding house of the future Queen of the Comstock.

In a few years there was a semi-permanent camp at the southern end of the Virginia Range. Men disappointed in California stayed a few weeks or months to pay their way home by panning, though with little hope of finding much on this desolate Sun Mountain. Only the Chinese, who had come in from the coast to dig irrigation ditches for the Saints, had the patience to pan steadily for the small returns. The camp of the whites moved slowly up the canyon and the Chinese trotted behind. The settlement merged and the whole was known as Johntown.

These original Johntowners weren't happy, only chagrined, at the discovery of silver on the Comstock Lode. To them it was just "blue stuff, blasted blue stuff."

In 1850 silver mining was comparatively a new industry in the United States. There were no silver miners among the men who rushed to California in '49, but there were Mexicans in Gold Canyon who had worked in the silver mines of their native land. One Mexican, "Old Frank," was a friend of Ethan Allen Grosh and Hosea Ballou Grosh, two young miners who entered Gold Canyon in 1851. It was possibly he who showed the Grosh brothers the silver ledges.

By 1858 the prospectors were working along Six Mile Canyon with values lessening as they approached the upper levels. They didn't think of lode mining and refused to give up the placer search. Early in 1859, Old Virginny, Pancake Comstock, and the rest of the partners struck the surface diggings. Matter of fact, they claimed the ground for placer, ignorant of the fact that under this thin crust lay the fabulous wealth of Crown Point, the Yellow Jacket and Kentuck mines.

One day a Mexican miner came to work for them in their placers. He could speak no English, but he gestured and loudly announced to his employers, "Bueno!" The miner from Mexico pointed dramatically toward Sun Mountain and directed, "Mucha plata! Mucha buena plata!"

The Johntowners knew no Spanish, but to them the Mexican was saying "Gold." Not entirely disregarding him, they worked on doggedly, recalling only afterward that his words were "Mucha plata! Mucha buena plata!" Again a peon, upon seeing them throw away buckets of "blue stuff" remonstrated, "You keep one dollar and throw away two."

Meanwhile, the two Irishmen, Pete O'Riley and Pat McLaughlin, were trenching a ravine to follow the placer rock. To impound water for their rockers, they set about digging a tiny reservoir and at four feet struck the stratum of the Ophir and were astonished at the results shown in their pannings.

But it remained for a rancher, not a miner, to explore the possibilities of the blue mud. Augustus Harrison of Truckee Meadows took a chunk of this new kind of ore over the Sierras to a friend, Judge James Walsh, in Grass Valley.

An assay proved the ore ran to thousands of dollars a ton in gold and silver. The answer was plain now, the "blasted blue stuff" Old Virginny and his pals had piled in waste dumps was fabulously wealthy in silver. Harrison and his friend agreed to keep it secret, but each had a few personal friends who gleaned the news. This assay had been run late at night, but by nine o'clock the next morning the rush to the Washoe was on.

The Grosh brothers might have been considered the Comstock discoverers had not death struck twice in 1857. But it isn't probable. Henry De Groot credits the brothers with discovering silver ore, but says:

"It is obviously a mistake to say that they discovered the Comstock unless we consider the ore channel that passes through the present Dayton claim (at Silver City) as being the main lode. For there can be no question that they obtained their best specimens from that neighborhood . . . the fact is that they never found any ore like the rich silver ore at the Ophir."

201

Nor did any of the old-time Comstockers believe that the brothers discovered the Comstock—although there has always been controversy in the matter. The struggles and sad fate of these brothers before they could organize a stock company in El Dorado County has aroused the sympathy of thousands. In August, 1857, Hosea Grosh, while prospecting, struck his foot with a pick. The injury did not seem to amount to anything, but when a menacing red line ran up his leg, he began treating the wound with compresses. This treatment was ineffectual, and the inflamation and fever mounted. After suffering agonizing pain, Hosea died September 2. His brother Allen was overwhelmed with sorrow. After he had buried Hosea (the grave may be seen now in the Silver City graveyard) and had paid his debts, he boxed up their papers, books, and tools, and left them in the stone cabin in American Flat Ravine.

With Richard Bucks, a friend, Allen Grosh set out in late November for California. An early winter had laid deep snow in the Sierra Nevadas and the two men trudged on with the burro on whose back they had packed their food and some of the samples of their ore. Soon it became necessary to throw away their belongings and they had to kill the burro for food.

They struggled through waist-deep snow and crossed the summit, continuing down the western slope. When they stumbled onto the cabin of a Mexican miner, both men's legs were frozen to the knees.

Bucke, who consented to have an operation that amputated his legs, lived to be an old man; but Allen Grosh refused, saying he would die before he would go through life with no legs. After this, he lived only a few weeks and he was buried in a little graveyard at Last Chance mining camp.

One man's poison is another man's wine. The Grosh misfortune was good fortune for Henry Tompkins Paige Comstock, a drifter into Gold Canyon in 1856. He was too lazy to make bread and was nicknamed "Old Pancake." Just how Comstock came into possession of the Grosh boys' cabin isn't known. He told different stories and claimed they gave him the cabin, and that he was their partner. At any rate he took possession of it and came on their papers, letters, and assay reports.

Comstock kept this knowledge a secret. He didn't know silver veins, but he waited around hoping someone would make a discovery.

Although "Old Virginny" Finney has been the butt of many writers, chiefly because of his convivial habits, it would seem he has been remembered more for his weaknesses than for what he did accomplish. Old Virginny was known to be the best judge of placer ground in Gold Canyon, and he located the first quartz claim on the Comstock, February 22, 1858. He is credited with the discovery of the placers below the Ophir in 1857, and it was Old Virginny who led three others up the canyon January 28, 1859, to locate the Little Gold Hill placers. It was obvious that early miners of Virginia City realized their debt to him by naming the town after him, and the mountains above the town were known as the Virginia Range.

Grant Smith in his *History of the Comstock Lode* reported that money meant little to Old Virginny—and generosity was second nature to him. He gave Little French John nine feet of his Gold Hill claim "for tending me through a spell of sickness," and received less for his Comstock interests than any other locator. After he was killed by being thrown from a horse June 20, 1861, the people of Dayton, then known as Nevada and as Mineral Rapids, gave him an appropriate funeral and passed a resolution.

"Resolved: That in the death of James Finney, the people of this Territory have lost a man to whom more than any other they are indebted for the discovery of the mineral wealth of this Territory.

"Resolved: That while we humbly bow to this dispensation of Providence, we recognize it not less a matter of propriety than duty to give our testimony to the virtues of the deceased; and whilst acknowledging his faults, faults common to mankind, we deem it not complimentary but just, to say that James Finney was ever known among the people of this Territory as a generous, charitable, and honest man."

It can be seen that Old Virginny was well liked by his partners in Gold Canyon.

The little original Gold Hill mines were placer claims. The three James Finney took with him as he made the locations were Alex Henderson, Jack Yount, and John Bishop. Each located a placer claim fifty feet in length along the hill and extending 400 feet across the gulch in accordance with the placer location rules of Gold Canyon. They called the new diggings Gold Hill to distinguish them from the placers down below.

A few days after this discovery, Lemuel S. "Sandy" Bowers, Joseph Plato, Henry Comstock, James Rogers, and William Knight came up from Johntown and located an adjoining fifty foot claim which they later subdivided, each taking a ten foot strip across the hill and the gulch.

The new diggings had been discovered on a Saturday, and the next day the rest of the male inhabitants of Johntown trooped to the head of the canyon "to pass upon" the new mines. The majority of the rest of the citizens of this mining metropolis of one dozen small houses sagaciously shook their heads over "Sandy" Bowers' find and "figgered their claims below prospected better."

But this was what sanctimonious, predatory Henry T. P. Comstock had been waiting for. Full of stolen knowledge from the strongbox of the Grosh brothers, he wasn't far behind the rest of the Johntowners and had more reason for taking this strike seriously than the rest of the boys. He came along toward evening, riding a strayed pony, his long legs dangling into the sagebrush.

When he saw the gold, he dismounted in an instant and "hefted" some of the glittering scales. In his loud-mouthed manner, he began bullyraging the rest of the miners "for taking gold out the land I'd located here for a ranch." Besides, he argued "me and Manny"—Emanuel "Manny" Penrod—"own the spring." In addition to this, he added prolifically, there were other men who formerly worked there who had claim on the ground.

Old-time Johntowners seldom quarreled over ground—it had all played out too quickly; so although O'Riley and McLaughlin knew Old Pancake for an abundant liar, they took him in.

CHAPTER SEVENTEEN

Virginia City

So it was born in storm, hope and trouble—the biggest boomer of the Great Basin, center of the greatest mining activity in North America—Virginia City.

During this first severe winter in 1859, animals died for lack of feed, flour sold for eighty dollars a sack, and buzzards pecked at frozen carcasses.

While those who had made it in lived miserably in slimy dugouts, half-frozen and half-starved, more thousands jammed the pass near Placerville waiting for the break in the weather that came in March, 1860. The trail to the Comstock was a crawling snake of humanity as the silver seekers charged to the new strike. But the Washoe was hard country, barren, inhospitable and uninviting, and the lot of these first inhabitants was pitiful as the first winter closed in on them.

By November, a tortuous street followed the line of the Comstock ledge running north and south over the Divide and down the Canyon. It became main street of Gold Hill and Silver City and passed through Devil's Gate, meeting the overland trail at Dayton. It detoured, meandered, and zigzagged to avoid the cabins of miners who refused to move over. Following this zigzag were flimsy cabins, canvas huts, and mud huts serviced by rusty stove pipes. Some drove coyotes from their lairs and took possession. Mackay and O'Brien, future "big boys" of the Lode, lived with ten others in such a dugout. Their food was bad, the water vile, and hundreds became ill. In the spring of 1860, the Sun Mountain dwellers emerged, dripping, wind-chilled, undernourished, but determined. They had run the Washoe gauntlet and lived through the worst winter in history.

Virginia City was born as all the big boomers are born—sprawling, pawing aimlessly for foothold, full grown, and completely unable to walk.

The Comstock finally resumed contact with the outside world as "Snowshoe" Thompson brought in the mail. Our chief source of information concerning these miners is from news items furnished by John A. "Snowshoe" Thompson to the *Sacramento Union* from January, 1856, to March, 1858, and from the letters of "Tennessee" to the *San Francisco Herald* 1857 to 1860. "Tennessee" was marooned in the small town of Genoa and kept contact with the outside world by writing letters to the city newspaper.

Thompson, a Norwegian farmer living on Putah Creek, California, heard that the settlers in Carson Valley and the placer miners at Gold Canyon were without mail and necessary small supplies in winter and would pay well for such service. In the fall of 1856, he fashioned a pair of skis, such as were used in his native land, and carrying as much as sixty to eighty pounds of mail and express, would cross and re-cross the untrodden Sierras as often as thirty-one times in one winter. Snowshoe never carried a blanket or other covering save his common winter clothing. When night overtook him, he kindled a fire by a dry stump or tree top, laid down by its side, and slept. Thompson took the bitter Sierra winters casually, and Myron Angel wrote of him:

"He was never lost in the woods or in the mountains. By observing the trees and rocks, he could tell which was north and direct his course accordingly. He was a man of great physical strength and endurance, and of such fortitude of mind and spirit that he courted rather than feared the perils of the mountains."

The presence of thousands of hungry newcomers to the Comstock had the Indians in a turmoil by 1860. The miners had killed the game, hacked and burned the pine nut trees, and driven them from their retreats. In the spring, the natives of the region, largely Paiutes, gathered at Pyramid Lake in war council. Up until this time, trouble with the Indians had been confined to wagon train shooting matches, stage station attacks, and battles with marauding parties; but the Bannocks, Shoshones, and Paiutes sensed the calamity that Virginia City was bringing upon their nation.

From these assembled chiefs there was only one who was friendly to the whites. He was named Numaga. This young chieftain attempted to point out to his people that war with the whites would mean eventual destruction of the Indian nations. He fasted for three days to express his sorrow until the old chiefs began listening to his earnest explanations that they would surely be driven to the desert to meet starvation, that the Indian could not win against this white man who kept coming. But it was too late. News came to the council of the Williams' Station attack, and Numaga sat down sorrowfully, knowing that now the Paiutes must fight.

James Williams, a trader living about twenty-five miles east of Carson, had been burned by the Indians; three white men were shot, and two others were burned to death. The generally accepted version of the cause of this first attack was that one or more of the whites had stolen two young Bannock squaws and thirty of the Bannock tribe had joined the husbands in recapturing the women and punishing their captors. The news of this attack sent panic up and down the valley, and one hundred five men hastily volunteered under the command of well liked William M. Ormsby, who took command of the Carson unit. Assisting Ormsby in command was another popular leader, Henry Meredith.

Men from Virginia City, Carson, Silver City, and Genoa were in the number under this command, and though experienced fighters, the four companies marshalled under Ormsby were untrained and marched on with no pre-arranged battle plan. They paused at Williams' Station, where they buried the murdered whites, then they picked up the trail north toward Pyramid Lake.

The volunteers moved in swift march to the Truckee, hoping to find the war party unprepared to meet them. As Ormsby's small army advanced, they saw a thin line of braves on a mesa just ahead and out of rifle range. Major Ormsby ordered a charge and almost immediately realized that he had been tricked into

207

ambush. From all sides, Paiutes rose from hiding places, closing off every line of retreat.

Ormsby saw his only chance was to rally his men and fight a slow retreat. He made his way to a small knoll and signaled his panic-stricken volunteers, but as he reached the knoll, he suffered the bad luck of having his saddle turn and throw him.

Before the Major could regain his feet, an arrow struck his heart. Leaderless, the volunteers escaped as best they could, running all ways in wild disorder. The howling Indians from the Black Rock country made the most of their victory, and slaughtered every man they overtook and the white volunteers met utter defeat.

The return of these survivors threw not only the population of the Washoe, but also the whole population of the Far West, into a panic. It looked like full-fledged Indian war with the safety of all the whites in western Utah and along the California mountain fringes in danger.

In all the settlements, women and children were quartered in the strongest stone buildings in each town, and sentinels were stationed at vantage points. Volunteers from all Nevada gathered and were soon joined by others from Downieville, California. San Francisco raised money and arms and the governor of California sent muskets and ammunition.

Major Warren Wasson volunteered for the dangerous mission of running the Indian lines alone from Carson City to Honey Lake Valley to deliver an order commanding the cavalry stationed there to proceed to Carson City. Without changing mounts, Major Wasson rode the one hundred ten miles in fourteen hours, and the cavalry from Honey Lake immediately rode south to join the expedition.

The Washoe regiment of eight infantry and six cavalry companies was under the command of Colonel Jack Hays, an experienced Indian fighter. Major Daniel Hungerford and Captain Edward Storey, who headed the Virginia Rifles, were placed on the staff. The Third Artillery from Fort Alcatraz and the Sixth Infantry from Benicia Barracks came from the coast to join the volunteers. This was an organized, well disciplined army that met

First six-horse stage pulled into Rawhide, October 22, 1907.

Sixteen-mule team delivering 21,000 pounds of liquid freight to Tex Rickard's Northern saloon at Rawhide, Nevada, in 1908. *Photo by Ned E. Johnson, courtesy Nell Murbarger.*

Selling water at five cents a gallon, Rawhide, 1907.

Humboldt House, Humboldt County, Nevada.

Part of the crowd of 20,000 at the single-jack and double-jack drilling contest at Goldfield, Nevada, about 1906. These contests were a major part of every mining town celebration, and miners cheered (and bet) on their favorite teams. *Courtesy Nell Murbarger.*

Main Street of Goldfield, Nevada, January, 1904.

Sacking ore at Red Top Mine, Goldfield.

SANDY BOWERS   **MRS. BOWERS**

Photographs of the original paintings of the two who became millionaires overnight from a 20-foot claim on the Comstock Lode, which yielded over $15,000 a week. Paintings on display at the Bucket of Blood Saloon, Virginia City, Nevada [378]

The Bowers mansion as it was originally constructed, before the addition of the third story.

James W. Nye

Abe Curry, father of Carson City, Nevada.

Lithograph of early Virginia City, Nevada.

Virginia City before 1875.

A saloon in early Virginia City.

Ore train on the Virginia & Truckee.

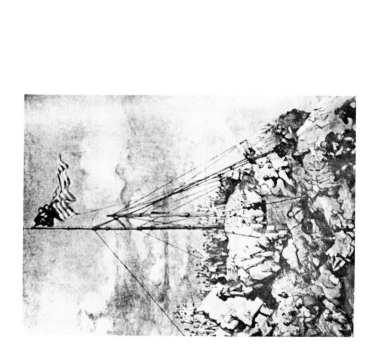

Flag raising, Mount Davidson, Virginia City, 1878.

Gold Hill, Nevada.

Exterior view of Harolds Club, about 1935.

215

Harolds Club's famous Silver Dollar bar with its background of western murals and whiskey waterfall.

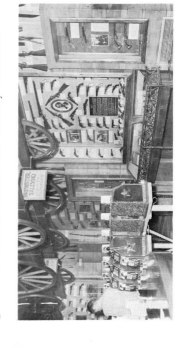

Part of the early western gun collection displayed in Reno's Harolds Club

Exterior view of Harolds Club, Reno, Nevada, 1962.

216

at the Big Bend of the Truckee on the last day of May. Advance scouts reported about three hundred Indians advancing, and the regulars and volunteers went forward to meet them. The Battle of the Truckee lasted for three hours. The Indians fled at dusk after an estimated loss of forty-six men. Three white men were killed and four wounded. The main force followed the Indians, but they had disappeared. After this, the Indians continued raiding Pony Express and stage stations and interrupted service to San Francisco for ten days. It was because of this outbreak that Fort Churchill was established on the Carson trail. This was the last time the Indians seriously menaced the whites. The majority of them fled into the deserts where they nearly starved.

The Paiute War had demonstrated to the Comstock the inefficiency of the civil authority they were governed under. They wanted to be Californians. Anyway, they said, it was California, and not Utah, who had sent troops to their aid.

A notice was posted announcing that Virginia City was going to form a provisional government for Sun Mountain. They would not be governed by Utah, and Salt Lake City was too far away to be concerned with their problems—and they wanted some kind of reliable government.

The Comstock absolutely refused to recognize their Utah authorities, thus ending any hope of reorganizing Carson County under Utah supervision. They sent an appeal to Washington, and this appeal fell into the hands of the Mormons and they were bitterly denounced by the hierarchy of the Mormon Church.

"Since the first organization of the Territory," read the scathing letter, "Washoe has been a most unremunerative burden upon Utah. What is she now? A worthless unaccountable scab . . . a scab which cannot find a place in any honest vocabulary. So let her remain . . . dried up, buried, forgotten. . ." (*Sacramento Union* December 22, 1860. *Territorial Enterprise* June 13, 1872.)

All of which scolding rolled off the backs of the hard rock miners. Besides, they argued, Mormons didn't drink and who could stand the water they had? "Give us whiskey or give us death," answered the Comstock.

Many fortunes were made in these boomers of the Great Basin

. . . and a substantial number of them were not made in mining. Carpenters in some of these fast building camps of the West made as high as thirty dollars a day, many more fortunes were made in saloons and hotels. *Pioneer Nevada,* published by Harolds Club of Reno, tells of one:

In March of 1860, shrewd John L. Moore loaded up $1,600 worth of whiskey and left San Francisco for Hangtown. Finding the mountains still impassable with snow of the previous winter, he secured a pack train and headed for Virginia City.

Moore trundled over the Sierras with two hundred blankets, tin plates, brandy, gin, whiskey, rum, and wine totaling 2,100 pounds. Twenty-five days later, his starved mules staggered up the main street of Virginia City. Cheer after cheer followed the pack train all the way, and a miserable populace hungry for something better than salt mule followed the sound of tinkling bells. Gold Canyon sighed with relief to be reunited with the outside world, whiskey, and food.

Moore unloaded his pack train and immediately set up a 15 x 52 tent saloon. A battered sideboard from an emigrant wagon was hastily erected to serve as a bar. Lanterns were hung and candles lighted and the stock of liquor was arranged at the back. At a given signal the crowd surged through the blocked doors, and the first combination saloon-hotel was opened on the Comstock to the loud hurrahs of a mob of thirsty miners. Flour at this time sold for five dollars a pound and the hungry mixed it with snow and ate it raw.

That night, thirty-six guests of Moore's "hotel" paid a dollar each for a pair of blankets which they spread out on the ground. Some slept on hay ticks with the stuffing at fifty cents a pound. Shavings from construction jobs were collected and added to the hay, but these unguarded bundles were quickly devoured by the starving mules.

Other supplies came in . . . shovels sold for nine dollars each. But liquor was ever the most popular cargo. It made fortunes in nearly every mining camp where recreation and entertainment were scarce.

The camel caravans of the Comstock were perhaps one of the

trangest sights on the Big Bonanza. Lyman, in his *Saga of the Comstock Lode* reported that Comstockers fresh from a night in saloon fell to their knees and began telling their beads at the ight of the coming "resurrection," so overpowered were they at he sight of a caravan of camels swinging out of the night. Mount-d on the back of the largest one in the lead sat a red turbaned Turk, and swaying upon the back of each camel were white locks that glistened in the moonlight.

These Bactrian camels had been purchased in Mongolia and vere used between Placerville and the Nevada mining camps. They eventually came to serve Virginia City and Carson River nills, transporting salt from the Esmeralda marshes for use in the lattering pans of the reduction centers.

Virginia City residents followed with a glass the progress of he salt-laden caravans as they made their way across the sands of Forty Miles and Twelve Mile toward Six and Seven Mile Canyons. t was a sight that never failed to cause excitement.

The camels took to Sun Mountain, as it bore a resemblance to heir native habitat. Lyman reports that when they were relieved of their painful burdens, they would roll and play in the warm ands like giant kittens. But the camels hated the alkali. The alty earth was a torture to them. It turned their nostrils, reddened heir eyes, and irritated the raw spots on their backs.

Horses and mules were "plumb scared to death" when they caught the strange scent of the camels, and for a mile ahead, coaches, freighters, ore teams, and pack freight trains were bolt-ng pellmell in terror while cursing drivers were forced to hold the heads of their teams until the camels passed by. For this reason, it became necessary to bring the camel caravans into Virginia City at night over trails that were more or less unfre-quented. They moved through the dark over the back thorough-fares following the back streets of the camp to a rendevous above the Paiute camp on Sun Mountain.

One grizzled old veteran who led this band had attained a can-tankerous reputation. This camel was the patriarch of the herd and had a magnificent mane more than four feet long.

There had never been any particular love lost between the

people of the Comstock and their governing body in Salt Lake City, for reason previously given. This was particularly so after the Mormon letter was published condemning everything on Sun Mountain from one canyon to the other and naming her camp centers of vice and sin. If this was so, it was the way Nevada wanted it. In retaliation against this attack, the sultan of the caravans had been nicknamed "Old Brigham."

One of the local bronco busters cast an envious eye upon the long mane of Old Brigham and decided it would make a good lariat for his mustang. The cowboy urged his frightened and unwilling horse near enough to get a lariat over Old Brigham, but as soon as the camel felt the rope tighten about his neck, he turned threw back his ears, displayed his teeth, and full of fight charged straight for the cowboy. The horse fled in panic with Brigham thundering after. Just in time to save his life, the would-be thief of Old Brigham's mane snipped his lariat from the pommel and rode for his life. The camel kept the chase up for another mile then proud, haughty, and still undefeated, returned to his family circle.

The camels required little care and liked the acrid greasewood They willingly ate all kinds of grasses, thistles, or cactus. Despite this, the bullwackers and mule skinners were unsympathetic to the animals and took a hatred to the ungainly beasts.

The sharp edges of the quartz-filled roads they were forced to walk bruised and tore at the soft pads on the camels' feet, and the caravans left a path of blood in their wake. The packs which shifted because of the steep climbs chafed and blistered their humps to the raw, and the alkali dust worked into the raw sores until the great beasts cried with the pain. Although the drivers were kind to mules and called them "their Washoe canaries," they flogged the poor camels up the trails with vicious three-thonged whips. The dislike between the camels and their handlers was mutual. The usually mild-mannered beasts were aroused by the ill treatment. They spewed their cuds into men's faces, they became vicious, kicking, biting outlaws to surpass any army mule outlaw. The treatment shown these animals was reported by Goodwin in his *As I Remember Them* and Lord's *Comstock Lode*.

he substitution of camels for mules was never any pronounced uccess, as they continually refused to walk the stony paths in pite of curses or blows, and they were eventually turned loose o wander a strange desert. For generations to come these camels vho wandered the open range provided tall tales and were stock n trade for the old time storytellers.

CHAPTER EIGHTEEN

Mines and Men of the Big Bonanza

Meanwhile, the great mines of the Comstock were opening up

From Henry DeGroot, who lived in the canyon in 1859-60, we have the names of the principal Comstock mines, most of whom were named after their early locators: The Gould & Curry, Hale & Norcross, Best & Belcher, Savage, Chollar, Overman, Belcher the Sides and the White & Murphy (which later became the Con Virginia). Writing of them later, DeGroot said of these original locaters: "More than half of them are dead, those living are either in moderate circumstances or very poor, none rich. Most of them were brought to this pass by liberal and improvident habits. . . ."

John W. Mackay, who became the Comstock's richest miner was among the first to reach the "Ophir Diggings," as it then called. He had come from New York to California in a ship he had helped to build as an apprentice, and he had arrived a Downieville in 1851 at the age of twenty. In 1859 Mackay and his partner Jack O'Brien read of the discovery of rich silver mine and packed their rolls over the mountains one hundred miles to the new camp.

"All I want," Mackay told his buddy, "is $30,000; with that can make my old mother comfortable."

Jack O'Brien looked down at the beehives of activity they were approaching and turned to his pal.

"John," he said, "have ye any money? I'm broke."

"Yes," Mackay answered, "four-bits."

"Hand it over, thin," was the demand, and Mackay passed the last of his money to his partner.

O'Brien took Mackay's last fifty-cent piece and threw it far down the hillside where it was lost in the sagebrush,

"Now," he stated, "we'll inter this city loike gintlemen."

Years later, Mackay confirmed the story stating, "That's what Jack did with his money all his life."

Nearly all the men who became leaders on the Comstock arrived in 1863 or earlier. The mine superintendents were among the first and remained the most constant. Among them were John W. Mackay, Phillipp Deidesheimer, Robert Morrow, Charles Forman, Roswell K. Colcord, Samuel G. Curtis, C. C. Stevenson, Charles L. Strong, Adolph Sutro, H. G. Blasdel, Isaac L. Requa, Robert N. Graves, Albert Lackey, Harvey Beckwith, H. H. Day, Enoch Strother, and I. W. James.

Phillipp Deidesheimer was the inventor of the "square set" method of mining on the Comstock. "Square-sets" consisted of short, square timbers, four to six feet long, mortised and tenoned at the ends so that they could be put together in a series of interlocked cribs and built up in a continuous row or block to any height or width. The idea was to fit the whole chamber of a mine, building it up as the ore was removed.

The earth below Sun Mountain was crumbly as dry cake. Cave-ins were frequent and more and more the men complained about lack of safety in the mines. The pumps could handle the water, but no one could control the falling earth. Miners picking at the face of a drift would suddenly be buried alive. The demand came for adequate protection. Where other engineers had failed, Deidesheimer succeeded by building a timbering set as bees support a honey-comb. By building up and extending his square sets, Deidesheimer extracted the Comstock ores from wall to wall. Great forests of the Sierra pine found burial places in the dank, disintegrating caves below Virginia City, but the men of the mines were able to mine in safety.

The leading lawyers in 1862 were William M. Stewart, Moses Kirkpatrick, Richard Riding, J. Neeley Johnson, William H. Clagett, Jonas Seeley, Thomas E. Hayden, Dighton Corson, Martin White, and C. H. S. Williams.

A picturesque group handled the newspapers, *The Territorial*

Enterprise was published by Joseph T. Goodman and Denis E. McCarthy, William Wright—"Dan DeQuille"—a humorist who served as reporter for thirty-two years, and Mark Twain, who worked there as a reporter for twenty-one months. Rollin Daggett became an editor on the *Enterprise*, and C. C. Goodwin became editor of the same paper in 1874. *The Virginia Daily Union* was started by John A. Church, James L. Laird, and Samuel S. Glessner. Philip Lynch started the *Gold Hill News* October, 1863.

The churches of Virginia City were first represented by Father Patrick Manogue, pastor of the Roman Catholic Church. Rev. Franklin D. Rising was rector of St. Paul's Episcopal Church, followed by Rev. Ozi W. Whitaker. Rev. Whitaker became Bishop of the diocese of Nevada and later Bishop of Pennsylvania and Presiding Bishop of the Church of the United States. This original group of men built the churches of Nevada, founded schools and other institutions, and were in the forefront in the development of the territories.

The methods of mining on the Comstock were rude in the extreme. The ore bodies had been exposed by wide trenches for a length of three hundred feet through the Mexican, Ophir, and Central claims. George D. Roberts, one of the early arrivals, reported: "This rich ore, worth from $3,000 to $4,000 a ton, is found in irregular veins one to four inches in thickness, enclosed in a large vein from 10 to 15 feet wide. Deidesheimer stated that on November 1, 1859, at a depth of 30 feet, the vein of silver sulphurets was 4 to 15 inches thick. Maldonado began to smelt some of his rich ore in little adobe furnaces after the Mexican fashion."

Gabriel Maldonado was a Mexican of Spanish descent who purchased one-half of the Mexican mine from Penrod for $3,000. Comstock had received $5,500 for his half interest from Francis J. Hughes.

"Old Pancake" Comstock's braggart tongue had attached his name to the lode, although he was not one of the original discoverers. This eccentric and ragged nabob talked his waspish way into ownership and like a bull at the gate alluded to the entire deposit as "Comstock's Lode." He wandered indiscriminately over

Sun Mountain staking out everything that took his fancy and calling it his.

Old Pancake "staked out" the Chollar and gave it to Billy Chollar. From Carson, he brought back Old Daddy Curry and put him and one Alvah Gould in possession of the sultan-rich Gold and Curry property. He "staked out" the Savage, then presented it to old man Savage. He claimed to own the Hale and Norcross and said he "kept Norcross around for a year to work on that ground."

According to Johntowners, Old Pancake "was one hell of a liar."

The first Californians to arrive were experienced quartz miners from Grass Valley and Nevada City, and they soon bought the majority of the interests in the Ophir and the adjoining claims. Others from the same region purchased nearly all of the little claims at Gold Hill. Others from the Bay region bought into the Gould and Curry and the Savage.

Judge James Walsh, in behalf of himself and his partner, Joseph Woodworth, bought Old Pancake's one-sixth in the Ophir, one-half of the old California, and other interests for eleven thousand dollars, and Penrod's one-sixth of the Ophir for $5,500. J. A. Osborn sold his one-sixth to Donald Davidson and General Allen, and Patrick O'Riley received $40,000 for his one-sixth from J. O. Earl of San Francisco.

George Hearst, who was one of the first to come, summoned his friend Almarin B. Paul. Hearst took an option on McLaughlin's one-sixth for three thousand dollars. This was the basis and the start of the fabulous Hearst fortune.

A list of the early bonanzas of Virginia City includes The Ophir, The Gould and Curry, the Savage, the Chollar-Potosi, the Yellow Jacket, and the original Gold Hill bonanzas. The fame of the Comstock during its first five years was based on these six silver gushers, of which the Ophir was the most famouss. The Ophir was one mine which was really operated in a grand, free-handed manner. It was a glorious wonderful possession and there was no need for economy. Who cared what anything cost when one owned a mine this rich? Mills and surrounding buildings were built without regard to expense. Some of the structures were of

225

cut granite. To save one three-mile haul around the lower end of Washoe Lake, the wagon road was grandly carried straight across for a mile and a half on a piling bridge.

But a bonanza can be a boomerang. The mill was a failure from the first day of its operation, and the company became involved in no less than thirty-seven different lawsuits with adjoining mines. Then the ore body narrowed, gradually decreasing in size and value. The reckless waste had opened a Pandora's box of troubles and the Ophir only had three prosperous years—1862-64.

The Mexican mine was part of the Ophir Bonanza and, like her sister, had nothing but hard luck. Both were fortune's children born on Friday.

During 1860-61, Gabriel Maltonado borrowed $170,000 from Alsop and Company of San Francisco to build a mill. He was unable to repay this huge debt and after a lawsuit and compromise, the mine was taken over by the Alsop firm. The Mexican's mill caught fire and burned in 1863, and the mine suffered two disastrous cave-ins later in the year. This dangerous condition brought about a sullen attitude on the part of labor, and the narrowing of the wedge-shaped Ophir bonanza added to the plague of woe cutting the Mexican out of ore at the depth of three hundred feet.

This mine was unique on the Comstock in that it was worked only by Mexican miners who worked after the fashion of their country during the first two years of operation. Instead of hoisting the ore, they packed it up the incline shaft in rawhide buckets slung from their foreheads by thongs. For ladders these Mexican miners used notched logs. Although the Ophir installed square-set timbering in 1860, the Mexican mine adopted a practice of leaving pillars of ore in the stopes to hold up the roof. After sporadic ups-and-downs, the Mexican was absorbed by the Ophir in 1867.

The Gould and Curry was a consolidation of the Gould claim owned by Alva Gould and the Curry owned by "Old Abe" Curry. Curry had located the El Dorado croppings located on the highest point of the Comstock Lode. Gould followed along taking the mountainside real estate below him. Both of these claims shortly passed into the hands of twelve men—chiefly San Franciscans who organized the Gould and Curry Mining Company on June 25, 1860. Among the incorporators and trustees were George Hearst, Lloyd Tevis, John O. Earl, Slepheus Bull, Thomas Bell, A. E. Head, B. F. Sherwood, and William Blanding, all of whom became California millionaires from their start in the Gould and Curry.

It wasn't until 1861, when the "D" street tunnel penetrated forty feet of solid ore, that the mine began to overshadow the Ophir; but instead of continuing downward, the ore body pitched southward into the Savage where it was equally rich. Neither Gould and Curry nor Savage found another ore body in all its history.

The Savage was called Virginia City's "child of fortune." Gould and Curry development work located its first great ore body for it. Four years later Hale & Norcross performed a similar service for the Savage by finding the neighboring body on the other side. Further development work in 1865 disclosed the rich "potosi strike." This, in addition to the Hale and Norcross discovery, gave to the Savage three years of large production during which time it was the great mine of the Comstock with a yield of eight million dollars. The Savage hit hot water in 1876 on her 2200 level and this gusher flooded her workings as well as Hale and Norcross.

After the discovery of the Crown Point bonanza in 1871, John P. Jones and Alvinza Hayward took over control of the Savage and ran the mine for the benefit of their mills. Hayward "boomed" the Savage stock in 1872 by giving out mysterious reports of a rich new strike and by confining his miners underground. This was an old and much practiced trick on the Comstock. The miners sat it out below, comfortably living on the fat of the land while Savage stock went from $62 a share in February to $725 by April. This was a cold-blooded stock manipulation that hurt many people.

The Chollar-Potosi mine was a consolidation of the Chollar and Potosi claims effected in 1865, accomplished after four years of the notorious Comstock litigation. Neither the Chollar nor Potosi claim had ore until the latter part of 1861, when Potosi discovered an ore body that dipped into the Chollar. Chollar brought suit by its attorney, William M. Stewart, and the fight was on. After two trials, Chollar won a verdict and the decision was affirmed by the Supreme Court.

Chollar then found ore dipping into Potosi, which in turn, brought on some lively action. It this instance the courts ruled against Bill Stewart and he was furious. Stewart was never known to take kindly to any kind of defeat.

Meantime, A. W. "Sandy" Baldwin had become his partner, and Bill Stewart kept fighting. The conduct of some judges was questionable, to state the case gently, and the controversy resulted in the resignation of three judges of the Supreme Court.

Chollar-Potosi then joined Hale and Norcross along with the Savage in 1875. This was for the purpose of sinking the Combination Shaft. In order to do this, they levied heavy assessments which continued until the shaft was closed in 1886. This asssessment totaled no less than seven million dollarrs. Some of the Comstock assessments were out and out graft, and were levied for no other purpose than enriching a few chossen ones selected for salvation when the time came for chopping off heads.

The Yellow Jacket was located south of the Little Gold Hill group in 1859 soon after the placer miners had uncovered Old Red Ledge. The Princess and Union claims were located lower down the hill adjoining Yellow Jacket on the east. There was peace between the two until Union tunnel discovered a fine ore body ninety feet beneath the surface. The Yellow Jacket then shifted its claim on down the hill, calmly moved in on the new ore body, and brought suit by its attorney William M. Stewart. After this trial, Yellow Jacket put down a shaft from its north line and moved into the deposit known as the Gold Hill bonanza. This mass of ore was two hundred feet in length and four hundred in height and was worth more than six million dollars.

William Sharon took control of this company and from that time on things were popping and the management of Yellow Jacket was highly questionable. While annual reports of the other important mines on the lode went into great detail, those of Yellow Jacket were slight and gave little information. Only the management knew when the heavy assessments were to be levied, only they knew when a dividend would be paid; and for them, the price of Comstock scales rose and fell conveniently.

William Sharon's philosophy was "sell when they're high and buy 'em when they're low."

Grant Smith's fine *History of the Comstock Lode* published by the University of Nevada reported that John B. Winters, Sharon's mine superintendent from 1864 to 1870, said he had lost his self-respect doing dirty work for Sharon. "To feed his mills, I've mixed waste rock with Yellow Jacket Ore until it would scarcely pay for crushing," he claimed.

When William Sharon wanted to go to the United States Senate in 1874, he purchased a newspaper with the cold-blooded design of furthering his ambitions. Editor Joseph T. Goodman of the *Enterprise* had displayed a notable lack of enthusiasm for Sharon. On one occasion when Sharon returned to Virginia City to push his political buggy, the *Enterprise* published a "welcome" to him:

". . . your expected return, Mr. Sharon," said Goodman, "has offered no opportunity for public preparation, and you will consequently accept these simple remarks as unworthy but earnest expression of the sentiments of a people who feel that they would be lacking in duty of self respect if they failed upon such occasion to make a deserved recognition of your acts and character. You are probably aware that you have returned to a community where you are feared, hated, and despised.

". . . your character in Nevada for the past nine years has been one of merciless rapacity. You fastened yourself upon the vitals of the state like a hyena, and woe to him who disputed with you a single coveted morsel of your prey. You cast honor, honesty, and the commonest civilities aside. You broke faith with men whenever you could subserve your purpose by so doing. . ."

When Sharon failed to obtain the coveted election by the legislature, he organized a company and bought Goodman out. The paper then changed its tune and the prose ran mad with praise for Sharon.

Alexander Toponce, well known cattleman and freighter of the times, affords us an interesting sidelight into the character of

William Sharon and handed to the banker the sort of by-play and retaliation the forthright mining towns relished. French Alex Toponce was accustomed to the rough frontier where it took a diamond to cut one. The story comes from his book of reminscence, Chapter XLVI:

"About the last of September, 1867, I started for California with near 6,000 head of cattle all in one big herd. We had eighty horses and four wagons with oxen to haul supplies, and a force of twenty men.

"We followed the old stage route most of the way—Fish Springs, Deep Creek, Steptoe Valley, Egan Canyon, Austin, on the Reese River, Mammoth and Walker Lake. The feed was fine all the way and we had no trouble with Indians.

"When we reached Walker Lake, I found that heavy snows had fallen earlier than usual on the passes over the Sierra Nevada range, and decided to winter in Nevada. I rented the Walker Lake Indian Reservation for the winter, paying one thousand dollars in gold as grass money.

"As I needed only about four men to watch the cattle during the winter I decided to pay off the balance and went into Virginia City, Nevada, with the Indian Agent to get my money. I telegraphed for money to John W. Kerr. All my money was tied up in the cattle. Word came back from Salt Lake that Kerr was not in town. He was at the Silver Reef mine down in southern Utah.

"So I went to the Bank of California to borrow, $2,500. The President of the bank was named Sharon. The Indian Agent identified me. I told my story and asked for the $2,500. I was a pretty tough looking specimen after six weeks on the trail. Sharon looked me over, then he chopped me down.

" 'I can't let you have it,' he said and turned away and walked from the counter.

"Then the cashier, who sat near, called me as I was going out. 'Come on in tomorrow morning,' he said, 'I'll see if I can fix you up. I've got that much money myself.' His name was Webster, and the next morning I got the $2,500 and paid off my men who all came up to Virginia City to work around the mines.

"But I got even with Sharon. I had brought with me two trotting horses I had picked up in Utah, that could do a mile in about three minutes, also a $400 buggy I had trailed behind a wagon. I brought the horses and buggy up to Virginia City and put them in Church's Livery stable.

"Sharon kept a team of fast steppers in the same stable and every day he drove them out to Gold Hill and back . . . taking with him distinguished visitors and lady friends and customers.

"I waited till my team was rested up and fed up and then every time Sharon ordered out his team, Church would harness mine and send for me. I would take the Indian Agent or some other friend and hustle out to Gold Hill and catch up with Sharon. Coming back, I would lay my team right along side of him until we got back into town, and then I would let my trotters go and they would sail right around Sharon and give him the dust for three blocks, right through the business part of town.

"This pleased me, and it tickled the people of Virginia City immensely. It got to be a daily spectacle, and when my team came in ahead of Sharon's, the crowd would cheer. They lined up every afternoon to see the horse race between Sharon's steppers and the team owned by 'that cattleman from Utah.'

"Sharon would get mad and touch his team up so hard they would break gait, and then he would jerk and saw, and lash them and go red in the face. And the madder he got, the louder the people would cheer.

"Finally, Sharon got so sore he would not order out his team and after a few days I got a tip that he would send a man around to buy my span from me. So I saw him coming first, and held the price stiff for $3,000 for horses, harness and buggy, and got it. After that, Sharon drove my team on his trips to Gold Hill . . . I had no trouble paying the bank back what I owed it."

In the next chapter, Alex Toponce tells how he made one hundred thousand dollars on his cattle deal. John W. Kerr and Governor Durkee, his partners, each made the same. Toponce also got himself mixed up in the Indian war at Walker Lake, then in a change of pace tells how everybody at Virginia City gambled on the stock exchange.

After describing the gamblers, tinhorns, swindlers, prostitutes, etc., all buying stocks, the old frontiersman makes this expressive remark:

"There was no underworld. Vice and all kinds of sin were open and above-board and were the rule of the day and not the exception and nobody seemed to be ashamed of anything."

Then the volatile Frenchman takes a final crack at William Sharon:

"Just before leaving Nevada, I took one last whack at my friend, Sharon. He had an expert look over his pair of trotters—the ones he drove before he bought mine. This expert told him they were getting old and that their grinder teeth no longer met and that the front teeth should be filed down . . . which was all true. So Sharon told Church to have their teeth fixed. Church asked me to help him. I helped Church with the job and then made out a bill to Sharon for fifty dollars, for 'expert horse dentistry.' I told Church to tell Sharon I would sue if he didn't pay up. Sharon was astonished at the size of the bill and paid it not realizing that it was meant for a joke."

But Alex took the money.

CHAPTER NINETEEN

Life on the Comstock

The most disastrous fire on the Comstock Lode occurred in the Yellowjacket mine on April 7, 1869, when fire raged out of control 800 feet beneath Gold Hill in drifts, chutes, and winzes. Nothing is more feared underground than a fire. Fire is an insidious danger, smouldering for days, months, or years, and a mine fire stamped to death in one spot will craftily erupt in another, burning for as long as seven years.

It was believed that one of the relay shifts of the Yellowjacket, off at 4:00 o'clock in the morning, probably left a candle sticking in a timber. Three hours later, nearly a thousand men were lowered to the various levels of the three mines in this area. Almost immediately flames were discovered and there was a scramble back to the shaft, but smoke was so bad that some were unable to escape. At Crown Point, many were overcome by the fumes as they ascended in the cage. As they fell they were crushed between timbers and cages as the overcrowded hoists were drawn upward.

Men trapped in the farthest drifts were well aware that the underground gas made escape impossible—and that to stay meant being cooked alive. Water boiled beneath their feet from the heat of the red-hot tunnel walls, and by 9:00 that night, fire had gained the 700 foot level and was burning furiously.

On the third day, the shafts of the Yellowjacket were covered and steam was forced into the deep levels. Four days later, the steam was shut off and rescuers went into the depths to retrieve more bodies. Two months after the outbreak, workers succeeded in cornering the worst flames and sealing them off where they continued smouldering for three years longer.

Ten hours was a work-shift during the early years on the Comstock, but the conditions underground became intolerable and the hours of the men were reduced to eight. Politics helped. The four-dollar-a-day wage for eight hours work was not enforced until John P. Jones needed votes for the U.S. Senate in 1872 and ordered that the eight-hour day, four-dollar wage should apply to all men working underground in Crown Point mine. Most of the other mines of Virginia City were by this time controlled by Sharon, and Sharon wanted votes as well. He followed suit, adopting the same rule, which thereafter prevailed as working conditions on the Comstock.

Comstock miners were then elevated to the role of lords of the labor market of the time. But the luxuries of the camp did not apply to these people, many of whom had large families to support. Generally, a Comstock miner lived well, but very simply.

Death was a daily hazard of the mines and accidents were considered a risk of the employment. The record does not indicate lawsuits for bodily damages, although men were killed and injured every week. The men worked in temperatures ranging from 100 to 125 degrees. Never had mines encountered such heat and scalding water. Grant Smith in his *History of the Comstock Lode* reported that the men suffered stomach cramps from the heat on the lower levels.

It was in an attempt to drain these waters of the Comstock Lode that Adolph Sutro made himself known to history. Sutro made his first appearance on the lode as a cigar store clerk, but he became one of its best-known citizens despite the fact that for thirteen years he was be-deviled about his "coyote hole."

This cigar clerk was a showman, however, as well as a capable engineer, and he foresaw the need for a tunnel to drain the deep mines below Sun Mountain. High water was a consistent roadblock to Virginia City production, and pumping was a costly operation.

In 1865, the legislature of the new State of Nevada passed a bill incorporating a tunnel company and the following year Congress chartered the corporation. In the meantime, Sutro had incurred the enmity of William Sharon, who opposed him and his project bitterly. Sutro was forced to travel to France in an attempt to obtain money, only to have his hopes there riddled by the threat of war.

Adolph Sutro recognized that the topography of the country around Sun Mountain could be engineered for the construction of a deep tunnel, and that the Comstock should be mined from the bottom up. His idea was to tunnel into the hills, then sink shafts to meet it which would insure drainage and ventilation.

But the Yellowjacket fire was his big break, and all the drama came out as the little showman took full advantage of the frightening situations that prevailed in the mines below. He took to the stump and earnestly called upon the miners of Virginia City to support his program as an opening wedge in a future mine safety program. He exploited the situation to the full, and the frenzied and demoralized miners, with the memory of the recent disaster still fresh in their minds, rallied behind him. This was really the thing—political presssure once again—that put the Sutro tunnel over. The indignation of angry men forced consideration from those who had previously shouldered the idea aside.

Sutro's project called for millions and he met solid opposition from the kings of the Comstock, Mackay, Fair, Flood, and O'Brien. They referred to his dream as "Sutro's Coyote Hole." At the time when Sutro considered himself almost beaten, he was amazed by a sudden loan that came through for two and a half million dollars from McClamonts Bank of London.

Thirteen years after the beginning of his project, Sutro put the Comstock tunnel through. It cost five million dollars and the Comstock had passed its peak of production. Even so, it paid off in royalties and in one year drained two billion gallons of hot water from Virginia City's mines.

Meantime, this great boomer was any fool's paradise. A man couldn't help but get rich on the Comstock.

Money poured freely, the best singers sang for Virginia City, the finest actors played, and the best orators of the day held forth from the rostrum. Oysters from the Coast, strawberries from Lamoille Valley, and squab were reported daily fare at public dinners. Champagne was imported by the case. The miners preferred whiskey but this was the Comstock, so champagne was in order. Youngsters made twenty dollars a day running errands, and no saloonkeeper was expected to give change for a five dollar gold piece. Change of any kind was seldom bothered with.

The dark-eyed, socially ambitious Seeress of the Washoe, Eilley Cowan, had divorced her second husband and was now leading the third, innocent and mild-mannered "Sandy" Bowers, on an uncomfortable jaunt about Europe where she collected loot for the Bowers Mansion. Ivy from England's Windsor palace, marble to be shipped around the Horn and then freighted a slow way over the western American mountains, Spanish tile, Venetian mirrors, and Moroccan bound books—which poor Sandy couldn't read—were added to Eilley's collection.

The Bowers Mansion, which stands today near Virginia City, between Reno and Carson City, turned out to be a Mediterranean, Victorian, Scottish combination; and Eilley Bowers, who was known as the Queen of the Comstock, ruled upon her throne of silver from the Ophir shaft. Theirs was a sad story, however, and wealth disappeared as rapidly as it had come. When Sandy died in '68, Eilley was involved in continual litigation over the Ophir.

This litigation drained her and she lived her last years reading fortunes for others in the crystal ball from which she had predicted her own rise. Washoe County now preserves the Bowers Mansion as a recreation area.

Labor troubles entered the Comstock along with the railroads when in 1868 Nevada miners and laboring men saw themselves threatened by an influx of thousands of Chinese coolies who were being brought into this country by the shiploads. The labor on the construction of the Central Pacific Railway through the high Sierras and down through Reno was supplied by these great gangs of coolies.

William Sharon brought them into the Washoe, and the Chinese were employed to lay the rail for the V. & T. Railway down the Carson River Canyon. The Miners Unions of Gold Hill and

Virginia City viewed this situation with alarm and saw themselves out of work when these Chinese were turned loose from railroad construction to descend upon the mining towns looking for work.

Within the year, vast hordes of Chinese were laying rail on the very slopes of Sun Mountain and the construction gangs moved closer to Virginia City with each passing day. Irish and Cornish, who already labored within the heart of the Comstock in scalding hot water for wages shamefully insufficient, saw an added threat to their insecure lives. They banded together in a move for common survival and resolved on direct action before the Chinese infiltrated their territory.

On September 29, 1869, a column of men 350 strong marched from Gold Hill and Virginia City down the Divide to the camps of the Chinese labor gangs. The sheriff of Storey County halted them and read a proclamation to disperse. When the men refused, the sheriff read the riot act.

The miners were patient with him and good naturedly allowed the good sheriff to finish his speech. They then gave him a rousing cheer for effort and another cheer for the United States of America and proceeded with their businesss. Militantly, to the beat of a drum and the shrill of a fife, the miners marched on the Chinese camp. As the small army approached, the Orientals threw down their picks and shovels, seized their belongings, and raised their heels in the direction of Carson Canyon. Thus was the "enemy" of the Miners Union and Virginia City routed—without bloodshed, without incident. The miners marched back, happily victorious.

They then negotiated with Sharon and it was eight days before they would allow him to bring back his Chinese crews; and then only after informing him that he could do it "Only as a privilege . . . not as a right."

Sharon was forced to agree that no Chinese should be hired in the area after the completion of the V. & T. Railroad. After this, the Chinese from the construction gangs scattered and there isn't a mining community in the West that doesn't have a record of them, their interesting customs, and a Chinatown.

These Chinese who thronged the Western mining camps of the sixties were lost and bewildered in the ways of the white man. The customs of the Chinese, on the other hand, were equally puzzling, if not senseless, to the white inhabitants. An amusing item regarding the method of obtaining a court oath from a Chinese appears in *Pioneer Nevada*.

When it was found necessary to call Chinese into court, it was soon discovered that they had no regard whatsoever for any oath taken over the Bible. The Book meant nothing to the "heathen" Chinese. But they took an oath seriously if it was made over a freshly-killed fowl! This ritual had to be accompanied by the burning of punk and squibs generously sprinkled with references to "sacred ancestors."

Nevada court procedure made no allowance for this peculiar practice . . . but there was many a trial held in Nevada courts that followed the custom. When a Chinese witness was to be sworn, the baliff or clerk brought in a squawking chicken, wrung its neck to the delighted grins and frank comments of the spectators, and placed it beneath the hand of the Chinese on the stand. During this time, other attaches of the Court busied themselves burning punk and squibs, and lighting firecrackers. After proper attention to this mumbo-jumbo, the lawyer could then try to obtain some information from the oriented Chinese.

The first of the Chinese laboring men came to this country in 1852, and in the first year more than twenty thousand of them arrived. By 1869, more than one hundred thousand had arrived on the Pacific Coast. They overflowed into Nevada. To this day it is said you can pan gold where a white man worked—but you can find nothing where the Chinese worked a placer.

The queue was sacred to the Orientals and was a source of amusement to the whites, many of whom exploited, mistreated, and tormented the helpless foreigners. The sheriff in Elko County at one time cut the pig tails from four Chinese. The Orientals turned the tables by promptly suing him!

At one time a bill was proposed to the state legislature prohibiting the Chinese his pig tail. After much ado about nothing, it was decided to live and let live and John Chinaman kept his queue.

No record of the Comstock could be complete without Bill Stewart.

It has been said that when Bill Stewart saw how the Comstock Lode was located, he laughed and laughed. Base to peak, Sun Mountain was one overlapping claim after another. There was more land claimed for these Virginia City mines than the whole Washoe could account for. Claims were three, four, five deep . . . deliberately so, and this was done many times just so someone could bring a blackmailing lawsuit.

American mining law permitted a miner to follow his vein on its dip into the earth even though it might penetrate beneath other men's mining claims. The American system had its origin in the early placer camps of California when there was no federal law permitting miners to go upon public lands and locate mining claims. The Comstock mines were located under district mining rules similar to those of California. The several veins which appeared on the surface of the Comstock were located as separate mining claims more or less conflicting with one another. This is what brought about much of the famous litigation the lode was embroiled in for five years.

The deeper workings in the various mines then showed that these parallel veins united at a depth of five hundred feet to form the Comstock Lode, and the courts awarded the full width of the lode on the surface, and underground as well, to the first locations made, which were those owned by the large companies. This controversy was known as "The many ledge theory against the one ledge theory." Local feeling in Virginia City newspapers favored the many ledge owners, as they were far more numerous. The big question of the Comstock was settled by Referee John Nugent in August, 1864, after its adoption by the courts. That decision settled the right of the owners of the main lode to follow the lode on its dip which had been claimed by each of the separate parallel veins.

It was upon the basis of the regularity of the strike and dip of

239

the Comstock Lode that Stewart was enabled—when he became a Senator—to pass the congressional mining laws of 1866 and 1872 which perpetuated the extralateral right and provided for the patenting of mining claims. Until 1866, the minerrs were without legal rights upon the public domain throughout the West.

William Stewart was a rough and tumble fighter, born and bred to the lawless period he lived in the Washoe, and he made a bare-knuckle way to power in politics. He was one of the first pair of Senators sent to Washington by Nevada, and he served in the Senate for twenty-eight years.

James G. Fair, a contemporary of the times, was another Comstock millionaire who went to the Senate, but he was sent from California. He was principal stockholder of the Nevada Bank of San Francisco in the days when the banks pretty much made up their own rules.

James L. Flood, another success story on the Comstock, was a former saloon keeper who made his money by speculation in shares.

John P. Jones, another of the newly rich, became United States Senator from Nevada for thirty years and can be mentioned as running neck and neck with William Sharon for honors in clever manipulation.

CHAPTER TWENTY

Characters in General

However, all the lawlessness wasn't under the guise of Victorian dress and manner nor the sedate black broadcloth which clothed the dignity of the time.

The "601" Vigilantes took over in Virginia City in 1871 when the citizens decided to put a stop to killings which had become the rule rather than the exception. Guns, more commonly knives, were daily used to settle the smallest disputes and the Comstock had a rough reputation from one end of the country to the other. The secret organization of the Six Hundred and One, a masked group, took over and dispensed justice without the wait of court and jury.

Methodically, this organization taught the seamy side of the Comstock to behave. On midnight, March 24, 1871, a few late hour Virginia City citizens saw the 601 in action when Arthur Perkins Heffernan, who had shot and killed another man in cold blood, was taken from the jail at the rough command, "Come out, we want you."

Heffernan wasn't given time to put on his boots. He was escorted to a shaft near the Ophir mine works. A noose was suspended from a hoist frame cross-bar, and he was made to stand upon an old timber placed over the shaft. When the signal was given, the plank was yanked away, and Heffernan, who had anticipated the action, leaped high into the air at the same time in order that the force of his fall would bring him quick death.

When the body was cut down, it was found to bear a note marked "601".

It was the custom of the group to present undesirables with "tickets of leave"—and it wasn't wise to ignore these exit invitations—as one who returned to the Comstock found out. The morning following his arrival, his body was found from the end of a noose and a similar card was pinned to his shirt.

It was men like "Fighting" Sam Brown and "Farmer" Langford Peel, who had no small part in the motivating forces behind such organizations as the "601".

Sam Brown was known not only on the Comstock but also up and down the Pacific Coast as "a big chief." But there were others. Such dregs as "El Dorado" Johnny, "Sugarfoot" Jack Davis, and Sam himself floated West from the Mississippi basin to become a plague on the life of the early camps.

Like many others of the "big chief" class, Sam Brown was a bully and, at heart, a coward. He was loathsome in appearance, coarse and dirty. He wore a beard which had been allowed to grow so long and unruly that he parted and tied it under his chin rather than to trouble trimming it. Sam boasted that he had personally filled a good sized section of the cemetery in any mining town he had ever been in, and his first night in Virginia City he picked a fight with a tipsy miner upon a flimsy excuse and ripped the man open with a bowie knife, killing him immediately. Casually, Fighting Sam wiped the blood from the bowie, stretched out on a bench, and went to sleep. The frightening brutality of this killer had a telling effect and the boys on the Comstock gave Sam a wide berth.

Upon one occasion, Fighting Sam heard that one of his pals was to stand trial over in Genoa. He confidently mounted his steed and rode down, fully intending to terrorize the court into submission and walk out with his fellow rascal in tow.

But he ran into Bill Stewart, and Bill Stewart wasn't known for backing down. Bill—Senator Stewart at the time—had been assisting in prosecuting the case. When Fighting Sam walked into the court room, confusion reigned supreme. Spectators took leaps out windows while others scurried like prairie dogs for holes under benches, but Bill Stewart whirled back upon the "chief" and covered him with two Colt pistols.

"Now, *Mister* Brown," Stewart told him, "you've been bragging you'd come down here and swear the defendant free. I'm here to tell you that if you attempt any of your gun play, or give false testimony, I'm going to blow your fool brains out."

Stewart then cross-examined Brown and made him admit that the defendant had a bad reputation. Duly impressed after the trial, Fighting Sam turned about and retained Bill Stewart as his attorney to defend him in a coming Plumas Couny action.

But Fighting Sam was disgruntled and plain mad at the world on his way back home to Virginia City. He hadn't liked being humbled so publicly and took pot shots at passersby as he went along—until he found one who shot back.

As Sam passed Van Sickle's Station, he shot at the owner, and Van Sickle decided that he, and all Washoe, had had enough of Fighting Sam. He reached for his shotgun and overtook the now now fleeing chief, riddling him with buckshot.

It was a day of retribution for Fighting Sam Brown of the Comstock, the day he died and the day two of his bluffs were called.

A verdict was handed down from a coroner's jury that read: "Samuel Brown has come to his death from a just dispensation of an all-wise Providence . . . it served him right!"

This verdict became a western classic.

"El Dorado" Johnny met his come-uppance at the hands of Langford "Farmer" Peel. With Sam Brown's death, there was considerable speculation on the Comstock as to just who would be the next "Big Chief" on the Washoe. The two likely candidates were El Dorado Johnny and Farmer Peel.

Peel, who reportedly rolled in from Salt Lake City, was blue-eyed, mild-mannered, and pleasant. He wore a soft blonde beard and six notches in his gun when he came to Virginia City. Maybe Langford Peel didn't mean to become a "bad man" but one thing just seemed to lead to another and a man had to defend himself. His first notch had been cut in self defense and the next five were direct results of the original blast. At any rate, Langford Peel was a dead shot.

El Dorado Johnny came into the Comstock about the same time

Peel did and didn't waste any time in making the local Who's Who in Virginia City. So, he walked into Pat Lynch's saloon and inquired if there were any "chiefs" around.

Peel, lounging at the bar, spoke up, "Guess you mean that remark for me?"

"Anybody can take it that likes to," replied Johnny.

Langford Peel was polite about the whole thing. "Very well," he said in a kindly manner, "let's settle it now. Come into the street."

Johnny walked from the door with a confident smile on his face only to die in the middle of the road when he turned to meet Peel. Peel didn't bother to go beyond the saloon door as he deemed El Dorado nothing but "small fry," and he dropped him from there. The body of El Dorado Johnny was treated respectfully and when he was "laid out" in a saloon it was agreed that he looked "real nice."

The former bad man was lowered to the earth to the tune of "When Johnny Comes Marching Home Again."

For reasons unique to the Comstock, the law didn't bother Peel about these various little adventures. Rather, he was regarded as a useful one-man clearing house. One after another, the friends of El Dorado came to Virginia City and sought out the new "chief," demanding justice in the name of their departed one. Peel obliged to the tune of five more—for which he was not even arrested.

The way the boys in Virginia City saw it, each one he notched off added to the general serenity of the whole community.

Peel had imbibed too freely upon one occasion, however, and was making a huge nuisance of himself. This day, he was so obstreperous that the police and a few indignant citizens hauled him before Police Judge Davenport, the Mormon justice of the peace who demanded one hundred dollars for his bad behavior.

"All right," Peel agreed, "just give me some time to get the money."

Judge Davenport granted the request, whereupon Peel proceeded to his familiar hangouts. Within thirty minutes, he had refreshed himself with another supply of whisky. As he drank, he dwelt upon the injustice of the courts. Suddenly, he stomped back to the courtroom, knocking down chairs and benches that stood in his way. He reached the judge and announced, "I'm back now, Judge, to settle up on that fine."

"Very good of you, Mr. Peel, very good of you," the judge answered as he stretched forth his hand to receive the expected money. Quick as a flash, Peel grasped two hands full of the judge's beautiful beard and began pounding his head against the wall until the poor jurist was almost dead. Then, releasing his hold, Peel strode from the courtroom.

No one laid a hand on him. Such was life in Gold Canyon.

From the first, Virginia City displayed a lusty appetite for entertainment of the filling kind. On the heels of the rush to the silver mountain, a theatre was constructed in the new rough city as early as 1860. Two more quickly followed, and within three years the town's entertainment was as famous and as fabulous as is that of today's Las Vegas.

Weighty Shakesprearean drama, six or seven variety shows, vaudeville song and dance, were common fare for the evenings. Virginia City was the cultural capital of the west—even San Francisco couldn't dispute it. But Adah "The Menken" opened their blasé eyes.

Piper's Opera House was responsible for much of Virginia City's entertainment fame. This theatre was managed by David Belasco and from its stage the Comstockers heard the voice of Adelina Patti and saw General Tom Thumb. Edwin Booth, Clara Morris, James O'Neill, Frank Mayo, and others were common diet for theatre goers.

The Menken appeared as Mazeppa and rode a horse across the stage of Piper's Opera House—clad in pink tights. It was as much of a shock to the viewers of the times as the first strip tease was to ours. But Virginia City came back for seconds and gave the Menken a bar of bullion worth two thousand dollars as a bonus of appreciation.

Nothing satisfied this fervent and intense city but the new, the daring, the sensational.

Whether Virginia City was at play or at war, it was in earnest, as its vigorous action during the Civil War proved. The sentiment in Virginia City favored the Union, and two regiments were raised and sent to Fort Churchill. There were, of course, Southern sympathizers, and there was trouble when the proprietress of the Tahoe House shot a man in the act of raising the Stars and Stripes over her hotel. No section of the United States contributed more liberally to the soldiers of the Civil War than Virginia City, and when news came that Lee had surrendered, the Comstock went frantic. Mine whistles blew, dance halls went wild with music and cheering, one hero after another was pledged, saluted and toasted until nobody could remember what started the whole celebration.

Despite a final war debt of $2,500,000,000, the Union dollar never fell below a specie value of fifty cents. The South lost the West and her silver and gold treasures that gave the United States of America her international standing and credit. This led President Lincoln to say "I would rather have Nevada in the Union than another million men."

This was the tremendous and real importance of the Comstock bullion to the Civil War effort.

It is impossible in a short version to tell much about the large mines, but the Big Bonanza, found in 1873, became the wonder of the world.

Although the Crown Point and Belcher mines were still extracting rich ore and millions rolled out in dividends, shares in Comstock mines continued to decrease steadily in value under prophecies of doom from those who declared such fabulous wealth could not continue to pour from the shafts of Virginia City.

Then came the Big Bonanza! It was the richest body of gold and silver ore ever found on the face of the earth. Within a year, the stock of Consolidated Virginia and Con. California had a total stock exchange value of $159,000,000. Mackay, Fair, Flood, and O'Brien—known as "The Big Four"—controlled these two mines. For a price of only one hundred thousand dollars, these Bonanza Kings, only two years before, had purchased the discovery. In 1870, the Consolidated Virginia had 11,000 shares of stock listed at one dollar a share, and two small claims adjoining it, with 300 feet on the Lode that were later part of the reorganized Consolidated Virginia, considered too worthless for regular listing.

Especially because of the Big Bonanza, there was never a camp like the Comstock, although the life was repeated time and time over on a smaller scale all over the West. The spirit of such times could live but once. A reading of Big Bonanza history leads one to understand the words of Arthur McEwen, whose newspaper life began in Virginia City: "The life of the Comstock in the old days never has been written so that those who did not share it can understand it. It never can be so written."

Maybe not.

We come back in the record to William Sharon, the Comstock's Johnny-on-the-spot. He was at this time an avowed candidate for the U. S. Senate and had one or more fine reasons to blow up the new boom on the Bonanza.

After Editor Goodman had flayed him in 1872, Sharon bought the *Enterprise* in order to have a champion. His next move was to obtain control of the Ophir in order to use the stock to further his political campaign. The mine itself was promising to develop an extension of the Con. Virginia bonanza, which Sharon figured to add to his prestige as well as to furnish ore for his mills.

But the Ophir was in control of E. J. "Lucky" Baldwin, who was every bit as shrewd as Sharon, and "Lucky" was content to let the stock ride along quietly. He had Sharon over a barrel and it became necessary to acquire over one-half of the 100,800 shares before December 13th in order to elect a new board of trustees.

Sharon started to buy quietly. On August 11, 1874, Ophir stood at twenty dollars a share. Con. Virginia was eighty dollars and California was forty. A month later Ophir was up to fifty-two dollars a share. Sharon bought James R. Keene's block of Ophir, then employed him to manipulate the market.

"Jim" Keene was good, but he wasn't good enough to pry Lucky Baldwin loose. Sharon was willing to pay a high price for stock and agree to sell it back within ninety days at a lower figure. He was hungry for votes for Senator.

But Lucky Baldwin withstood all of Sharon's wooing and

Sharon was forced to pay his price for the stock, one hundred thirty-five dollars a share for twenty thousand shares!

Sharon took over control at the Ophir election but kept boosting this stock until he was safely a Senator. Meantime, the speculators had gone mad. January 8th, the bottom fell out, and Sharon was charged with "unloading" at high prices and then "shorting" the stock to recoup his expenditures.

The San Francisco Chronicle, then the leading newspaper of the Pacific Coast, and holding the largest circulation, led all the rest in extolling the riches of the new strike and the supposed and imagined virtues of the men in charge of it. This newspaper played a leading and alarming part in boosting the stock market to tottering heights; then, in later years, it went into complete and mysterious reverse and hounded the Bonanza Firm with a vitriolic vengeance. Its denunciations were used in connection with the lawsuits brought by Squire P. Dewey against Mackay and his associates—which were inspired and supported by the *Chronicle.*

It has been said that the change of heart of the *Chronicle* was ascribed to the unsuccessful attempt of Charles deYoung, chief owner and manager of the *Chronicle,* to induce the Bonanza firm to make good his losses on Consolidated Virginia stock.

It is true that this boom was started by Sharon and those in control of unprofitable mines, but speculation in this important discovery on the Comstick was considerably aided by the cupidity of the gambling public.

Two other papers, the *Call* and the *Bulletin,* printed editorials warning the public against this dangerously inflated market. The *Chronicle* sneered back, and the people of the Pacific Coast merrily continued rushing to market to buy a fat pig.

An example of what happened to many can be illustrated by what happened to one. Dr. Bronson, a noted Comstock surgeon and inveterate stock gambler, made $500,000 in the Crown Point boom in the spring of 1872, then was caught in the declining market and had to go through bankruptcy. In January, 1875, he had 1,000 shares of Consolidated Virginia bought on margin account and could "clean up" over half a million dollars.

"Sell that stock for a beggarly price of seven hundred dollars a share!" he said indignantly. "I would rather kindle a fire with it and I will before I'll sell it for less than $3,000."

Dr. Bronson, along with countless thousands, again went into bankruptcy. It was thought and believed at the time that this stock would actually reach three thousand dollars a share.

Virginia City's hills had gushed silver for so long and so fabulous were the shipments from the Comstock, that people believed it an unending source of the white metal. Its profits built railroads and pipelines, established banks, and dictated the commerce of the time. It established the stock exchange in San Francisco and constructed monuments of marble and mansions on Nob Hill.

The hard impact of American wealth against the rest of the world was a little too good—and the great ore bodies rocketed into international significance resulting in foreign pressure to demonetize silver. This brought about what was known as "the crime of '73."

While the Comstock drove deeper into Sun Mountain, France and England viewed this tremendous silver production with apprehension. These countries commanded top drawer position in world money circles and were dependent upon the gold standard. Sir Thomas Gresham warned England she must make money scarcer. Gold was on the decline and silver was increasing rapidly. If silver could be demonetized, then U. S. Civil War bonds, held by France and England, would be worth more.

Emperor Louis Napoleon sent an emissary to study the Comstock mines and his report only furthered the anxiety of France. In 1867, the United States sent John Sherman to the world monetary conference in Paris. As a result Sherman introduced a resolution at the conference which pledged representatives to establish the gold standard in the respective countries.

The outgrowth of all this was the so-called "Mint Bill" introduced in Congress in April, 1870. Its aim was to revise minting and coinage laws of the nation. The silver dollar was somehow omitted from the bill and was the start of a controversy that is still a hot one in the West.

While this bill was on the floor of Congress, a group of financiers made a trip to Virginia City. Among the party of seventeen were representatives of the Rothschild interests. The next fall 1872, the Mint Bill in final form was introduced and in 1873 it was passed. This was the beginning of the decline in the price of silver. Twenty years later, the price of silver was half of what it had been and the "goldbugs" were ruling as kings.

Then hard times descended on the mighty Comstock, on the "never ending" wealth of Virginia City, and there were soup kitchens on the Big Bonanza.

When the Consolidated Virginia, greatest of the Comstock, failed to pay its regular monthly dividend of $1,080,000 in 1877, the market crashed, and thousands of prosperous citizens were reduced to begging in the streets. People were starving and desperate in the once-rich camp, and robberies were common until the threat of mob violence was a reality.

Pioneer Nevada tells of two women in particular who did much to relieve the suffering in Virginia City. They were Mrs. Mary Mathews, who ran a lodging house, and her close friend, Mrs. Beck. These women knew that good food was being wasted in restaurants and arranged to obtain this food for a soup kitchen. They converted an old carpenter shop into a kitchen and obtained clean left-over food from restaurants, broken food packages from grocers, wilted vegetables, and meat scraps. A dairy donated milk, and the bakeries gave their day-old bread. These generous women fed five hundred people a day, keeping entire families alive on the Comstock, and many of their soup kitchen patrons were women and children. What surplus they had from their meals was given to the starving Paiute Indians and the Chinese who were in pitiful need. When the camp saw what these two women were doing, the whole town pitched in to give help. Even with this assistance the two women still rose before daylight and worked into the night preparing meals.

When the time came for the soup kitchen to close, the two women put up hundreds of lunches for men to carry as they left Virginia City for other western camps seeking work. The churches and other organizations then organized to assume this burden of caring for the poor on the Big Bonanza. Even at the height of its prosperity, this big boomer had its cabbages in the garden of the silver kings.

Other disasters were visited upon the town from the forces of nature. Virginia City was destroyed by fire in October of 1875. There had been no rain for months and a strong wind poured over Sun Mountain. Four hours after the city had been roused from its bed, the greater part of the town and the Consolidated Virginia and Ophir hoisting works were in ashes.

Goodwin in his *As I Remember Them* states that when a church took fire, an old Irish woman rushed over to the Consolidated Virginia shaft to Mackay who was working like a madman to save his mine and implored him to save the church.

"Damn the church," Mackay replied. "We can build another if we can keep the fire from going down these mine shafts."

Mackay made good his promise and contributed largely to the rebuilding not only of churches but also of the whole town.

As soon as the news sifted over the mountains, and San Francisco learned that the Con. Virginia and Ophir were on fire, everybody began to sell and stocks crashed to new lows.

Stockholders of Comstock shares were much more interested in market than in management, and elections of trustees meetings were usually sparsely attended. However, there were times they aroused themselves. There was a hot time in 1877 at the Con. Virginia meeting owing to the vitriolic criticism of Squire P. Dewey who was destined to become the nemesis of the Bonanza Firm.

If Bonanza could have foreseen the litigation and troubles Squire Dewey was going to visit upon their firm, they couldn't have paid him the fifty-two thousand he demanded from them fast enough. Dewey claimed he lost this money through misinformation given to him by Flood; and Dewey intended that somebody was going to make good, or else.

Dewey came to this particular meeting backed by Mr. James White, an English stockholder, and between the two of them they aroused Mackay and Flood to an indignation of response that was reported by the hostile *San Francisco Chronicle* as follows: "Mr.

Mackay's attitude toward Mr. White was something that might have been expected from a scrub, who, raised from nothing, had attained to nothing except dirty purse pride."

So up and down, and around after the brass ring, went the mad merry-go-round that was the famous Comstock, and the story of the litigation would of itself be a book. The sudden switch of the *Enterprise* from its extravagant praise of the Con. Virginia and its managers to its bitter condemnation has previously been mentioned. Both Squire P. Dewey and the men who owned the paper had lost great sums of money and both intended that the Bonanza Firm was going to make restitution.

"Blackmail!" was the answer from the Big Four. "We'll pay no blood money."

No one halted the word duels long enough to realize that the Big Bonanza had hit barren rock, that hundreds of levels beneath Virginia City lay deserted, dank, unproductive, deep in mould and sunk in sumps of water. The members of the Bonanza Firm continued in their efforts to find new ore bodies, but they were unable to do so.

Dewey, who worked hand in glove with the *Chronicle* in this pressure-squeeze, and was the man responsible for the suits, had grown rich dealing in San Francisco real estate. Thinking he was entitled to special information, Dewey asked Flood if the dividend would be paid following the fire in which the Consolidated Virginia works had been destroyed. Flood referred Dewey to his secretary for information as to cash on hand. The secretary gave Dewey the amount of cash—but not of bullion—on hand. Dewey assuming that the dividend would not be paid, sold a large block of stock, thinking the price of stock would go down. But the dividend was paid and the stock rose; thereafter, Dewey maintained that Flood was responsible for his financial losses. It was from this incident that suit was brought against Bonanza in behalf of the stockholders.

The glory of the Comstock had passed by the year 1880, and many of the men who were to make names in other famous camps of the West had moved on to other fields. Among them were

Marcus Daly and David Keith, both of whom had been Comstock mine foremen.

Daly became founder and manager of the great Anaconda Copper mine at Butte, Montana, to which many of the old Comstockers followed along. Keith was one of the organizers and principal owners of the rich Silver King mine at Park City, Utah.

Although the Comstock made many millionaires, the San Francisco stock brokers were more uniformly successful than any other class connected with the riches of the Lode. More than fifty of these brokers made substantial fortunes, and they came off, generally speaking, better than anybody else on the Big Bonanza. It is said that the following acquired more than a million dollars on the exchanges: James R. Keene, John D. Fry, Colonel E. E. Eyre, John W. Coleman, George T. Marye, Sr., B. F. Sherwood, James Latham, and C. W. Bonynge.

The Comstock isn't only a legend, it is a romance, one of the last epics of the West. Life for those who left the village below Sun Mountain was never the same adventure again, because the thing that had made it so had rolled into history . . . and, in the words of one of the brightest stars on the Comstock, John W. Mackay, manhood was at its best beyond the Rocky Mountains.

CHAPTER TWENTY-ONE

Red Men, and Yellow

"Volent et Potens," willing and able, read the motto on the Territorial seal of Nevada. A miner leaning on his pick, upholding the flag of the United States, expressed the two ideas of this rugged, independent one hundred thousand square miles of desert. First, that Nevada was loyal to the Union; second, that she had the wealth to sustain it.

From the northern border in the Washoe and Humboldt to the intersecting state line and the mighty Colorado River, these boom camps of the Great Basin carried on the tradition.

The weary mileage that is most of the Basin is today as it was yesterday, seen by the tourist in a cyclorama of endless blue sky, thirsty rock, and occasional ruins mottled by sage, as it was seen by the emigrant of the rutted wagon trails, just as dry, just as dull grey, just as uninspiring—unless one loves the desert. Strangely enough, some do, and the lonely reaches of the West have a special call for those who have known them.

But the way stations of today cater to speed, and are a far cry from the time when J. Ross Browne rode sedately along in his wagon behind his driver, Timothy, notebook in hand and propped as comfortably as possible against bundle and baggage, umbrella above his head for protection against a withering sun. Obtaining any type of comfort along the dusty routes of yesteryear was a scratch compared to the red-carpet treatment Nevada affords the traveler of today where at a simple service station with "OK'd" rest rooms, a plunger spray will dispense a full and generous squirt of White Shoulders, Chanel No. 5, or My Sin for one dime!

J. Ross Browne was a familiar figure in the life of the Great Basin, and his interesting "Peeps at the Washoe" in *Harpers Magazine* were nationally known. Browne has quite a following among students of Western Americana and is considered by some of them to have been a more entertaining writer than Mark Twain. He was an ex-government officer who found himself in San Francisco with an empty purse. He saw no remedy but to visit the newly discovered silver regions which were then making a big stir on Front and Montgomery Streets. He traveled into the Washoe, aided by a commission to explore some mines which had no existence in this world nor the next. He footed it over the mountains, pack on back, to Carson City and began writing his impressions of the country. He was never an enthusiastic booster and couldn't have made the local Lions, Kiwanis, or Rotary of the day. He deplored the wild speculation that took place in the stock exchanges and mocked the mines, men, and management of them, warning people to keep their money in the bank.

For this reason, when he considered returning to the Washoe, he was humorously warned by his friends that there were various threatening characters on the sharp lookout for the writer who had slandered the Washoe in public print. Special mention was made of a ferocious Irishman known as "Dirty Mike" who watched for Browne near the crossing of the American River armed with a tremendous shillelah in his right hand and a copy of *Harpers Magazine* in the other.

Also waiting vengeance upon this early day roving reporter of the plains was another Man-about-the-Washoe who was going "to get that fellow that showed them up in print." The "them" in this instance being a vicious local character and Bull, his dog. It seems that Browne had cast a slur upon the foul condition of this man's cabin which might have been overlooked, but what "the writer feller" said about Bull could only be wiped out in blood.

Undaunted, our brave Browne came back into the Washoe, making his inky way among men who had slung firearms since their infancy and some of the most hilarious stories of the West came from his running "the Washoe gauntlet." His story of the labor troubles between the Chinese and the Indians is not only entertaining, but also factual history.

The Celestials traditionally occupied the neglected nooks and corners of these mineral regions where they bore their share of adversity and disaster. Enmity between them and the dispossessed Indian tribes was a never ending see-saw type of cold war and frontier incidents without the soothing balm of any intervening diplomatic corps.

The first Chinese to enter Nevada were fifty Orientals engaged by John Reese to dig ditches in Carson River Valley in the mid-fifties. After this, five thousand more were brought into the valley to work the railroad grades. Prior to this, the Indians had chopped the wood for the many mining camps and their squaws hauled it into the towns to sell. The squaws had performed all the laundry work as well, but after the Chinese moved in, they took over both the laundry and the woodcutting business. J. Ross Browne gave a word picture from the times:

"Whenever a Chinese struck a good claim, it belonged to a white man. He may never have seen or heard of it, he may have abandoned it and gone elsewhere, but if Johnny Chinaman struck it rich, he came back or sent his partner to take possession."

The Indians learned a great lesson of civilization from their American benefactors. They also were driven from gulch to canyon and saw that "Melican man" claimed mines and minerals on general principles, and like him, they despised what they considered an inferior race. They hated the Chinese because "Chinaman squaw, no kill Indian like Melican man."

They seemed to look upon the Chinese as a base imitation of the Indian race—but without the redeeming quality of their bravery; hence the Diggers were singularly bitter in their hostility to the Chinese and began to tax them without mercy and kill them whenever they got a chance.

It is related by Browne that one Indian chief and his band made several thousand dollars in one summer by following up the

Chinese and compelling them by force of arms to pay taxes for the privilege of working in the mines.

"John Chinaman was taxed by the state, by the government, by every white pilgrim who jogged along with a pick or a shovel, by his own people, and finally by the Digger Indians."

The conversation when red skin met yellow skin went something like this:

"Say, John, what you do here?"

"Me workee—who you?"

"Me Piute Cappan—me kill plenty Melican man. This my land. You payee me, John, you payee me."

"No gottum."

"Me killee you."

"No got. Vellee poor Chinaman. How much you want?"

"Fifty dollar."

"No got fifty dollar. Vellee poor. Melican man he catchee Chinaman. He makee Chinee pay. No got fifty dollar."

"Melican man . . . Melican man . . . damn Melican man. Me no sabee Melican man, me a Paiute Cappan. You no pay me fifty dollar, me killee you."

Generally, after many protests and lamentations the Chinese paid the money. But if the Digger force was small, and the Celestials were in the majority, the cry of battle was raised and then came a tug of war.

Browne continued: "When Greek meets Greek the spectacle may be very impressive, but when Chinaman meets Digger, it is absolutely gorgeous. Negotiation has been prolonged without issue, the English language has been exhausted, the fight is inevitable. From every hole in the earth, the valiant Celestials rushed forth armed with picks and shovels, tin platters, gongs, and kettles . . . everything that could be made available for war-like purposes in the emergency of the moment. They beat their pans, blew their wind instruments, shrieked, shouted, laughed and made horrible faces and performed the most frightful antics in the hope of striking terror into the ranks of the enemy and foe. In every conceivable way, they taxed invention to make themselves hideous, poked their tongues out, doubled themselves up, hopped on one leg, squatted on the ground like frogs and then rushed furiously at the enemy. The hills and the forests resounded with the barbarous cries, the clatter of tin kettles and gongs."

In the meantime, the Digger Indians didn't stand about idle. More adept in the arts of barbarian warfare than were the Chinese laborers, they were not in the least frightened by the clownlike theatricals and mock warfare put on for their benefit.

But a pistol or gun shot was different and as long as the Chinese confined the war to one of loud noises, the Indians stood firm for their "fifty dollar." Tired of waiting for the Chinese to hand over the demanded tribute, the Diggers would tear in with war club and spear, bow and arrow—usually, however, a few pricks and a show of blood speedily ended the mock battle and the Chinese paid the demanded amount. Once in a while the Chinese had mustered up an old shotgun or pistol and returned fire when they fought with a desperation against being pushed over the border edge of starvation. These incidents teetered back and forth, with victory at times on the side of the Indians, other times for the Chinese.

As for the mines and mining properties Browne had been commissioned to report on, the eminent historian Bancroft seemed to support Browne's opinion that most of the speculation was a humbug: "I wish I could say that Comstock ethics were likely to mend; but the truth must be told, which is that the managers when they had appropriated to themselves the Bonanza, erected a multitude of mills, and kept on reducing the lower grade ores at a cost to themselves of five dollars a ton, but to the other stockholders of fourteen dollars, when perhaps the rock only yielded fourteen . . . or at any rate, was reported at that figure. A thousand Comstocks at this rate would be of little value to a state."

This seems to indicate that the author of the Washoe papers had "the big boys" pegged.

CHAPTER TWENTY-TWO

Dayton

Spafford Hall arrived from Fort Wayne, Indiana, and set up his trading post at a spot where Gold Creek flowed into the Carson River and the post was known as Gold Creek until 1854 when he sold out to James McMarlin. In 1856, a crew of Chinese laborers were brought in to construct irrigation ditches. They settled here, and it became known as Chinatown, later Johntown, so named from "John Chinaman." After the discovery of the Comstock Lode, this, one of the oldest towns in Nevada, became known as Dayton.

Nevada's first dance was held here on New Year's Eve, 1853, when Spafford Hall's log store was lighted for the celebration which was attended by 150 men and nine women. Miners, ranchers, and station keepers from fifty miles around cavorted until the wee morning hours to the popular ditties of the day while a curious band of Indians who were viewing the white man's celebration from outside decided to hold their own party. They drove off the white man's stock, slaughtered two of the horses, and had a fresh horsemeat barbecue.

When this first dance broke up, tired revelers were surprised by the sight of empty wagon tongues and cut ropes dangling where horses had been tethered the night before. Open corral gates and tracks in the alkali told the story. It was late the next day before they succeeded in rounding up their stock which had been left to wander by the well fed Indians. The Indians had discreetly disappeared into the hills, possibly averting a new series of Indian wars.

The Washoes inhabited the eastern Sierras and made the stealing of cattle belonging to the settlers both a business and an amusement. They roosted on the tops of the mountains waiting an opportunity, and whenever the whites collected for any purpose the Washoes seldom neglected to swoop down from their hiding places, gathering up and driving away anything they could find. Their fast retreat could generally be found marked with the remains of roasted horses, for which they cherished a great fondness. The Indians considered this New Year's caper a big joke and after such tricks upon the white man there was laughing in the Indian campoodies.

It all seemed to even itself out in the end. Just as the Indians considered the stock of the white man legitimate prey, so the traders regarded the "pilgrims" who traversed their routes. A continuous stream of wagon trains rolled across Nevada up the Carson River Pass on their way to California, and they were, without exception, exhausted, threadbare, and out of supplies by the time they reached these first trading stations operated by two Salt Lake City men, H. S. Beattie and Captain DeMont, along with others.

Business was terrific and Beattie and his partners made numerous trips into California for supplies which they floated across streams on rafts of logs, bringing back to Mormon Station sacks of flour, bacon, sugar, and coffee. If business was terrific, profits were fantastic. After the wicked desert crossings, travelers were willing to pay anything to avoid being marooned without supplies and equipment they needed. Beattie got a thousand dollars for a single ox the emigrants needed for beef; the standard price for a few loaves of bread became one good saddle horse. In no time Mormon Station had collected over 100 head of fine horses. The close of the first "tourist season" sent the first traders back home well-heeled from hitting the first Nevada jackpot.

Dayton is the area where "Old Virginy" of Comstock fame is buried. Before the site of the Dayton cemetery was designated by L. L. Crockett and Judge Calvin, several interments had been made at the foot of the hill. One of these was Old Virginy. The location of this grave was vouched for by an old Paiute Indian.

He saw the miner thrown from a bucking mustang he was trying to ride while under the influence of liquor. Virginy was pitched head first upon the ground, received a fracture of the skull, and died a few hours later. Said the Indian: "Well, you see, he die down to Dayton long time ago. Old Birginey, he all time drink too much whiskey. One day he bully drunk, he git on pony; he run, he buck one bully buck and Ole Birginey go over Pony's head. One foot stay in stirrup and pony drag old man on ground and kill him. Me help dig one grave, bury Old Birginey down Dayton by Carson River."

This Indian had previously worked a rocker for Old Virginny in Six Mile Canyon and his statement was accepted as history.

When in 1862-63 the Indians saw with alarm their game as well as their pine nut forests disappearing in the wake of mine and miner, their leader Numaga came into the camp of the wood-cutters. He eloquently set forth the complaints and conditions of his people and asked as a matter of justice that the natives be reimbursed for some of this devastation.

In order to avoid trouble, the woodmen agreed to pay four hundred dollars to the tribe for the privilege of cutting trees on their section of land. They raised half the amount then, agreeing to pay the balance three months later. At the appointed time, the Indians reappeared and were paid the balance of the agreed amount, which averted trouble for the time being.

DUTCH NICK'S

Dutch Nick's was a famous landmark in this area where the Overland Emigrant stage route met the banks of the Carson River three and a half miles from present Carson City.

The original owner, Nicholas Ambrosia, recorded his claim to this property in 1855, and it was known as Dutch Nick's. The people of this early settlement, the people of Johntown, were a jovial and gregarious lot, fond of any amusement they could scare up. Nearly every Saturday night a "grand ball" was held at Dutch Nick's saloon. Among the partners who "made up the set" was Sarah Winnemucca, the Paiute Princess, daughter of Winne-mucca, chief of all the Paiutes.

Nick Ambrose moved along up Six Mile Canyon and followed his customers. He didn't come to mine but set up a large tent which was a combination saloon and boarding house. He charged fourteen dollars a week for board, and the boys "slept themselves." That meant they provided their own blankets and rolled up in the sage.

With the discovery of the Comstock Lode, Dutch Nick's boomed. When the Virginia and Truckee Railway was built, this became one of the most important settlements along the east fork of the Carson. Although the Mexican, Morgan, and Brunswick mills were located here, milling was only secondary to the thriving logging business.

Dutch Nick's was located on a wide, lazy curve of the Carson River and made an ideal spot where the huge timbers could be guided shoreward and loaded into waiting flat cars to be sent to the mines of the Comstock. The lumber, cut in the Sierra Nevadas, was rafted for eighty miles to this depot of the wood business. It required forty days to bring the lumber from the Carson headwaters to the landing.

On the map of this country it is seen as Empire—which it was called after its survey for a townsite—earlier, and more romantically, it was known just as Dutch Nick's.

WASHOE CITY

The boom business of the 1860's was the building of mills for the ores of the Comstock which were hauled in freight wagons from Virginia City and Gold Hill down the Ophir grade and over a causeway built across the southern end of Washoe Lake. The Ophir, largest of the mills, was on Ophir Creek on the west and a town was built near the mill. Washoe City became a mill and freighting town on the north end of the lake.

Later, when the Virginia & Truckee Railroad was built from Carson City to Virginia City, these mills were moved to the Carson River. There were, at one time, forty mills operating on this stream. Washoe City was the county seat of Washoe County. From 1869 to 1869, this was a busy valley. Horse and mule teams pulling ore laden wagons from the Comstock returned to Virginia

City with loads of wood and farm produce. During these years, there were approximately 5,000 people in the Washoe Valley, but that was when it was an inflated community owning churches, schools, and sawmills. Washoe City itself dwindled down to a population of 70 by 1875.

Uncensored, sarcastic frontier editors often printed articles that were considered rank affronts by some, and one such incident led H. F. Swayze to kill Editor George W. Derickson of the Washoe City *Times* on January 23, 1863. Swayze, of nearby Ophir, had "palmed off" a plagiarism on the *Times* and Derickson wrote:

"ICHABOD. A tall, gawky greenhorn, dressed in a buckskin suit, stepped into the Times offices yerterday, and handed us an article, which he was very anxious to have published. He said he had spent a great deal of time in getting it up, and wanted a dozen or so copies of the paper, containing his article, to send to his friends. The article was headed HOW I GOT MY WIFE, and was signed Ichabod. The said greenhorn, whose real name, he informed us is H. F. Swayze, is hereby informed he can have a dozen copies of the Times, containing his article by calling at this office and paying for the same. His article, which he says cost him so much trouble and study was published in the second number of the *Times*, word for word, we have the same for sale ..."

When editor Derickson was attending a dance at Steamboat Springs, he heard Swayze was looking for him and he armed himself. They met the next day in a Washoe City saloon and from there went to the office. Swayze demanded that Derickson retract the charges printed against him and Derickson refused, saying the paper had printed the truth.

"You're a damned liar," Swayze charged, and as Derickson retreated through the open door, both men fired simultaneously. Guns blazed several more times and one ball lodged in Swayze's mouth, cracking the jawbone and carrying teeth with it, but editor Derickson was mortally wounded. Swayze was jailed, while local residents who had liked the popular editor were incensed to a near-lynching fever.

There were many such instances on record in western history where disputes were settled "by the gentlemanly form." This was a carryover from the customs of the many southerners present in the boom camps in Nevada. Dueling became such a fad in the sixties that it was outlawed, but legality never curbed the desire for this kind of satisfaction on the field of honor, and many a party met on a hillside or in a ravine in the grey dawn. Usually, a wound was deemed sufficient payment for a personal slight, but not always so.

Before dueling had been outlawed, a duel was fought between Joseph T. Goodman, editor of the *Territorial Enterprise,* and Tom Fitch, editor of the rival paper, *The Virginia Daily Union.* The verbal blasts these papers fired at one another kept the Comstock highly entertained.

Goodman and Dennis McCarthy, journeymen printers, San Francisco, arrived on the Comstock and invested their money in the run-down *Enterprise* which they built into the finest and most successful paper in the pioneer west.

When Tom Fitch of the *Virginia Daily Union* likened "the logic of the Eenterprise to the love of God," Goodman was at first complimented, but when the reporters of the *Enterprise* located the quotation in the Bible and learned that the love of God "surpasseth all human understanding," fine furies arose and Goodman challenged Fitch to a duel with pistols. Fitch accepted enthusiastically. Fitch at this time was in his thirties, Goodman, twenty-five.

The duelers met at dawn of the day set for the shooting match, firing at a given word. Goodman shot low and Fitch shot high. The latter missed, but Fitch was wounded in his knee and remained crippled for life as a result of this fight. But it ended the quarrel and both men went on to be famous as writers. Fitch aided Gridley to raise funds for the Sanitary Commission, which was the equivalent to our present day Red Cross. He was a man always in demand as a speaker and finally served as congresssman from Nevada in 1869-70-71.

And it was trouble over a duel that finally got Mark Twain into such hot water that he had to leave Virginia City.

Twain, energetically filling his boss's shoes for a few days, decided he must prove himself capable of the trust placed in him. He therefore proceeded to tear into the editor of the rival *Union*, James Laird, for "failing to contribute for the Sanitary Sack of Flour Fund," and slammed an ink lecture at the local ladies' group in Carson City for diverting some of these funds to other use. He really stirred up the bees. Rival editor, ladies, and husbands of said ladies were outraged, and Mark Twain was in trouble up to his famous neck. Although neither reporter really wanted to slug it out on the dueling range, Mark's friends egged him on until he challenged Laird; and Laird, equally cornered and unwilling, was forced to accept. The reluctant champions of the press met in the grey hills of Nevada May, 1864. Twain's second, Steve Gillis, was a good shot. Twain couldn't hit even a target a few paces away, and he was in a state of acute panic. Fate intervened. A small bird flew overhead and Gillis casually shot its head off. As it fell, one of Laird's seconds picked it up asking how such a fine shot had been made. Gillis calmly lied, "Why, my man here did it, of course." Not wanting to face this pistol expert, Laird backed out.

But this incident had repercussions of a serious nature. The authorities determined to make an example of Mark Twain for violation of the anti-dueling law. Also, various husbands who belonged to the insulted ladies were descending upon Virginia City, pistol in pocket, challenging Twain to more duels than he could rightfully handle. Trouble added on trouble, and it was then that the two good friends, Steve Gillis and Twain, boarded a California-bound stage—and fame.

What these early newspapers lacked in news, they made up in imagination. They created hoaxes and stories that were read and believed across the nation, making Nevada Territory notorious if nothing else wherever they found their way. Local liars clubs filled columns when the editors lacked truth and originated a carefree style of writing that swept Western philosophy and journalism into generations of American print.

Entertainment was scarce. Nevadans showed originality there

too. *Pioneer Nevada* tells the story of the Washoe Lake Ice Boat.

Winter months in the camps were particularly dull, so a few imaginative and adventuresome souls at Washoe City designed and built an ice boat which became the talk for hundreds of miles through the territory.

It is reported that the best engineering minds on the Comstock had a hand in designing and building the Washoe Sail Boat—and there is no question that some of the best minds in the nation, engineering, legal, or otherwise, found their way to this center of fabulous wealth. At any rate, the winter of 1863 found Washoe Lake frozen hard and the ice boat constructed and ready to make the most of the sport. The fame of the strange craft spread and it seemed that everybody in Nevada wanted to ride on the ice boat whose speed was reported to have ranged from sixty to one hundred miles an hour. As the Washoe Zephyr is a constant and terrific wind, it is quite possible the boat did attain such speed.

When this craft was loaded, the boat would skim Washoe Lake then, without warning, her skipper would pull hard on the tiller, and whip the boat around in a tight turn that broke the grasp of every passenger on deck. Pioneer sports, fun, and humor were rugged and the treatment the guests received aboard was no exception. They would be torn from the boat and hurled out across the smooth ice for a distance of fifty yards. That there were no fractured skulls or broken bones was nothing short of a miracle. The skipper would drop the said and pick up his bruised and battered passengers who hobbled painfully back to the accompaniment of loud guffaws by the crew.

After this ritual, the passengers would be loaded back on the boat and the party would skim back to the Lake House at Washoe City for the standard remedy of hot toddies. Then peace was made between crew and passengers, many toasts were drunk to friendship; and these toasts led to more incidents and more stories that rivaled the ice boat stories themselves.

GALENA

Galena and other camps which supplied lumber for the Comstock from the Sierra slopes to the west of Washoe City provided an endless stream of bullwhacking traffic on the Ophir grade as they hauled the giant "sets" and spiling to Virginia City.

In 1860 this lumber town had eleven sawmills and a sash factory, while loggers, millmen, bullwhackers, woodcutters, charcoal burners, and teamsters swelled the burly throngs along the crowded streets. This was a busy and influential camp, and while it lasted, it produced millionaire lumber barons, but within a few years the mountain slopes were stripped of timber.

"Stuttering" Jim Mathews became a legend among the bullwhackers. He was a well-known character of the ox team days. On his way from Thomas Canyon, Jim would find his heavy load bogging down deeper and deeper while the thirsty oxen halted mid-stream for water. Normally, Jim had a speech impediment which somehow disappeared when he became angry. After many unsuccessful attempts to get the yoke pulling together, he would mount a stump and begin an oration to the team which would relieve his pent-up feelings. He never halted until he was out of breath and in one last gasp would wind up by calling on the Apostles to "come on down and help me cuss them cattle." It worked, like witchcraft, and this midnight blessing moved the wagon right along as the oxen answered with a successful pull.

After the railroads were built, these boomers declined, although some lumber was still floated down the river to Carson. Washoe City and Galena died in the wake of the steel rails when faster and easier methods of supplying the Comstock were employed.

The name of Warren Wasson is encountered so frequently in the folklore and history of the Western section of the boom towns of the Great Basin, that one's attention is captured by the many incidents in which his name continually reappears.

Warren Wasson took his first stand in Genoa, where he spearheaded a movement aimed at the "land grabbers" who claimed more land than they could place under cultivation, but he came into prominence during the time of the Indian troubles in West Nevada and is closely connected with the story of Fort Churchill.

Nevada has been termed "battle born" for many reasons. The Civil War was being fought during her territorial period, and Nevada was taken into the Union as a hasty measure because she was a saving financial support. But there were many southerners here, and keeping Nevada loyal to the Union during the war was a very real problem with which the early government had to deal. This was one reason Governor Nye proclaimed that anyone who was disloyal would be punished.

Indian troubles were another problem for the battle-born territory. Indian strife brought the establishment of military outposts to protect settlers, surveyors of government routes, and the overland traffic.

Fort Churchill, near Wabuska, was constructed in 1860 after a general uprising of the Indians all over Nevada. Damage done to Pony Express stations cost that company seventy-five thousand dollars to repair. Still, the mail was interrupted by persistent outrages. The soldiers were then used to police the overland routes.

Warren Wasson became Indian Agent and one who was known to respect the rights of Paiute and Washoe. He learned their customs and language and treated them with an honesty and consistent policy which won their respect.

During the Pyramid Indian War, Wasson served with the Nevada volunteers, and when the regulars withdrew to Fort Churchill in 1860, Wasson was left as agent at Pyramid Lake to organize an Indian reservation. He posted notices defining these boundaries and warned the whites to leave the area.

In December of this year, he freighted supplies into the Walker Lake fisheries for the Paiutes. There Wasson and his men handed out clothing to the Indian men and needles, thread, and materials to the women. It was bitterly cold, and the last of the clothing had been distributed when one old Indian hobbled up for his gifts. Everything had been given, and the Indians stood quietly to see what Wasson would do. Without delay, Wasson removed his own clothing and handed it to the old man.

Warren Wasson made an impression that day that lasted as long as any Indian present remained living, and it was an action that placed in his hands an almost legendary power to prevent

Indian uprisings, raids, and massacres. Without him the history of Nevada would today make different reading.

For troubles certainly came. By 1861 the Indian tribes of Nevada Territory were reduced to starvation. Crews of woodcutters made no distinction in a forest, and their axes stripped the pine nut forests which were food for the tribes as well as hunting reserves. The game was driven away and the streams polluted, and Governor Nye, becoming concerned over the gravity of the situation, wrote the Commander of the Pacific for food. Supplies were loaded at Fort Churchill, and teamsters started out with a huge load along the Overland Trail.

Warren Wasson went on a whirlwind tour to keep peace. He contacted the Indians at Smith Creek, Roberts Creek, Simpson's Park, Dry Creek, and Grubs' Wells, assuring them that food was on the way. He found in each instance that the Indians were being kept alive by stage station employees.

He reached Ruby Valley December 22 and found one hundred Indians who had again been kept alive by the stage company. This way, Wasson went through his routine, keeping the peace, and assuring the tribes that relief was on the way. No estimate was given of the number of Indians dying from starvation or malnutrition, but Warren stated that they were "without horses or dogs."

But during April of 1861 serious trouble arose and about 1,500 war-minded Paiutes assembled at the fisheries near the mouth of the Walker River. Wahe, half-brother to Winnemucca, was the guiding genius behind this new offensive.

Wahe planned the murder of Warren Wasson, scheming that with the death of this popular Indian agent he would be able to seize the rifles and powder at the agency, and that by concealing these weapons under blankets and rabbit robes his braves should filter into Fort Churchill in small groups. His plan was that, at a given signal, the Paiutes would rise and slaughter the garrison from the inside. With the guns and arms of Fort Churchill at his disposal, Wahe intended to arm the entire Paiute nation.

This plan and the warning of the plot against his life were related to Wasson by a young interpreter, and Wasson met the

269

danger alone. He had no time to alert Fort Churchill. Alone, Warren Wasson strode down to the crowds of Indians at the fisheries where he boldly called the chiefs and sub-chiefs together.

Sitting among them, he told them that their plan would fail. He recounted past history to them and called to mind their disastrous defeat at Pyramid, warning them of the white man's vengeance which would surely follow another Indian uprising. He watched calmly as the band restrained Wahe and he kept up his argument, gradually winning the Indians away from war with his logic.

Wahe left the region for Oregon and peace was returned to Nevada Territory through the efforts of this one amazing man. Wasson's move was particularly providential. Fort Churchill had been stripped of men by the press of the Civil War and was in a dangerously vulnerable position. When Wahe returned to Nevada, the Indians had lost their fear of his dread magic as two chiefs who beat him to death with their war clubs demonstrated. To make sure he was good and dead, they chopped his body into tiny pieces and scattered the bloody fragments far out over the lonely desert.

CHAPTER TWENTY-THREE

Ranches, the Capitol and More Mines

This cattle country where there was some mining is still going strong.

Ranches in Nevada are *big*, for two resons. First, although the public domain stretches endlessly, water to irrigate the land is scarce, necessitating huge acreage to support a ranch. Second, Nevada early fell into the hands of land-grabbers and a clique of cattle moguls who tied up all the land bearing creek, stream, or mountain seepage. The names of Henry Fred Dangberg, of Westphalia, Germany; Colonel T. B. Rickey from Ohio; Colonel John Tinnin and John Sparks; the families of Walsh, Huffaker, Keough, Kenyon, Sadler, Molini, Lambertucci, and Henry Miller of the famous Seven S Brand are burned into the hide of Nevada, and were well remembered by countless hundreds of smaller ranchers who were forced out of business so that the big ones could get bigger.

Henry Fred Dangberg arrived in Dayton in 1853, purchasing a small farm near the town of Mindon which became a ranch of 36,000 acres in Carson Valley and was used for the grazing of thousands of cattle and sheep. His ranch was the scene of early experiments in irrigation, with new ideas in the growing of crops, and Dangberg is said to have been the first in Nevada to cultivate alfalfa. To increase the yield of wild hay, he built dams and ditches to water his lands. These holdings have been kept in the same family and remain one of the great ranches in Nevada.

Another district that drew in the stock raisers was the Mason Valley. The trading center of this district was Pizen Switch. Jim

Mills moved into this country, taking up land on either side of the Walker River. When the Central Pacific Railroad was built in 1869, Henry Miller, already a cattle baron of the firm of Miller and Lux in California, came in to build up a domain that stretched from the Oregon line to Pizen Switch.

Then sheepmen moved in. They were called "trespassers," didn't accept this definition of their presence on the range, and fought back; then Nevada saw cattleman-sheepman wars. The cattlemen were bitter against the Basque sheepmen whom they termed "tramp ranchers," as they owned no land and paid no taxes, and their flocks overgrazed the land. But the Basques stayed on, managing to acquire water rights and eventually to establish a sheep country that encompassed an area three hundred miles wide from Winnemucca to Oregon.

Cattlemen fought private feuds, tied up rights of way, poisoned other stock, "dry-gulched" sheepherders, and forced out smaller men. Miller was in there with the rest of them and drove his rivals out. After this he sued his contemporary, Tom Ricker. Ricker planned to use a natural reservoir for storing Walker River water in order to irrigate his land, but his plan meant that little water came on down to irrigate Miller's lands and Miller sued for water rights carrying his case to victory in the United States Supreme Court.

HAWTHORNE

Hawthorne, at the south end of Walker Lake, was the terminus of the Carson and Colorado Railroad and much of the freighting of the mining camp of Bodie was done through Hawthorne. A former county seat, it lost out to Goldfield in 1907.

Nevada had its "ghost counties" as well as its ghsot towns, counties which were created and later either had their names changed or were abolished as county units. Carson, Desert, Greasewood, St. Mary's, and Shambip once formed parts of Nevada. Short-lived mining towns and migratory miners account for the boom and bust, and mining left broken-down towns putting up a futile battle against newer and more vigorous boomers which drained away the original political importance. So it was that Pioche replaced Hiko, Reno took over from Washoe City, Winnemucca from Unionville, Tonopah from Belmont, Yerington from Dayton, and so on.

Early Pizen Switch had derived its name from an enterprising saloon keeper who kept his whiskey potent by means of plugs of chewing tobacco flavoring one original supply of XXX firewater. This saloon was constructed of yellow switches, and when it first opened for business, was given the name of "Switch" by the miners and cowboys who met at this crossroad. Never did one barrel of whiskey last so long—it was watered, colored, doctored, and nursed along until the patrons, who knew this drink didn't deserve the name of whiskey, called it Switch's Pizen. The town which later became Yerington was thus first known as Pizen Switch.

NEVADA'S CAPITOL — CARSON CITY

"A mere accident, occupation of the inhabitants, waylaying strangers bound for Virginia City; business, selling whiskey, and so dull that men fall asleep in the middle of the street going from one grocery to another. Productions: grass and weeds on the Plaza." Thus wrote J. Ross Browne in 1861, "A Peep at Washoe," in *Harpers'*.

Abraham V. Z. Curry was the father of Carson City. The capitol of Nevada was built where he envisioned it, on the Plaza. He built the state prison and sold it to the state. All the stone for these buildings came from the Warm Springs quarry; all was sold to the builders by the same Abe Curry.

This man came to Carson City because he wouldn't pay the price asked for land elsewhere.

"The' hell with it," remarked the doughty old timer, "I'll start my own city." And start it he did.

Abe arrived in Carson from Mormontown and was later joined by B. F. Green, F. M. Proctor, and J. J. Musser. They purchased land that was at that time known as Eagle Ranch and in September of 1858, Curry proposed to his partners that they survey for a townsite. They obtained a reluctant surveyor—Jerry Long from Dayton. Jerry looked over the project and instantly suggested they abandon it, but Curry insisted that he do the work. No argument could deter Curry from this seemingly rash enterprise, and in the face of all who looked upon this plan as foolish, the site of Carson City was laid out. The surveyor refused land in Carson in payment of his work saying he would rather have Curry owe him than take such stuff in compensation for his skill and labor. So confident was Curry of the future of this empty piece of real estate that as the Plaza was being surveyed, he made the statement that in years to come, the capitol would be built upon that square.

It must be remembered that at this time the territory now comprising the state of Nevada was Utah Territory, Carson County. At this visionary date, Abe Curry saw a future when Utah Territory would be divided and the western portion given over to a new Territory, which would, in a given time, assume the proportions of a new state in the Union. So it was that the Plaza, or square, was fully designed by Abe Curry to be a future capitol.

An equal division of the townsite was made, and in September 1858 the four partners took equal proportions. Curry all the while was busy making adobes for this city which wasn't. Lots were given to those who would guarantee to erect buildings, and others were traded for such legal tender as pairs of boots, twenty-five pounds of butter, ponies, etc.

No rapid influx of population came despite the frantic promotion by this local boosters club. Carson found that the population went, willy-nilly, where the gold was. A minister, the Reverend Mr. Bateman of the Methodist denomination, arrived in 1858, standing alone, as it were, a sober and judicious influence in a frontier town that gave little concern to The Great Future.

Such mixed and migratory population as there was felt the need of law and regulation, and on the 11th of June the city fathers agreed among themselves to adopt certain simple rules of conduct and to enforce them upon others. This action, taken by many of the early boom camps, was known as "The Miners Code." One element of the code stated: "For offenses such as murder, hanging, wounding, robbing, cattle thievery, or other crimes, the punishment was set as the miners jury should determine."

The notorious "Murdering Sam" Brown of the Comstock visited Carson City long enough to commit its first murder when he killed one William Bilboe. Sam was never tried for this murder, his deadly reputation intimidated many a jury who might otherwise have meted out punishment. The *Carson Appeal* also recorded an early vengeance killing. A young man named Ashim killed one of three brothers named Perasich. As a result, the other two Perasich brothers shot up a Carson stage in an attempt to kill Ashim who was in it.

Under this first law, two men named George Ruspas and David Reise had their ears cut off for stealing cattle. This pair had appeared in the Washoe Valley with cattle for sale at a low price, and an investigation revealed they had been stolen from a Dayton rancher. The miners jury who tried them met in the open under a big pine and handed down a sentence that the pair should have their left ears severed.

Jim Sturtevant was appointed executioner. With a quick motion he parted Reise with his ear, but when he lifted Ruspas' long hair he found this gentleman had already given up his ear for some previous offense. Ruspas, who was bound, laughed up at Sturtevant, but Jim Sturtevant, not to be denied, took a firm hold of the remaining ear and as he severed it he tossed it back to the jury with the statement that, "now you got you a right and a left." The two men were banished from the district and told upon pain of death never to return to the Washoe.

So while mine owners bought and sold and speculated in mining ground at Virginia City and Gold Hill, others bought and sold building lots in a town they had determined would be a future metropolis. Carson City made a good beginning and in 1860 had an able and flourishing newspaper, the *Territorial Enterprise*, a water company, seminary of learning, telegraph office, stage line, mercantile houses, hotels, and other business places. The leading hotel of Carson City was the Ormsby House, where Major Ormsby had invested in his share of Carson. Here, conventions of both political parties were held. Both the Pony Express and the telegraph station were at the Carson Inn. J. Ross Browne observed Carson's growth upon a second visit: "Leaving the lake at the Glenbrook Station, we begin to ascend the last of the Sierra Nevada Divides. After a long pull and heavy descent we enjoy a fine view of the pretty little town of Carson. An hour more, and we are safely landed at the express office of Wells Fargo and Company from which point we can diverge to any number of bad hotels, by selecting the worst, you will possibly not be disappointed.

"Carson City has enjoyed a very wholesome kind of prosperity since my first visit here if I might be allowed to judge by a casual glance at the new buildings about the Plaza, and many pleasant residences in the suburbs. The plethoric condition of the stock market in San Francisco, and the fact that capital has been pouring through the various passes of the Sierras into the Washoe Valley, had led me to expect that wonderful improvements must be the result—nor was I disappointed. The number of saloons in Carson City, and in fact all along the route, manifested to a remarkable degree the rapid progress of civilization. The splendid stone penitentiary situated a couple of miles from Carson presented another striking evidence of moral advancement."

During the winter of 1859 and the spring and summer of 1860 numbers of Californians came into the Washoe. As these new arrivals had no affinity with the first settlers, the Mormons, the cause of those wishing a separate territory was considerably strengthened, and on March 2, 1861, President James Buchanan signed a bill creating the Territory of Nevada. It became the task of President Lincoln to appoint the new territorial officers and James W. Nye, a lawyer and politician of New York City, became Territorial governor. Other officers came in, among them Orion Clemens, of Keokuk, Iowa, bringing with him his brother Samuel L. Clemens. The future Mark Twain was disappointed in his ambition to become his brother's secretary, and that, along with his failure as a miner, turned him in the direction of the *Territorial Enterprise*, where his writing career began. Twain, finding the appointment under his brother carried no salary along with the honor, decided he preferred a job he got paid for.

The new governor, James Nye, took a ribbing from Carson City when he arrived at the Capitol. A band of fifty Chinese "musicians" had been hired to serenade him, and Nye, who understood their music no more than he did their language, listened to a horrible caterwauling which he seriously applauded. He was new to the West and anxious to please, and it wasn't until the Carson folks could no longer keep a straight face that the new governor realized he had been tricked. He then joined in with a hearty guffaw which won him friends and got him off to a fine start in the frontier territory he was to manage.

Abe Curry's town gradually shifted out of low gear and got to rolling on his Eagle Valley Railway. When his dream finally came true and legislators were assembling at Carson, it became evident there was no place with room available for their sessions. Curry offered the third story of his Warm Springs Hotel, rent free. His offer was accepted, but the legislators were still faced with the problem of transportation. Abe then offered free transportation for the law makers from Carson to Warm Springs, and in order to make good his offer set about building Nevada's first streetcar. This consisted of a flat car and a windowless passenger car with benches for seats, and the vehicle was pulled by two mules. Abe then hauled the legislators from Ormsby House in Carson City to Curry's Warm Springs and back to Carson over the railway. The legislators rode up front on free passes while Abe hauled his stone from Warm Springs quarry on the flat car behind and sold it to them to build Carson. The city today owes its existence to this early day hotshot from the local chamber of commerce.

During this time when sober citizens were busy building towns to last, political kettles in opposite warring camps boiled while "secesh" and Union man circled for a showdown of power. Feelings were bitter in 1863 in Nevada Territory where the Civil War was a much more personal isssue than it was considered in Utah. Many southerners had gone West, and Nevada ran fifty-fifty, Confederate and Union, in population which might have swung support in either direction. The West was in chaos, and early elections were strong-armed through by either side who could swing the biggest fist.

The election of August 31, 1861, illustrates the tension prevailing in Nevada Territory. Only people who had been living in the territory at the time it was established were supposed to vote, but there were large numbers of soldiers stationed in Nevada who didn't go along with this thinking. The soldiers, being Union, feared there were too many "secessionist" scattered among the old timers, and on this occasion trooped into Carson City from Fort Churchill, officer in command, non-coms alongside. The civilians of Carson objected strongly to the soldiers voting but they were outnumbered. There were many irregularities in the first election which were allowed to pass; for Unionists, and only Unionists, were placed in office. As for the Federal authorities, they maintained a discreet tongue-in-cheek attitude and looked assiduously in the other direction. With the nation threatened by secession, no one was much concerned with the political niceties and they held control. But with the passing years, the turbulence settled, and Carson became the friendly, pleasant, tree-lined town that it still is today, open as always.

Nevada has always been a wide open state with a liking for the lusty life and not much use for "blue laws." The Reverend Henry Ward Beecher, leading temperance advocate of his day, was pilloried on every possible occasion in Nevada. The people liked fighting, and as in Alta, Utah, where citizens openly stated "a little blood-letting was a fine thing," so long as combatants didn't use bullets, they would watch any kind of a fight. They fought badger against bulldog, jackass against jackass, and man against man, and they held the effete East in contempt where the Beechers and their ilk had made prize fighting illegal.

Nevada miners might not know the name of the president of the United States, but to a man they knew that John L. Sullivan was the heavyweight champion of the world, and they considered "the Boston Strong Boy" the greatest fighter of all time. John L. could whip more men, and drink more whiskey, than any other man who ever lived—and that made him an honorary citizen of Nevada!

Then, one bleak day in New Orleans in 1892, in an illegal, speak-easy sort of place, the great John L. Sullivan was over-

278

thrown by an upstart San Francisco bank clerk called "Gentleman Jim" Corbett, a fancy-Dan boxer who jabbed and feinted the champ of champs into a state of helplessness and knocked him out in the twenty-first round.

It just didn't seem right, somehow, for a non-drinking dude to hold the championship. But Corbett proceeded to beat all comers whenever he could bootleg a fight, including the great Negro pugilist, Peter Jackson, whom he wore down in a sixty round match off the coast of San Francisco.

Nevada's interest was somewhat impersonal until it suddenly dawned upon the sports that Nevada was one of the two states in the Union where prize fighting was legal, and they learned that there were capitalists who would put up money to bring a championship fight to Carson City.

Nobody would give the challenger, "Ruby Bob" Fitzsimmons, of Australia, much of a chance, but he was the sentimental favorite. He was the middleweight champion of the world, and although he would weigh in at around a hundred and sixty pounds, he would still be nearly thirty pounds lighter than Corbett.

Fitzsimmons had one asset—he could hit with the kick of a mule. Corbett was grace personified and freckle-faced old Bob, older than Gentleman Jim by some years, was a physical anomaly. His youthful years as a blacksmith had given the Cornishman from Australia shoulders like a gorilla atop a slender body and thin, bird-like legs. And like a gorilla, his arms were unusually long. However, against Corbett, he was as slow-moving as old John L.

Dan Stewart of Carson City undertook to promote the fight, and it cost him fifty thousand dollars to get the combatants into the ring. A new industry called motion pictures was in its infancy, but pictures had been taken of a fight between Corbett and Charley Mitchell, the champion of England, and a British firm, pulling for a fellow citizen of the Empire, offered the two gladiators $200,000 for the picture rights—provided the fight went twenty rounds—thus giving the battle an international flavor.

Interest in the fight was at fever height all over the nation and the eyes of the world were on Carson City, Nevada. Not since the mighty days of the Comstock had the big desert attracted

279

so much attention. The fight was set for March 17, 1897, and Carson City took on the appearance of a national convention city a month before the contest. Carson's main street was bedecked with banners proclaiming the headquarters of the leading newspapers of the country. The wires were kept hot as the sports writers of the nation kept sending out minute accounts of the condition of each man and long personal interviews with the principals. A unique touch was added when it was learned that Mrs. Fitzsimmons would be in her husband's corner as a second. Although old Bob was the sentimental favorite, the smart money was on Gentleman Jim. Many Nevadans recklessly wagered their money on Fitzsimmons, though privately conceding that he would probably lose. The population of the town soared as special trains pulled in, one after another. Fitzsimmons, like many another fighter, had a secret weapon, the solar plexus punch. Boxing in orthodox style, with left hand extended, he would sometimes shift position and bring his lethal left to the stomach.

The fight proceeded much as had been expected with the dancing master jabbing and hooking the challenger's face into a bloody mess, and with old Bob ploughing in and boxing as best he could. In Fitz's corner, his wife screamed so loudly for Fitz to "Kill him, Bob!" that with a grin, the confident Corbett remarked, "Why don't you have your wife fight me, Bob, she might do better."

Suddenly, it happened. In a moment of carlessness, Corbett failed to notice the Fitzsimmons shift until old Bob drove his terrible left into the nerve center called the solar plexus. Paralyzed for the moment, Corbett had no defense for the ex-blacksmith's right which landed on his unprotected jaw. Down went Gentleman Jim in the fourteenth round, and though he made a valiant effort to rise, the count of ten was tolled over him and Carson City went wild.

If the agreement to pay $200,000 for the picture rights was ever made, Ruby Bob was willing to forget it when the opportunity arrived to use his Sunday punch. For once in its life, Carson City, little more than a village by Eastern standards, was the center of the eyes of the whole world. It had put Nevada on the map.

A year or so later, Fitzsimmons lost his championship to Jim

Jeffries, the burly young boiler-maker from Los Angeles who in turn was to retire undefeated, but was inveigled into a match with the first Negro champion of the world, Jack Johnson, as a "white hope" only to be knocked out in the fifteenth round. Gentleman Jim Corbett was Jeffries' chief second, and he must have remembered the way he had taunted Bob Fitzsimmons that day in Carson City when Johnson called to him in the middle of a round, "Ah wish Ah had you in here, Mista Corbett."

Ruby Bob continued fighting until he was well into his fifties but never could regain the championship he had lost. Neither could Gentleman Jim, who finally gave it up and became a popular vaudeville monologist on the American stage for many years. But the great fight at Carson City did much to popularize boxing, and it soon became legal in most states of the Union.

The lonely search of the Great Basin continued on, and the prospectors walked the sands of the desert in search of the shadow dancer, who now and then by a flick of her skirts revealed an outcropping, a ledge, a soft shoulder of malleable rock that turned out to be pure silver. Most of the prospectors were laid to rest on the prairie before the dance was ever over but they died still dreaming of the search.

CHAPTER TWENTY-FOUR

Shooter Towns

BODIE AND AURORA

The unsurveyed boundary lines between California and Nevada Territory caused two disputes—one fought with votes and one fought with guns.

A hundred miles southwest of Carson City the early mining town of Aurora was county seat of Mono County in California in the year 1861. The same year the territorial legislature met at Carson City, Nevada, and created Esmeralda County, likewise honoring Aurora as *their* county seat. This is probably the only instance in the nation where a town served simultaneously as a county seat for two counties in two different states. The dilemma was highlighted by a special election in 1863.

As the boundary was still in question and hadn't been surveyed as far south as Aurora, the exact status of the town was as much a quandary as ever. Terms of office for officials elected in 1861 had expired and it was time to elect successors. A brilliant idea was conceived. They would hold *two* elections! Accordingly, full tickets were nominated by both Republicans and Democrats, making four in all, two for each county.

This election was lively and hilarious. Polls for the Esmeralda election were held in Armory Hall, and those for Mona in the Police Hall, a friendly distance down on the same street. Folks just voted in both, and good feeling prevailed as citizens trooped into one place, passed on down the street, and voted at the other, making sure "that if I don't hit it on the one side I'll get it on the other." Republicans were successful in both contests.

Twenty days after this election was held, the survey party reached Aurora and passed to the southeast leaving Aurora in the land of Nevada, much to the disgust of some of the strong adherents of California who charged that the surveyors ran the line around Aurora in order to leave it in Nevada. There are adherents of this view today who claim there is a jog in the state line.

J. Wells Kelly in the first directory of Nevada Territory, published in 1862, gives credit for the discovery of Aurora to J. M. Corey, James M. Brady, and E. R. Hicks. Corey and Brady were residents of San Jose who had been in the Washoe in the spring of 1860 on a prospecting tour which contemplated exploration of a wide range of country but found themselves confined to the Virginia City area by Indian troubles. While they were in Carson River Valley, they fell in with Hicks, who had been prospecting in Oregon. The three, having similar objects in view, formed a partnership and continued their search south along the Pine Nut range of mountains to the West fork of the Walker River. Bending a zig-zag course east, they came to the mountains between the forks of the Walker, working down to Mona Lake. From the Durado district back to the ragged hills west of Walker Lake they met no encouraging prospects and determined to push their journey into Arizona or even Mexico. For the purpose of getting an extended view of the surrounding country and a mapping out of a future course, they ascended a high peak which since has been named Corey's Peak. Having determined a route from this elevated positions, these partners entered boldly upon what promised to be a long and toilsome journey through one of the most fearfully barren sections of the Great Basin. It wasn't long until they met the challenge of the desert, lack of water. This deflection in their course, which forced them west, led Hicks to the discovery of a quartz ledge. The three partners halted and examined the neighborhood, finding the hills ribbed with quartz veins impregnated with precious metal.

Thus mining began early in the Esmeralda mining district and the town of Aurora by 1864 had a population of ten thousand, seventeen quartz mills, and a production of over sixteen million.

Mark Twain lived here in at least seven different cabins, all of which are "the one." Here he made his famous statement that "A mine is a hole in the ground with a damn liar at the top."

Civil War troubles ran riot here in 1862 and climaxed one Saturday night when a "secesh" element decided to put to a test the recent orders threatening punishment for any show of disloyalty. This is the town where the "Johnny Rebs" were marched in the square and forced to kiss the Union Flag, after which they took the Oath of Allegiance—or else.

Generally, emigrants on their way to California through these Nevada towns never made display of their political feelings as they could never be sure which stronghold they were approaching. J. Ross Browne encountered one group, however, who hauled out the Union Flag, displayed it on their wagon, and rode through a southern infested town.

Stories of the demimonde weave in and out of the silver camps and one who first appears in the records as early as 1854 was known as "Madame Moustache."

Madame Moustache was a generous gambler, and it was said of her that no luckless miner who asked her for a stake was ever refused. The miners liked her because she paid off bets with a friendly smile. The towns where she had her establishments approved of her also. They liked the way she kept the peace, and she was respected enough to be able to break up a pistol-toting crowd merely by talking with them.

Through the fifties, sixties, and seventies, stories are heard of her in many of the boomers: how she drove a smallpox-laden river boat from Fort Benton at the point of her revolvers, how she kept a protective eye over the young and inexperienced, how she provided quality entertainment in the raw mining towns.

Her business ventures were highly successful, and Madame Mustache amassed a considerable fortune; but when she married, she purchased a ranch in eastern Nevada and turned her property and all her money over to her new husband, who promptly squandered everything, after which he left her. This woman had been known as striking in appearance, formerly petite and beauti-

284

ful, but it is told that the mental and emotional shock of losing the man she loved produced a physical effect upon her. Her features changed and coarsened and a growth of dark hair, which had never been visible before, appeared on her upper lip. She sought the death of a suicide and her body was found beside a bottle of poison.

The "601" previously mentioned in Virginia City were in evidence in all the boom camps, but one of the most celebrated cases in the history of the Vigilantes of Nevada took place in Aurora in 1864. Aurora had been terrorized for months by a gang of roughs who had inflicted indignities upon the populace. They rode the town, roughshod and rowdy, and punctuated their orders with gunplay. Juries were frightened and it was impossible to obtain convictions against these men for fear of retaliation from another members of the gang.

One brave citizen by the name of W. R. Johnson, who resided at Hoy's Station, had defied this group and had refused to disclose the whereabouts of a man named Rodgers who had killed a friend of John Daly, a member of this gang. These men waylaid Johnson, shot him, then cut his throat. When word of the murder spread through Aurora, three hundred fifty citizens decided they had had enough.

Three of the suspects, John Daly, James Masterson, and Three-Fingered Jack McDowell, were arrested, while a fourth, William Buckley, was located hiding out in an abandoned mine tunnel. The town of Aurora, intending to wipe the slate clean, erected a quadruple gallows. When Governor Nye wired officials requesting information of the affair, he was answered: "All's quiet and orderly. Four men will be hung in half an hour."

They were hanged, and on schedule.

This decisive action had a telling effect and resulted in a general roundup of miscellaneous undesirables who were given their walking papers from Aurora and threatened with a lynching if they came back to the town.

These mining camps never grew slowly, they raced along at high fever, just as suddenly passed a climax, and moved along to some new outbreak. These heterogeneous populations were migrant caravans who followed the mines and liked doing it. They were never too tired to pull up stakes and move on to the next El Dorado when a richer strike was heard of over the hill. And newspaper, merchant, Chinatown, Indian town, gambler, saloon keeper, and dance hall girl followed along. They lived as a group and moved as a group. So it was much of Aurora found its way into Bodie.

BODIE

Bodie, California, "the top of the world in Shooter's Town," and home of the famous and not so mythical "Bad Man from Bodie," lay deep in Paiute country of Mono Basin in the year 1859.

It was in this year that Dutch William S. Bodey panned dirt while his partners Doyle, Garraty, and Black Taylor followed along. But it was to his mule that the forty-five year old prospector addressed his confidence. "Say, old Peter, this looks like pay dirt at last, and if it is, you know and I know we came a hell of a ways to find it."

The four prospectors thought so well of the gold showings Bodey had turned up that they constructed a cabin in Taylor Gulch where in the winter of 1859 they suffered through blizzards and freezing weather. In November they had the misfortune to run out of food and it was necessary for them to leave the protection of the cabin to go to Monoville for supplies. While they were traveling, the two partners, Taylor and Bodey, were separated. Bodey was lost in the storm and frozen to death before Taylor could locate him.

In time, Black Taylor was the lone occupant of a cabin in a gulch at Benton where he was continuing further prospecting work. But Benton at this time was a gathering place for hostile Indians who were attracted by the hot springs of the area. They were on the warpath and in the dead of night broke into Black Taylor's cabin. Although he had been taken awares, Taylor fought at bay and, like a hero of the Alamo, took ten of his enemy with him before they could overpower him. The howling savages then dragged him from the cabin where they severed his head from his body.

There are many superstitions among miners—one of them is that the discoverers of worthwhile camps are star-crossed and doomed to tragedy. And it is remarkable how this type of history does repeat itself. Bodey's story and others like that of Sandy and Eilley Bowers of the Comstock, the tragic death of Old Comstock, Old Virginy, and others only add to this legend.

The name of the Dutchman was forgotten while the world was gasping over the marvel of wealth that was Virginia City. It wasn't until 1879 when the Standard and Bodie Consolidated Mines were ticking out mining history that the story and sad fate of the founders was recalled. This gold camp then became Bodie in a corruption of the original spelling, and her first claims were recorded in Mono District July 10, 1860.

Bodie claims were consolidated in March, 1863, in an attempt to interest outside financial backing. Leland Stanford, who was governor of California, was named president, Judge F. T. Bechtel, secretary, in the Bodie Bluff Consolidated. However, Stanford was advised by his "experts" to abandon any interest he might have in Bodie. Accordingly he gave up his share of this real estate, losing a fortune which possibly wasn't missed too much.

The properties eventually came into the hands of Essington and Lockberg and from them, in payment of a $950 overdue board bill, into the hands of a colored gentleman who possessed the one-hundred percent Irish name of William O'Hara. Essington and Lockberg redeemed their interest, however, by working off the board bill, and resumed work on the diggings. As they worked short of funds, the timbering in the mine was scanty. The result was a cave-in, but the same cave-in was the thing which accidentally revealed the fortune and put gold lining into the partners' pockets.

After this discovery, the two sold for $67,500 cash to Seth and Dan Cook, John Boyd, and William Lent. Bodie made all of them wealthy men.

By 1878 the word was out and the silver boys galloped back to a gold rush. By '79 the population had reached 12,000 and mining stock in Bodie rose from fifty cents to fifty-four dollars a share. Extravagant stories of Bodie wealth were circulated and enthusiastic miners forgot that the "inexhaustible" Comstock was running at a crawl. Anyhow, the new boomer was *gold!* Thus was born one of the wildest, maddest towns the West has ever known, the town of the legendary "Bad Man from Bodie." This notorious camp of the Great Basin was known as "Shooter Town" and stories of the life liver here have outfamed the wealth of the mines.

By 1879, Bodie main street was a mile long, packed solid with two-story frame buildings, every other one of which was a saloon. Her first newspaper was *The Standard Pioneer Journal of Mono County*, published October, 1877. This boomer produced about one hundred million, which placed her in there with the big ones. The principal mines: The Standard Bodie, Noonday and Mono Syndicate.

The "bad girls" of Bodie followed the bad boys and took up residence on Maiden Lane and Virgin Alley. Best known were Rosa May of "The Highgrade," Emma Goldsmith of "The Ozark," and the well known Madame Mustache along with one known as "The Beautiful Doll."

Bodie was a tough camp! It ranked with Butte, Montana, and anyone who has read the history of the country that produced Anaconda Copper will understand this meaningful statement.

Bodie's Boot Hill in the shadow of Potato Peak today swarms with tourists who come to view the famous cemetery of the lawless camp. If one would see the real Boot Hills, he'd not find them inside the cemetery; they're outside the fences.

People in these early camps were ruled by miners jury, and they sat in judgment over a death to see whether the deceased merited burial in a respectable place or whether he should be relegated to the Boot Hill section. Nor was there always a meeting of minds on the verdict. Friends sometimes objected to this type of ostracism and gunplay resulted over such technicalities which in turn has been known to bring at least two and maybe three more deaths in addition to the original one. Ella Cain in her *Story of Bodie* lists some of the graves in Bodie's real Boot Hill:

"James DeRoche, who was strung up by the Vigilantes for the killing of Tom Trelour. Dave Banner killed in a saloon row between sporting men. Neva Pyne who died from an overdose of opium. Harry Robbins killed by William Hawkins. James Kennedy killed by James Baker. Charlie Jardine shot through the heart by 'Piccche Kelly.' Dave Mitchell killed in an opium den—suicides—the graves of illegitimate children—all are outside the fence, as well as are the graves of several hundred Chinese."

It can be seen that Bodie's Boot Hill contains a sizeable population, and that the early undertakers were kept busy.

Most of these camp undertakers ran their "parlors" as a side line to some other business, and "Shotgun" Johnnie Heilshorn, a Cornish undertaker, was one who in addition to being town undertaker seemed to encompass within his evil personality all the tradition of "The Bad Man."

His final instructions to grieving ones were: "Come ye forth, all ye wee nickies and ye big nickies; come forth and take a geek at he before I screw 'im down."

Johnnie, reported Ella Cain, was "an undertaker by trade, a rounder by profession, a thief by inclination, a dope fiend by choice, and a scalawag by association." His best buddy was "Big Bill" Monahan, a fit partner. These two were hold-up specialists and while certain characteristics clearly revealed to their assailants who they were, no one was ever able to get a conviction on these ghoulish highwaymen. They continued merrily along on their road of crime and eventually took to robbing the graves of this famous Bodie cemetery.

Production in this camp climbed steadily for twenty years. In the meantime, the notoriety of the camp spread through the West, and so terrifying was its reputation for wickedness that the prayer of one child became a story repeated throughout the Basin. The young daughter of a God-fearing family, upon finishing her evening prayers, signed off with,

"Good-bye, God, we're going to Bodie."

"Not so," maintained the residents of Bodie.

"What she really said was 'Good, by God, we're going to Bodie.'" This hodge-podge of a boomer abounds in tales. One highlight of the town's entertainment was the thrice-weekly arrival of the jerk line freighters from Carson City where Bodie obtained its supplies. This Carson-Bodie fast freight was reported to be the best mountain route ever established. Experts at jerk line driving guided twenty horse teams by day and *night* through these tortuous mountain passes. These wagon trains consisted of large "lead wagons" and three "back action" wagons to allow for negotiating the turns. Every other span of horses throughout the twenty animal team was harnessed with high wooden hames from which lanterns were hung to enable night driving over the desert and mountain terrain. The description of these big trailer operations is a picture of romance and a phase in the epic of the Great Basin that arouses the deepest admiration and respect.

Hinds Hot Springs on the route of the freighters was an early well-known spa, milling center, and ranch. Freight trains put up for the night here since feed was available for their teams; the ore of the miners was hauled in by wagon load, and in the midst of all this were the visitors who came for rest and treatment. Years before the white men set foot along the Walker, these springs had been a favorite gathering place of the Indian tribes who also realized the curative powers of the waters.

Millions in gold bullion were shipped on the Wells Fargo stages from Bodie. The Fortuna Ledge was almost pure gold, worth thousands of dollars a pound; and miners had no scruples about hi-grading samples in their lunchbuckets, much of which found its way into the hands of Rosa May, Madame Mustache, and The Beautiful Doll. Wells Fargo messengers, gun in hand, rode up front to "shotgun" this rich cargo. Most well known of the Wells Fargo men were Oliver Roberts, Mike Tovey, Alex Montgomery, Eugene Blair, Alex Burke, and Aaron Ross.

Aaron Ross had been a Wells Fargo messenger at Elko, where, in the performance of his duty, he had killed two train robbers and wounded another three who had attempted to relieve him of a valuable cargo he was delivering to Ogden, Utah.

The central figure, of course, was the driver. These men became symbols along the various routes and names like Hank Monk and

"Old Charlie" were bylines with the stories of the swinging sedans. J. Ross Browne inquired of Charlie how he could keep on the road. Browne himself couldn't see beyond the horse's ears for dust. Said Charlie: "When the wheels rattle, I'm on hard ground, when they don't rattle I gen'rlly look over the side to see where she's goin'."

Browne asked about accidents and whether many people were killed on the route: "Some of the drivers mashes 'em once in a while," Charlie answered casually, "but that's whiskey or bad drivin'. Last summer a few stages went over the grade but nobody was hurt bad . . . only a few legs an' arms broke. Them was opposition stages—Pioneer as a gen'r'l thing, travels on the road. Gittaoup!"

Charlie drove the Western stages for years, and it wasn't until Old Charlie's death that it was discovered that Charlie was a woman. During her lifetime, she cussed as well, puffed a cigar as well, and drove a stage as expertly, as the best of them!

Aaron Ross, however, was famous as a messenger and like good drivers of the stages placed a great deal of confidence in the "horse sense" of the teams. "Watch the ears on the pointer team," he would say. "A horse can scent danger quicker than a human, and he tells you about it with his ears. He holds them erect with quick little jerks backwards. When you see this danger signal, put the butt of your gun to your shoulder and get the trigger cocked as only the fraction of a second may stand between you and death."

During World War I, Aaron Ross was the messenger chosen by the United States government to move thirty-two million dollars in gold and silver from San Francisco to Denver, Colorado, even though he was getting old.

During all these years of service with Wells Fargo, Aaron Ross never lost a shipment of bullion. He wounded or killed at least a score of bandits defending these shipments, coming out of the fights himself with only minor wounds.

The bandits most feared in this part of Nevada were the Small and McDonald gang, Vascus and Chavis, dreaded Mexican outlaws, and the lone workers, Three-Fingered Jack and Johnny-behind-the-Rocks. Johnny-behind-the-Rocks was a highwayman who had hit upon the unique method of robbing stages by rolling huge boulders down upon the stages from the mountainside, wrecking and then robbing them.

And Bodie had its Buffalo Bill! But what a Bill.

This character-about-town, whose real name was William Gross, was so nicknamed because of his long white beard and tall tales of how he had "fit Indians." In Bodie, Nevada, however, he was just plain Buffalo Bill, Old Buff, or just plain "Thievin'" Bill.

This human pack rat was such an accomplished petty thief that he even taught his old hound dog to steal. It was Bill's habit to throw anything he could lay his hands on down to his dog, who would obligingly make his way out the door with the loot and carry it home for Bill. Old Buff threw down a package one day which was later discovered to be a pair of ladies lace-trimmed white drawers. The package had come untied, but the dog was observed dragging them along the dusty road. Instead of the bone which was his usual reward, all the poor dog received was a kick in the head.

When this pile of loot from years of thievery was stacked from floor to ceiling, and he had no more room for stolen goods, Bill dug a cave back of his Bodie house and was back in business again. Paradoxically, this early day kleptomaniac didn't trust anybody else, and his cabin was locked fast and tight against the world with three different padlocks.

There was another Bill as well. Bill Monahan of Bodie was a happy-go-lucky Irishman, well liked and congenial. But one thing about Bill bothered the boys; he was a bragger, and Westerners are notorious for their delight in puncturing inflated egos.

Bill was always swaggering about how "Bill Monahan don't take any water from anybody." The boys were gathered in Murray's Saloon one evening and decided that for once and all Bill was going to prove all this courage. So they hit upon a plan.

A Chinaman's grave had been dug up south of the cemetery conveniently near a spot where Bill Monahan was in the habit of pasturing his horse. The bones of this Celestial had been shipped back to China and the boys in the saloon figured that one of them,

Chuck, should wrap himself in a sheet, get down the empty hole, and pretend to be the ghost of the departed one from China.

Bill tethered Pete, his horse, one dark night as usual, and swung the halter over his shoulder. At the moment Bill was passing the grave, Chuck jumped up before him, waving the white sheet and making menacing noises. Bill Monahan grabbed the halter from his shoulders and started landing on Chuck. "Get back down there in your hole, you yellow skin son of a B . . ."

To save himself being beaten to death, Chuck was forced to jump back into the grave, his head bloody, and blood all over the sheet.

Bill talked into the door at Murray's Saloon and told the crowd. "What'dya think, boys? They wouldn't have that old dead Chink in China and he's landed back here again. Shure, an' I put him in his place with my halter."

There was dead silence in Murray's. The boys just stood there looking blankly at one another. Then the bartender yelled, "Th' drinks are on the house!"

When the Chinese crews had completed their first task in the West—that of building the railroads and unwinding the coils of wire that ticked off the miles of the telegraph lines; when they had worn out their first issues of blue denim overalls and shirts— they reverted to their traditional occupations of restaurant keepers and laundrymen.

Bodie had one Chinese restaurant owner named Chickie. After the days of the telephone, Chickie reluctantly began using the instrument, having finally become convinced that the telephone would talk Chinese as well as English. It was Chickie's custom to call the Wells Fargo agent at Hawthorne to inquire whether his produce was there; when he did so, he invariably inquired about his sweet potatoes.

Jesters one day put three sweet potatoes in the battery box of the telephone and waited for Chickie to make his usual call. The agent at Hawthorne, in on the joke, received the expected inquiry and answered, "I'll send the sweet potatoes up by wire—right now."

The joksters then opened the battery box. Out rolled three sweet potatoes. The astonished Chinese dropped the receiver in amazement, grabbed it back again, and hollered into the phone, "Holy Gee! These come velly damn quick—send everything!"

CHAPTER TWENTY-FIVE

The End of an Era

TONOPAH AND GOLDFIELD

The discoveries of Tonopah and Goldfield forced a new, if grudging, respect for Nevada from an East whose newspapers at one time advocated that she be disenfranchised from the sisterhood of states.

Jim Butler opened up this last era, and Nevada prestige, battered since the days of the mighty Comstock, once again zoomed. Jim Butler was brought into White Pine, Nevada, at the age of thirteen and grew to manhood in the midst of the Eureka and Austin excitement. In later years, he lived with his wife at a ranch in Monitor Valley near Belmont, then the county seat of Nye County. He took many prospecting trips in between ranch duties, and it was on one such excursion over the Manhattan Mountains by way of Rye Patch, that he reached a point known to the Indians as Tonopah, meaning "waterbrush," and no spot was more inaptly named, for the future camp of Tonopah freighted in water which was sold for two dollars a barrel, twenty-five cents a bucket.

Modern Nevada has its roots in this boom camp, and many of Nevada's leaders got their start here. The lush days of Tonopah, Goldfield, and Bullfrog made the W. A. Clark, Charles Schwab, and Guggenheim fortunes.

This eastern capital moved into Tonopah in the 1900's. The railroad was then extended south and water piped in. By 1913 the camp had produced more than ten million, with Goldfield, Rhyolite, Wonder, and Rawhide to follow with additional millions in production.

Jim Butler was caught in a desert sandstorm while searching for his lost burro. Sitting out the storm under a protecting ledge, he chipped away at what appeared to be ore-bearing material. The date was May 19, 1900. It looked good and Jim returned with his wife who helped him prospect the country further. They located the Desert Queen, The Burro, and the Mizpah—which proved to be the richest real estate in the country. The other partners who came in on this find were those who helped him pay the cost of assay work.

An unusual feature in Tonopah history was Jim Butler's "oral leases." Butler granted more than one hundred leases on some of the most wealthy ground in Nevada and not one scratch of a pen defined any of them!

Management of this purely Western arrangement was in the hands of Tasker L. Oddie, one of Jim Butler's partners, and Oddie jotted down notes in a memorandum book. Hundreds of thousands of dollars in high grade were shipped from these one hundred leases, they were checked, recorded, and paid for by Oddie from his notebook, and never was as much as one dollar held in dispute.

Then came O. A. Turner, backed by Philadelphia capital, to examine this boomer. He purchased the eight original Butler claims for three hundred thirty-six thousand dollars. Jim Butler, however, still protected his friends, the leasers, by specifying that they must be allowed to finish out the time he had promised them they could have. From this purchase, Butler retained five-eighths of the payment. The remaining three-eightes were divided between Oddie and Wilson Brougher, another of Jim's partners.

Oddie took part of his payment in stock in the Philadelphia company, and the Tonopah Mining Company was formed with Oddie as first manager. Shortly after this, there developed the first battle of Tonopah between the established old timers and claim jumpers from Salt Lake City.

Nevada law of the time required that a shaft be down ten feet or an equal excavation on the vein proper. The jumpers had framed to jump a portion of the ground owned by the Philadelphia group. Tasker Oddie discovered that their shaft was down more than six feet. To block the jumpers from reaching the required ten, he jumped in the hole. He was unarmed and found himself facing the guns of the claim jumpers. But others, running up behind Oddie, had taken in the situation, and one of Oddie's backers spoke. "This ground belongs to the Tonopah Mining Company. You'll have to get off."

"Who says so?" demanded the leader of the Salt Lake City men.

"I do."

"An' who in hell are you?"

"I'm Wyatt Earp."

After Wyatt Earp's career as a peace officer in Tombstone had been climaxed by the battle against the Clanton-McLowery gang, he came to Tonopah, Nevada, where he started the Northern Saloon.

By 1901 business was booming. In addition to local business establishments, saloons were opened by Ole Elliott, Harry Ramsey, Wyatt Earp, Jim Butler, and Tom Kendall; and Jack Carey started the most famous of them all, the Tonopah Club, where the most sensational play of the time was conducted. First profits of the Tonopah Club, however, were from whiskey and beer freighted across the desert from Sodaville. It was in Tonopah that Nevada's famous George Wingfield got his start. He dealt stud and played draw and faro at the Tonopah Club. Thus was the beginning of "King George," who became the overlord of the political and economic life of Nevada, a boss who ruled with an iron hand from offices in the Reno National Bank Building.

In 1902, the moment the leasers had completed their work, the Black Death or "Tonopah Sickness" swept the camp. This dreaded form of mountain pneumonia killed over a tenth of the population of the mining town. This was possibly the same sickness known among the Indians as "pogonip." It was the custom among the tribes to stone the medicine man to death when his chanting rhythms and ministrations of herbs had failed them and three or more had died of the affliction.

During this terrible Tonopah plague, the care of the sick and the burial of the dead fell into the hands of the Miners' Union, and Tonopah history will never forget the union for their service.

Their officers were always available for burial duty, and their hospital, which was the only one in the camp, was overflowing. The Union Hall was the morgue, and its members were the only nurses and grave diggers. The Union president, Doc O'Toole, closed dead men's eyes and read the funeral services. These men were heroes of the day, for no one knew when this sickness was halted, nor whether it was contagious.

With the passing of this fierce epidemic, the town settled down to steady production and the opening of a new Western epoch. Tonopah carried on with a third phase of Nevada development after the California rush and the Comstock, which was similar to Leadville and Cripple Creek, Colorado, Tombstone of Arizona, Butte of Montana, and the great rush to the Klondike of Alaska.

Regular teamsters couldn't handle the immense volume of traffic and the company of McLean and McSweeney were bolstererd by local Nevada farmers who brought in their teams and wagons. Miles of ore trains snaked their way across the desert headed for the smelters. After the Tonopah Mining Company was organized, the Tonopah-Belmont, North Star Development Company, and the Montana-Tonopah Companies followed.

The essential need of the camp was water. Curtis and Lewis organized the Crystal Water Company in 1902, developing wells. They constructed a seventy-thousand-gallon reservoir and piped water to the saloons and business houses. Then all Tonopah took a bath to celebrate and drained the reservoir dry. But the company, sensing a new gold mine in water sales, promptly developed an additional supply of one hundred fifty thousand gallons a day from some deep shafts. From that day on, sniffed old timers, the camp became effete!

GOLDFIELD

Lack of a job during slump times in Tonopah moved Billy Marsh and Harry Stimler to ask Jim Butler and Tom Kendall for a grubstake. With this, they located the Grandpa Claim—later to become the town of Goldfield. Here, new Nevada gold waited, buried deep in the heart of Marsh and Stimler's Sandstone Claim,

Myers and Hart's Combination Claim, and Charley Taylor's Jumbo.

Goldfield became a boomer in the early 1900's, attracting people from all over the world. Her population had reached more than twenty-five thousand by 1906, and her post office did more business than any other post office in the West except San Francisco itself. There were two daily and three weekly newspapers, which were sent to every state in the Union and six foreign countries. The new towns of Nevada attracted brilliant men from all parts of the United States. George Wingfield followed along from Tonopah and with his partner, George S. Nixon of Winnemucca, bought several mines in Goldfield, forming the Goldfield Consolidated. This organization acquired the best mines in the Goldfield district and became one of the biggest producers in mining history.

This was the last big rush of the West—and this camp was like the one in Creede, Colorado, where "there was no night."

Wide open, a town that never slept, Goldfield grew with frantic haste. Day and night the sound of hammers was heard, punctuating the tinkling of pianos from the saloons with the staccato sound; fiddles played; there were shouts and songs from all-night revelers. Throughout the dark hours, small boys made good money holding lanterns for busy workmen, and Goldfield moved on, twenty-four hours at a stretch.

Two of the boys drifted out of town to look over the surrounding territory. They were "Shorty" Harris and Ed Cross. While prospecting near Beatty's Ranch, they found greenish-blue ore resembling the color of a Bullfrog, and the Bullfrog Mining District was born. Ed Cross and "Shorty" Harris, otherwise known as the Death Valley Terrapin, had an assay run and when the news was out, part of Goldfield, part and parcel, bag and baggage, loaded up and the prairie wagons rolled right along to the blue-green ore of Bullfrog.

Shorty Harris wrote of the rush: "I've seen many gold rushes in my time that were hummers, but nothing like that Bullfrog stampede. Men were leaving town in a steady stream with buck boards, buggies, wagons and burros. It looked like the whole population of Goldfield was trying to move at once. Timekeepers and clerks, waiters and cooks, they all got the fever and milled around trying to find a way to get out to the new strike.

"A lot of fellows loaded their stuff on two-wheeled carts, grub tools, and cooking utensils . . . and away they went across the desert, two or three pulling the cart and everything on it rattling. Men even hiked the seventy-five miles pushing wheelbarrows.

"When Ed and I got back to our claim a week later, more than a thousand men were camped around it, and more were coming in every day. A few had tents but most of them were in open camps. That was the start of Bullfrog, and from then on, things moved so fast it made us old timers dizzy."

The townsite of Bullfrog became hotly disputed real estate just like any of the good mining ground, and to save the fuss and furor, a lot of folks moved on over to future Rhyolite. This new spot made a good camp ground, and good living conditions prevailed here. There was water for drinking as well as irrigation, so trees were planted and gardens produced while nearby stone quarries furnished building materials. Rhyolite became established in its own right by 1906. It had a bit of political implication became most of the boys who came into here were from Colorado and had been members of the Industrial Workers of the World. They formed the nucleus of a radical labor organization which began the work of organizing Nevada and the scene was set for labor troubles to come.

The quick and easy money was done in Tonopah and prospectors began branching feelers farther out into the desert. Alva D. Myers, ore wise practical assayer from Cripple Creek, Colorado, followed Marsh and Stimler into the Grandpa country along with his partner, Bob Hart. Myers and Hart were grubstaked by a group of Tonopah men, Harry Ramsey, Jim Foreman, T. D. Murphy, C. K. Jarvis, Wesley Warren, Lathrop Davis, and Rutledge. Myers and Hart, who had left Tonopah May 20, 1903, named this the Combination Claim because it had so many backers.

Then in came Charley (C.D.) Taylor, carrying with him his worldly goods, a barley sack containing six loaves of bread and two cans of corned beef! Marsh and Stimler hadn't been able to dig up enough money to keep up the assessment work on the number of claims they had staked, so when Charley pulled in on his old crow-bait of a horse they pointed out the Jumbo Claim and said, "Help yerself."

Taylor did—to the multi-million Jumbo!

Swarms of humanity moved in. Grandpa became Goldfield. Rhyolite, Searchlight, Fairview, Wonder, Round Mountain, Greenwater and Rawhide came into being.

There are not many printed records which cover this rich decade in the history of the West Great Basin boomers. Files in the old newspapers are broken and yellowed. Information is sporadic and insufficient. The State Historical Society of Nevada, however, is gradually coming into possession of more pictures, records, diaries and papers that have been in the possession of relatives. These are being donated as old timers, who had treasured them, move along into the Great Beyond. The Society, as the material is obtained, is piecing together a complete history.

One bit of lost history which may or may not have been filled in at Goldfield is the legend of the lost Breyfogle Mine—most famous of the lost mines of the desert. Ore that came from the Jumbo Claim of Goldfield has been believed by some to be this lost ledge.

This legend from the Great Basin began in 1864, when John Breyfogle, a blacksmith from the camp of Austin, Nevada, left on a three-week prospecting trip. John's horses strayed from camp during one of the nights, and as he searched for them he broke some ore specimens from an outcrop and placed them in his pocket. During the search for his lost animals, John Breyfogle lost his own way and would have died of thirst in the desert had it not been for a friendly band of Indians who saved his life, nursed him back to health, and put him on the road to Austin with his own horses and his ore samples. Breyfogle placed this rich ore into the hands of the men who had grubstaked him, and they assayed sky high. His backers promptly sent him back on the search with a new outfit, but he could never relocate the mine which he had lost in the delirium of fever. In later years, Breyfogle ore samples were compared to the ore of the Jumbo. They were reported identical in character. It was possible the two mines were one and the same, yet many mining men maintain no ore to match Breyfogle's was ever found.

Next to the Breyfogle, the most famous lost mines of the West are the Pegleg and the Gunsight. The Gunsight was found in Panamint Mountais west of Death Valley by three Mormon emigrants seeking a way out for a party who were perishing at Bitter Springs. While climbing a cliff, one of the party knocked the gun sight from his weapon and substituted a temporary sight from some malleable metal he chipped off a ledge. When they reached civilization, the makeshift gun sight was found to be virgin silver. This mine has never been relocated.

The railroad from Tonopah reached Goldfield in September, 1905, and the population of eight thousand doubled to sixteen thousand. Many of these, however, came in for a three-day carnival being staged to celebrate the completion of the line. A gold spike was driven to commemorate the occasion, but when the Southern Pacific sought to recover the spike for their museum, they discovered some one had appreciated it quite as much as they and had drawn it neatly away, replacing it with an iron one.

The promotion of the mines of Goldfield was brisk. Some of this promotion was honest, most of it was not. First, and most reliable, of the companies was Patrick, Elliot and Camp; but a wildcatter, and the worst of the lot, was the L. M. Sullivan Trust Company organized and managed by George Graham Rice, ex-convict and crook, real name Jacob S. Herzig. This worthy was a graduate of New York State reform schools and the state prison before he graced the boomers of Nevada with his presence.

The companies organized by Rice were pure fraud, and the only legitimate property he ever promoted was in the Manhattan area. But he had no difficulty selling stocks in his make believe mines. Notorious as the Comstock had been for it, Goldfield surpassed Virginia City in fraud and chicanery. Rich mines like the Mohawk, January, Red Top, Laguna, Atlanta, and Jumbo made it easy for dishonest brokers to lean out a window and sell stocks to a clamoring crowd below who were willing to buy anything.

George Rice's partner was L. M. Sullivan, an illiterate keeper of a sailor's boarding house in Seattle, known otherwise as "Shangahai Larry." Shangahai Larry knew nothing of mines and mining and cost Rice some juicy prospects at one time. Larry was conducting prospective customers for stock over some of the firm's "properties" when he remarked: "Right now, I've got a whole carload of winzes coming in to rush development work on half a dozen properties."

Two years after the first shipment of ore from the Goldfield district, four years after the first shipment from Tonopah, stock was being purchased in this new boom area in every state in the union; and an East which had lost all interest in Nevada's "100,000 square miles of nothing to make a state in the first place" was showing great deference and respect to the everlasting source of the great fortunes of America—the West.

Goldfield liked this publicity, and sought even more when in 1906 the camp offered a purse of $30,000, outbidding competing towns, for the bout between Battling Nelson and Joe Gans for the lightweight championship of the world. Gans, Baltimore Negro, was thirty years old; Nelson, born in Copenhagen, was twenty-four years old.

Manager of the local committee was famous "Tex" Rickard. Before Tex Rickard came to Nevada and opened up the Northern, which was a combination saloon and gambling house in Goldfield, he had been town marshal in Henrietta, Texas, a sourdough on the Yukon, gambler in Circle City, Dawson, and Nome, Alaska.

This fight was scheduled for Labor day and 6,972 bought tickets. Nelson had been guaranteed a $20,000 purse and Gans $10,000. The Dane and Negro fought for forty-two rounds and the fight ended when Nelson gave Gans a foul blow. The victory was therefore awarded to Gans. Gans was said to have contracted T. B. from the grueling match and died a year or so later. Nelson fought many fights, always taking punishment but outlasting his opponent. He finally lost to Ad Wolgast. Nelson was weakened mentally and died poor while Wolgast died in a sanitarium.

Jack Dempsey fought preliminaries at Tonopah, where, presumably, he met Rickard. After Dempsey became champion,

Rickard promoted all his fights—the so-called "Million Dollar Gates."

Goldfield's production was hitting more than one million a month! In the midst of that much money, litigation was inevitable, and company fought company in legal terms over an old issue which has placed millions into the pockets of attorneys—the law of the apex.

While this was going on, high-grading miners working in these same mines were busy as bees carting out rich rock and joining up with the I.W.W. Goldfield, Nevada, was just too rich for its own peace.

So the mine owners consolidated for two reasons. To put the mines on a paying basis, they had to put a stop to the high grading; and in order to stop bickering which had been going on for five years, they had to find some way to an agreement with the workers. During these years, the American Labor Union had lost out to the I.W.W., and more conservative unions found themselves at odds with the International Workers of the World, but all the same helpless against them. So happened one of the first general strikes in America.

This strike and the Nevada troubles brought in some new "wild west" tactics on both sides. Pockets sagged with six shooters and the town was an armed camp. The union terrorized the town and companies brought in men like "Diamondfield" Jack Davis, union-hating gunman who walked the streets with a pair of .45's hooked over his belt. George Wingfield displayed the nerve that made him future "boss" of Nevada when he walked the streets selling the *Sun*, a newspaper the union had forbidden on the streets for calling them "wobblies." Wingfield picked up a six gun, dared them to stop him, and sold copies up and down the sidewalks.

Townspeople, weary of the whole thing, hit back, and guards patrolled the business blocks of the town. In the meantime the mines installed "change rooms" to compel workers to change clothing before they left mine property and eliminated the "corset covers" with which some had been accustomed to stealing rich ore.

After forty-one days a final vote ousted the I.W.W. from power, but the panic of 1907 brought more labor trouble when miners were paid part in cash and part in drafts on San Francisco and Salt Lake City banks—later in script from the company, which script bore no stated date of redemption. This caused another strike.

Fearful of a repetition of violence such as they had seen before, the Goldfield mines played politics and influenced Governor Sparks to demand federal troops from President Roosevelt charging that lives were in jeopardy and properties in danger of dynamiting. In December three companies of infantry were in the town, but there was no disorder and President Roosevelt, not so sure he hadn't been duped, sent a commission to study the history of the trouble in Goldfield. The President was not willing to keep troops in the state, and the infantry departed when Nevada established the State Police. Followers of Charles Moyer and Bill Haywood, known as Local 220, found themselves pegged in index files and the mines refused to have business relations with them, whereupon most of them moved on to California.

RAWHIDE AND RHYOLITE

Nevada boomers moved on, leaving dead towns strewn in their wake and rusty dumps behind. The trail breakers of the Great Basin aren't particularly known to fame, but it was Jim Swanson who made the first location in what became known as the Rawhide district on Christmas day, 1906. The next year, Swanson was joined by some other wanderers, Roseberry, Holman, McLeod, Dunning, and Carson. What became the main street of Rawhide was once the old immigrant trail where wagons crunched over ledges worth $1,800 a ton. The ore taken into Reno by the first locators caused such an influx of population that the old timers couldn't find where their tents had been located.

Rawhide reportedly was named by a cowboy who came over from Buckskin: "By, Gad, boys," he said. "There's a buckskin, and every other kind of hide on this map. We'll just name this one Rawhide."

For its size, Rawhide had a great collection of world wide celebrities, possibly as many as any in existence.

The first famous character to make his appearance in this boomer was "Swiftwater" Bill Gates of Yukon fame. His advent into the camp was productive as he operated the first stamp mill in the district.

"Diamondfield" Jack Davis came in, backing the district with his money and becoming a successful mining man.

Riley Grannan moved in and with Swede Sam purchased a half interest in Moss's Corner where they erected another clubhouse.

Tom Kearns of Utah was in the Rawhide mining picture, and the colorful Irishman was known in this Nevada camp as "Honest Tom." Even the old Overland Limited Stagecoach that had run the road from Wadsworth to Austin found new use in the Rawhide rush where it was pressed into service as a lunch wagon where buckwheats and java were served.

Rawhide was a camp more *speculated* into prosperity than anything else by the fine hand of George Graham Rice. Rice was tied in with Nat Goodwin, and the Nat C. Goodwin Company promoted Rawhide stock while the *Nevada Mining News*, a tool, backed it with the necessary publicity.

"Tex" Rickard came in on this boomer as well. Before Rickard left Goldfield, he placed a sign on a deserted church: "THIS CHURCH IS CLOSED. GOD HAS GONE TO RAWHIDE."

Rickard moved to Rawhide in one day, purchased an eight-thousand-dollar lot, and in ten days built a new Northern Saloon. To say that Rickard was a "doer" is an understatement. A disastrous fire burned down his Northern, and Rickard lost all he had made in Goldfield. He still owned mining claims, however, and sold them in New York for a million. Then a financial crash took away his second fortune. It was then he went into the fight promotion business backing the Jeffries-Johnson fight in Reno and moving on to the big time in prize fighting.

Riley Grannan, who died in 1908, was another prime mover in West Basin boomers and his funeral oration, preached by the famous W. H. Knickerbocker, was an embittered classic which brought tears to the eyes of the listening crowd.

Knickerbocker was a preacher who had been tried for heresy. He was acquitted but retired from the pulpit. His last words over Granman were: "And now . . . I will say goodbye old man. We will try to exemplify the spirit manifested in your life in bearing the grief at our parting. Words fail me here. Let these flowers, with their petaled lips and perfumed breath speak in beauty and fragrance the sentiments that are too tender for words. Goodbye."

Rawhide camp died the same time Granman did, for it was the same time that Rice, with his flowery orations on the stock market potentials, overreached himself by boosting a worthless mine. He had also made an enemy of Wingfield; and his tie-in with Goodwin and his past were exposed. The Rawhide boom collapsed, aided by bank failures and a fire that destroyed much of the town. The camp was never rebuilt.

From a Federal Penitentiary on Blackwell Island, Rice wrote a serial for a national publication entitled "My Adventures with Your Money."

He made money on that, too.

RHYOLITE

Rhyolite was a thriving camp in 1906. It had two banks, a newspaper, school, stores, and residences. A bank, jewelry store, and four other establishments occupied the ruins of the Overbury Block, and the stucco station of the Las Vegas and Tonopah and Tidewater Railroad became a night club for tourists.

Most of Rhyolite's early citizens came in from Colorado, where the closing of the mines there had forced them out.

Charles Schwab, Pennsylvania steel operator, had interests here in the Montgomery Shoshone Mine. Bill Stewart set up his law offices here when he retired from the U.S. Senate and William Clark of Montana helped finance the railroad; but the ore veins of Rhyolite were not extensive enough to sustain the town. It was interest in this section of the Great Basin, however, which stimulated activity in old camps like Olinghouse, near Wadsworth, Silver Peak west of Tonopah, Tybo in the central area, and Searchlight in the southern part of the state.

It is difficult to know where to draw any part of the story of the

Great Basin boomers to a close, yet those whose brief histories have been given in this volume were typical of the whole of this rich production basket of Utah and Nevada.

Western relics are different. The whole tone, timbre, and sight of them is a quiver of thrill, a memory of excitement. The breath is the nostalgia of sage perfume, the sound the lonely desert wind rushing down a ravine. The story, one of quick accomplishment, and quick death.

The boomers weren't meant to be boomers. Every camp was settled with full hopes for permanence. A few do survive. The enthusiasm of those who peopled them each time they packed up and trudged to a new digging is a monument to human hope, a fascination in history, a fiction that is truth.

But anyway you want to look at it, it was a Great Basin!

CHAPTER TWENTY-SIX

Mid Pleasures and Palaces—
Las Vegas and Reno

Las Vegas comes very near to being the amusement capitol of America, and one would have to think twice to name a place with a better claim. To some it is a symbol of freedom; to others, a synonym for vice. To the people who live there and go quietly about their business as they do in any other American city, it is a good place to make a living and raise a family.

Since it has drainage into the Colorado, Las Vegas is not technically in the Great Basin, but it has too many historical and spiritual connections with the Basin for it to be omitted, and it is the largest city in Nevada. It has a good climate, except in the summer time, and the heat is combatted with air-conditioned houses and many swimming pools. The city's neon light can be seen miles away from any direction, and the sky is full of airplanes from the nearby government base at Nellis Field, and from McCarren Field. It is accessible by railroad and excellent paved roads. It is up to the minute in every respect, including good daily newspapers, and it had at least one fighting editor who was willing to risk jail for his principles.

Las Vegas is not cannibalistic; it lives on the people who are passing through, not on itself. It is jammed with tourists as few cities are, and at times on the highway from Los Angeles and San Francisco cars may be bumper to bumper for miles, and there is a constant flow of traffic from Salt Lake and Phoenix.

The casinos are elaborate and lavish and are open twenty-four hours a day. The constant noise one hears is the rattle of the slot machines and the jingle of coins pouring out of the one-armed bandits; and every few minutes is heard the announcer over the loud speaker crying, "Jackpot on number . . ." The monotonous voices of the croupiers and dealers at various games of chance drone on, and the faces of the customers are either studiedly calm, or filled with excitement. Everywhere one looks are piles of silver dollars, keeping alive the tradition that Nevada is the Silver State.

From time to time bar girls come around inviting the customers to have a drink on the house, costing only the size of the tip; but anyone showing signs of intoxication is quickly and quietly ushered out of the place. One will not see any sign of movie or television type of gangster, and if anyone gets robbed or rolled it does not happen at the established places.

Hotels and motels are always crowded, and the wise travelers make their reservations in advance, especially over the weekends. There is zing and zest in the air, for the visitors have come to have fun and relax, or to satisfy curiosity. The natives rarely visit the casinos unless they work there or want to show the town to a visiting relative.

Then there is the Strip, with the best shows that can be seen in America, where gambling goes on much as it does uptown. The shows get the finest talent from New York and Hollywood, and it has been the salvation of many an aging actor or actress who can cook up an act. No Hollywood actor can claim he is somebody unless he can brag about his last Las Vegas engagement. The salaries are fabulous and nobody knows, or cares, how much of it goes back across the gaming tables. Even the burlesque shows are in good taste, unless one happens to be a puritan who thinks that the female form should be draped in a Mother Hubbard.

Many people go to the strip just to see the Hollywood stars and enjoy the entertainment. If one is not addicted to gambling or drinking, one may see a good show and get room and meals that are not ruinous to the average pocketbook. Generally speaking, the suckers, if there are such, are self made.

The most popular sight except, of course, those to be seen along the Strip, is Boulder Dam, a few miles distant. One hears it called Boulder more often than Hoover Dam. Second in importance is Lake Mead, where boating and fishing are popular. Visitors to Las Vegas are within easy driving distance of such scenic wonders as the Grand Canyon, Zion's, Bryce.

Some Eastern papers and magazines claim the city has been taken over by gangsters and organized crime, but there is no visible evidence of it, and it is strenuously denied by the regulatory agencies of the state, who scrutinize carefully every application for a license. To them, instead of being the sin capital of the nation, it might better be called a place where people can blow off steam harmlessly instead of having it simmer back home until it erupts in a violent explosion.

Las Vegas, of course, has a history, but a much less violent one than most of the boom towns listed in this book. The Spanish *las vegas* means the meadows, and in that hot, dry country a watered meadow meant a lot. It was on the old overland route from Salt Lake to Los Angeles, and was a welcome resting place for weary teamsters. There were mines here and there, but none of any great renown except at Searchlight, on the road to Kingman and Phoenix.

When Las Vegas began to boom, an enterprising promoter from the East planned to build a luxurious redlight district equal to San Francisco's famed Belladonna; but his scheme did not meet with public approval, and indeed so puritannical was the town that little, and far more liberal, Searchlight profited considerably from the stern morality of its big sister.

The colonizing Mormons were among the first to settle in Las Vegas. Their attention was more directed farther east toward Callville, or Call's Landing, which Brigham Young dreamed of making a great port of navigation on the Colorado. Steamboats such as the *Esmeralda* and the *Nina Tilden* did make it there from as far away as Matzalan, Mexico, but it was one of the few enterprises of the great leader which didn't pan out. After the Mormons had given up and gone, a San Francisco merchant chartered the steamer *Silver Heels and* delivered a cargo worth $30,000 at Callville, which remained there a year before the shipper could get wagons from St. George to haul the stuff north, selling

311

such goods as he could along the way to Salt Lake. When Brigham Young gave up on a project, other men were foolish to try it. Las Vegas, not Callville, was destined to be the metropolis of southern Nevada.

There is a story told in the *Deseret News,* June, 1869, that just before the abandonment of the wharf at Call's Landing three desperately pressed desperadoes arrived there and, finding themselves trapped, pried the doors from the warehouse to make a raft, which they launched down the treacherous Colorado—and were never heard of again.

From St. George, in Utah's Dixie, the Mormons moved southward and established colonies at Mesquite and Bunkerville, Nevada, which still prosper because of climate and favorable location. Hoping to control the road between Salt Lake City and San Bernardino, California, where they were already entrenched, the Mormons settled in Las Vegas and built a fort, but in those days of horse and wagon traveling they were largely baffled by high, dry Mormon Mesa, and little ever came of that early settlement, though today a large part of the city's population is Mormon.

The fort itself never amounted to much, and only a stone monument in the north side of the city marks its location. As in other scattered settlements, the Saints were called back to Utah during the Mormon War, and they didn't return until other people had built a town.

There was, however, another fort on the same site called Fort Baker, but its existence was only on paper. There was much talk of fortifying it to protect the overland route at the beginning of the Civil War. The Mojave Indians were giving trouble to the mail routes between Albuquerque and Los Angeles, and others were making it tough all the way from Laramie, Wyoming, to Sacramento. Three forts, Camp Floyd, Fort Halleck, and Fort Churchill protected the worst of the route there, so it seemed wise to build another one at Las Vegas.

Much political intrigue was going on, for General Albert Sydney Johnston, former commander at Camp Floyd, was now in command of the Department of the Pacific, and he was a strong

Southern sympathizer and delayed any action that might help the Union in the impending struggle. Lieutenant General Winfield Scott, in command of the U. S. Army, sent Brigadier General Edwin V. Summer to relieve Johnston, which he did April 25, 1861, and a company of soldiers, it was said, would be despatched to Fort Baker with ample supplies, after Secretary of War Cameron issued a call for California volunteers. But neither troops nor supplies ever showed up at Fort Baker, which remained a fort in name only.

At one time a part of the southern tip of Nevada was in New Mexico, later in Arizona. When Arizona Territory was created, the region was in Pahute County, and Callville was designated as county seat. As navigation decreased, the county seat was moved to the mining town of St. Thomas, which soon became a ghost with the depletion of the mines.

Eventually, Las Vegas found itself in Lincoln County, Nevada, with the county seat the old outlaw stronghold of Hiko, hard by Yucca Flats where some of the first important atomic experiments were conducted. These, of course, were supplied from Las Vegas.

With the fading of Hiko, the county seat was removed still farther north to Pioche, which started Las Vegas pressing for a new county. Finally, Lincoln County was divided, and Las Vegas found itself in Clark County, of which it is now the county seat.

Las Vegas is not likely ever to be known as an agricultural center, though some range cattle may be seen on the desert; but a few miles to the north is the fertile little Moapa Valley, which has become noted for its early cantalopes and other crops. Because of the early spring, the supplying of tomato plants to colder regions has become quite an important industry.

The men who pioneered the Great Basin would have popped their eyes at the sight of present day Las Vegas, but from what we have been able to learn from our research most of them would have thoroughly enjoyed it.

313

If one drives an automobile any place in these United States, and can read, he must be aware of Harolds Club. Fourteen hundred signs sprinkle the countryside. Two of the most common are:

HAROLDS CLUB OR BUST
IN RENO IT'S HAROLDS CLUB

Often, there is a picture of two old timers hurrying by boat down a swift river, which could only be the Truckee, unless they started somewhere on the Yukon; but there is a look of anticipation on their faces which implies they will use any kind of transportation to reach the Promised Land.

More people come by automobile, but wherever they are from, or how they come, there is implicit the promise of splendid adventure and something-for-nothing wealth. Of course the something is a myth. The casinos will all tell you that the percentages are in their favor, but that you *may* win—if you are lucky—and there are always enough people who think they are Lady Luck's darling to keep them coming.

There are many big casinos in Reno, though Harolds Club is undoubtedly the most widely known. It is famous enough for almost anyone to know what you are talking about. Yet it is typical of the big gambling places that make Reno a Mecca for the sports-minded. It is seven stories tall and has every game of chance the customer might ask for, and one can go up or down by elevator or escalator. One may eat at the club's renowned dining room, or get a drink at the any of the convenient bars. In one, The Silver Dollar Bar, the bar has 2143 silver dollars imbedded in its top—silver that surely came out of the Nevada hills.

One of the world's finest gun collections is on the second floor. On the top floor is a night club called Harolds 7th Floor Fun Room. Then there are the Covered Wagon Room and Roaring Camp. Somewhere, you will see almost everything connected with the pioneer epic. That is purely static history; but if one is historically minded Harolds Club publishes two large volumes called *Pioneer Nevada,* which are full of the history and folklore of the early days.

The club also distributes free a little booklet telling how to play every game of chance. It emphasizes the law of averages, which it illustrates by the fact that a coin tossed into the air ten times may come down heads seven times and tails three times, but that in ten thousand times or more the result would be about even. It tells of instances where customers have been unusually lucky, but never claims that everybody can win.

It advises customers to budget their money and divide it into small units, and play for small stakes until they have a winning streak. If one doesn't come, the losses will not be too heavy. But the most important part of the advice is this: "Before you start, set aside the total amount of money you plan to pay. When you hit a winning streak stop while you are still ahead. Never buck a losing streak too long, and above all, PLAY ONLY WHAT YOU CAN AFFORD."

Not all people take the advice, of course, and one of the big problems of any establishment is bad checks. The customers are not always scrupulously honest.

Most popular of all the gambling plays so far as tourists are concerned are the slot machines, and there are several hundred of them that take from a nickel to a dollar, though they are scorned by dyed-in-the-wool gamblers. Some observers claim that they are played mostly by rich old ladies—though they could be mistaken. The management claims that a jackpot is hit for every minute of the day.

At another place the coin goes into the bosom of legless artificial mannequins, but the customers usually avoid those out of modesty, or because they believe the percentages of pay-off are smaller.

The management of Harolds Club says the place employs more than one thousand people and pays more than a quarter of a million dollars in taxes. In the second quarter of 1961 Nevada gambling houses paid $2,140,000 to the state in taxes, based on $47,900,000 gross winnings the preceeding quarter; so it can readily be seen that gambling is big business in Nevada. Anyway, the state is pretty much dependent on it. The tax runs from three to five and one-half per cent on gross winnings. All the gambling in Nevada is controlled by the Nevada Gaming Commission, and everybody claims that no crookedness will be tolerated by either the state or the casinos. All the big houses, such as Harolds, employ detectives, and it would be bad business for them if any game wasn't strictly on the up-and-up.

Harolds Club maintains an ultra-modern parking building and also a luxury motel for the convenience of its customers. Nothing is overlooked.

The club was started on Virginia Street in 1935 by the Harold Smith family on a purported capital of five hundred dollars and equipment of two slot machines and a penny roulette game. In the latter game a mouse was released from a cardboard box at the center of the wheel, and scampered around it until it decided which of thirty-eight holes it would enter, and bets were as to which hole it would choose. The Smith family has now become a financial dynasty—a far cry from the carnival with which it started.

Just a few miles from Reno is beautiful Lake Tahoe, where the price of real estate is probably climbing faster than in any other part of the state. Its casinos rival Reno's, and its floor shows those of Las Vegas. Top names in the entertainment world appear there nightly, as they do in Reno's two first class hotels, the Mapes and the Riverside.

The winter Olympics held for the first time in nearby Squaw Valley made that fine resort internationally known. If there were no gambling and no sports events, Lake Tahoe would still be a popular resort both winter and summer, for there is no more beautiful body of water in the nation than this lake which once bore the prosaic name of Biglar. Prim and "civilized" California claims half the area, but there is little doubt that the Nevada part gets the more tourists.

Reno has long boasted that it was "The Biggest Little City in the World," and the visitor couldn't possibly miss the flamboyant sign proclaiming it.

Reno was the first city in the country to make a business of divorce, because six weeks residence was all that was required. For a number of years a large part of the population consisted of female transients, and it was a paradise for lawyers. That few of the ladies remained single is attested by the number of wedding chapels. However, Las Vegas began to take a good share of this business away from Reno, and now a number of other states have decided to get in on a good thing. Divorce in Reno may be said to be a minor and steadily diminishing industry.

Reno's location in a beautiful little valley at the foot of the Sierras is ideal. The valley was so lush that in early days it was known as The Meadows. It was a good place for the emigrants to rest their stock before undertaking the last arduous leg of their long journey. It was a natural spot for a trading post, but the original traders were so transitory that people who might want to bring back damaged goods were strictly out of luck.

It was in the heart of the mining country but was never famous for its own mines. Virginia City and the Comstock were only twenty-one miles away; all the riches of the Washoe were in its back yard. It had a vast area to draw from, but it was the railroad that made Reno, formerly the largest city in the state. Its favorable location will always make it a prosperous transportation center, even though sport may now be its leading business.

So sport-minded is Nevada that gambling is a naughty word. It is always "gaming." It is a harmless little hypocrisy which they seem to think will somehow be less frightening to more orthodox people than the accurate and descriptive word "gambing."

But Reno is a real sport center. There are always the old standbys, hunting, fishing and boating. Boxing and wrestling are popular, and some notable fights have been staged there. Golf and baseball are popular in the summer, and of course there is the fine skiing in the winter.

Away back at the turn of the century when bicycle racing was the craze, Reno was proud of its racing team. So were Sacramento and Salt Lake. A race still cherished in the memory of Renoites was their defeat of the champion Sacramento Olympics. The Olympic relay team, it seems, had a trick of staying behind over most of the five mile laps; the semi-vacuum created by the riders ahead helping to cut down wind resistance for the rearmost riders. Then on the last lap the less tired Olympics would suddenly spurt ahead to the finish line.

King Ryan, the trainer of the Reno Wheelmen, planned to outmaneuver this bit of skullduggery. The fourth rider of the Reno team, and their fastest racer, was a man named Peckham who rode a bicycle equipped with an extra large gear. At the pick-up Peckham pretended to have trouble; his bicycle wobbled, and he nearly lost his balance. Recovering himself, he fell in behind his competitor who was obliged to tow him in the vacuum until Peckham suddenly whizzed past him at forty miles per hour, opening up a wide gap which the other riders of the Reno team were able to maintain, outrunning the back draft, and winning the race.

Reno's most disastrous fire occurred March 2, 1879, and was accompanied by a blizzard raging down out of the Sierras. The fire broke out in the night, and the city was awakened by the town fire bell. Realizing the danger, the inhabitants fled to the meadows south of town. Four volunteer fire companies rallied and fought the conflagration valiantly, the wind blowing hot steam back in their faces and burning and scalding many of them. Two fire engines raced in from Wadsworth and Truckee in the gray dawn to join the fight, and the residents of Chinatown were pressed into service to man the pumps. But the town was not to escape without casualties. A woman dashed back into her house to retrieve something and was never seen again. Three tramps perished in a barn in which they were sleeping, and an Indian sleeping in a flour mill was burned to death. In four hours ten blocks containing 350 buildings were destroyed, while Reno shuddered.

The legislature appropriated $1,000 for relief, and all kinds of supplies were rushed in from Carson City and Virginia City. At the time both towns were larger than Reno, though now Reno could put them in its vest pocket.

Reno has never been too reconciled to Carson City having the state capitol, but the historic old town seems pretty likely to hold onto it. The U. S. Mint was once in Carson City, but was closed down by the government. It perhaps serves a better purpose as a museum, which contains an entire mining operation into which the visitor may enter from inside the building and emerge onto the street. Reno now cherishes Carson City as a beloved, slightly handicapped little brother.

In Nevada one seldom sees a dollar bill. The silver dollar is not only the common medium of exchange, but it is also the visible link between the hardships of the past and the luxury of the present. Nevada is still a great and freedom-loving state with a minimum of Thou Shalt Nots on its statute books. It has a thrifty, hard-working population, good schools and highways, and as many churches per capita as any other state. Its citizens mind their own business and look askance at meddling do-gooders. If tourists spend more money there than in other places, they come of their own free will because Nevada has more to offer, and it does its best to show them a good time. It tries doggedly to preserve some of the spirit of the Old West in which it played so prominent a part.

Utah, too, is a great and thriving state whose population is not as unitedly strait-laced as some would like to think. Its agriculture, on which it was founded, may be steadily diminishing, just as mining in Nevada has done, but its growing industries bring in a lot more cash. The old struggle between agriculture and mining lies in the remote past, and while the cleavage in customs and ethics may still exist, privately the two states get along very well, each rich in its individual history, and together they have kept the Great Basin from reverting to what it once was, The Great American Desert.

Table of Illustrations

320

Bibliography

Alter, J. Cecil. *Utah, The Storied Domain.* 3 vols. Chicago: American American Historical Society, 1932.

Bancroft, H. H. *History of Utah.* San Francisco: The History Company, 1890.

Bancroft, H. H. *History of Nevada, Colorado and Wyoming.* San Francisco: The History Company, 1890.

Brooks, Juanita. *The Mountain Meadow Massacre.* Stanford: Stanford University Press, 1950.

Browne, J. Ross. *Adventures in the Apache Country.* New York: Harper and Brothers, 1869.

Cain, Ella M. *The Story of Bodie.* San Francisco: Fearson Publishers, 1956.

Egan, Howard R. *Pioneering the West.* Salt Lake City: Skelton Press, 1917.

Glasscock, C. B. *Gold in Them Hills.* New York: Grosset and Dunlap, 1932.

Harris, Foster. *The Look of the Old West.* New York: The Viking Press, 1955.

Harold's Club. *Pioneer Nevada.* 2 vols. Reno: 1951 and 1956.

Howard, Robert West. *Hoofbeats of Destiny.* New York: New American Library, 1960.

Larsen, G. O. *Outline History of Utah and the Mormons.* Salt Lake City: Deseret Book Company, 1958.

Lewis, Oscar. *The Town That Died Laughing.* Boston: Little Brown and Company, 1955.

Lillard, Richard G. *Desert Challenge.* New York: Alfred A. Knopf, 1942.

Lord, Eliot. *Comstock Mining and Mines.* Berkeley: 1883.

McClintock, Jas. H. *Mormon Settlement in Arizona.* Phoenix: Manufacturing Stationers Inc., 1921.

Mack and Sawyer. *Our State Nevada.* Caldwell, Idaho: Caxton Printers, Ltd.

Mariger, Marietta M. *Saga of Three Towns*. Panquitch, Utah: Garfield County News, No date.

Mortensen and Mulder. *Among the Mormons*. New York: Alfred A. Knopf, Inc., 1958.

Murbarger, Nell. *Ghosts of the Glory Trail*. Palm Desert, California: Desert Magazine Press, 1958.

Smith, Grant H. *The History of the Comstock Lode 1850-1920*. Published by the Nevada State Bureau of Mines, Geology and Mining Series No. 37, Vol. XXXVII, July 1943, Number 3.

Stone, Irving. *Men to Match My Mountains*. New York: Doubleday and Company, 1956.

Thompson and West. *History of Nevada*. Oakland: 1881.

Toponce, Alexander. *Reminiscences of Alexander Toponce*. Salt Lake City: Century Printing Company, 1923.

Utah Institute of Fine Arts. *Utah Guide Book WPA Project*. New York: Hastings House, 1941.

Whipple, Maurine. *This Is the Place—Utah*. New York: Alfred A. Knopf, Inc., 1945.

Whitney, Orson F. *Popular History of Utah*. Salt Lake City: Deseret News, 1916.

Wilson, Lycurgus A. *Life of David W. Patten*. Salt Lake City: Deseret News, 1900.

Young, Levi Edgar. *Founding of Utah*. New York: Charles Scribner & Sons, 1924.

BULLETINS

Koontz, John. *Political History of Nevada*. Secretary of State of Nevada, 1959.

Lincoln, Francis Church. *Mining Districts and Mineral Resources of Nevada*. Nevada Newsletter Publishing Company, 1923.

Nevada State Historical Society Papers Volumes I, II, III, IV, V.

Nevada State Historical Society, *Third Biennial Report*, 1911-1912.

Salt Lake Mining Review, article by Murray Schick, 1936.

Utah Farmer, article "Miner Mike," 1946.

Utah Historical Quarterly, William R. Palmer article, "Early Day Trading with the Nevada Mining Camps." October, 1958.

Utah Historical Quarterly, Jack Goodman article, "The Shining Mountains—The Oquirrh Range," July, 1959.

Utah Historical Quarterly, William M. McPhee article, "Vignettes of Park City," April, 1959.

NEWSPAPERS

Beatty Bullfrog, Nye County, Nevada, 1905.

Bingham Bulletin, Bingham, Utah.
Daily Territorial Enterprise, Virginia City, Nevada.
Eureka Sentinel, Eureka, Nevada.
Humboldt Register, Unionville, Nevada, 1865.
Park City Record, Park City, Utah.
Pioche Daily Record, Pioche, Nevada.
Rawhide Rustler, Rawhide, Nevada, 1908, 1909.
Rhyolite Daily Bulletin, Bullfrog Mining District, Rhyolite, Nevada.
Reese River Reveille, Austin, Nevada.
Sacramento Daily Union, Sacramento, California.
Salt Lake Tribune.
Salt Lake Deseret News.
Searchlight, Searchlight, Nevada.

Index

Cache Valley, Utah, 10
Call, Anson V., 31
Call's Fort, 44
Call's Landing, 31
Camels of the Comstock, 218-221
Campbell, A. G., 131
Camp Floyd, 27, 391
Cape Horn, 19
Carbon County, Utah, 65
Carson City, Nevada, 273-281
Carson, Kit, 13, 95
Carson Valley, 195
Carthage, Illinois, 16
Casement, Jack, 42
Cassidy, Butch, 11, 192
Cathedral of the Madoline, 87
Cedar City, Utah, 21
Cedar Fort, 29, 32
Cedar Valley, 29
Chambers, Robert C., 88
Charcoal Burners Union, 184
Charleston, Nevada, **126**
Chief Tintic (Goshute Tribe), 91
Chinese Bridge, 85-86
Chisholm, Robert B., 67
Church of Jesus Christ of Latter-Day-Saints, 16, 140-142
Churches of Virginia City, Nevada—Roman Catholic (Father Patrick Manogue); St. Paul's Episcopal; (Rev. Franklin D. Rising); (Rev. Ozi W. Whitaker)
City of Corinne (ore boat), 44
Clark, W. A., 295
Clay, Dan, 57
Clegg, Charles, 181
Cody, Buffalo Bill, 44
Colorado River, 254
Committee of 601, 147, 193, 241-242, 285-286
Comstock, Newspapers of: The Territorial Enterprise, The Virginia Daily Union, Gold Hill News; Principal mines of: Crown Point, Yellow Jacket, Kentuck, The Mexican, Ophir, Gold and Curry, Potosi, Hale and Norcross, Best & Belcher, Savage, Chollar, Over-

man, The Sides, Consolidated Virginia
Connor, General Patrick E. (Father of Utah Mining), 43, 47, 61, 63, 66, 76, 90, 138
Cooke, Jay, 115, 132
Corbett, "Gentleman Jim," 279-281
Corey, J. M., 283
Corinne, Utah, 39-47
Cosmos, Utah, 43
Cottonwood Observer, 72-73
Coughlin, Patrick, 80
Courtney, Morgan, 151-152
Cove Fort, 139
Covey, Edward, 35
Cowan, Eilley Orrum, 199
Cox, Howard, 159
Craig, David, 11
Crandall's Canyon, 80
Crandlebaugh, Judge John, 33
Crystal Springs, 147, 160
Cuch, Jake, 11
Cullen, Matt, 131
Cumming, Alfred, Governor, 22, 23, 29
Curry, Abraham V. Z., **212**, 273-281
Cusic, Pat, 101

Dallin, Cyrus E., 63
Daly, J. J., 77, 86
Dangberg, Henry Fred, 271
Danites, 97
Davids, James, 31
Davis, "Diamondfield Jack," 306-307
Davis, Gad, 83
Dawes, N. E., 80
Dayton, Nevada, 259-271
De Groot, Henry, 201-202, 222
Deidesheimer, Phillipp, 223-224
DeLamar, Captain Joseph, 62, 111; town, **125**
Dempsey, Jack, 303-304
Denver and Rio Grande Western Railroad, 63, 84, 86
Dern, John, 111-112
Deseret, State of, 18, 27
Diamond Field, **127**
Diamond, Utah, 90

326

328

Raddon, S. L., 78
Rawhide, Nevada, **209**
Raymond, William H., 149
Reed, James, 14-15, 186
Reese, John, 195
Rhyolite, Nevada, **127**
Rhyolite Daily Bulletin, 146
Rice, George Graham, 302
Rice, W. V., 86
Richards, Willard, 17
Rickard, "Tex," 303-304, 306-307
Robinson, Maud, 74
Robinson, Utah, 90
Rockefeller, John D., 61
Rockwell, Porter, 92
Rocky Mountain Fur Company, 11
Rocky Mountains, 17
Rollins, James A., 115
Rose, Edward, 12
Rose, William, 95
Ross, Aaron, 290-292
Rossie Hill, 85
Roubidoux, Antoine, 11
Russell, Majors and Waddell, 23, 34
Ryan, Dennis, 131
Ryan, James, 131

Salt Lake and Mercur Railroad, 111
Salt Lake and Western Railroad, 101
Salt Lake City, Utah, 14, **54**
Savage, C. R., 42, 46
Scanlan, Father Lawrence, 92, 135
Schaefer, Jack, 113
Schenck, Robert C., 69
Schubach, James, 78
Schwab, Charles, 295-307
Semloh Hotel, Salt Lake City, 88
Shaver, Leonidas, 22
Sharon, William, 228-232
Shick, Murray, 131
Silliman, Professor, 69
Sinclair, Charles E., 33
Silver City, Utah, 90
Silver Reef, Utah, 135-146, **122, 123**; principal mines of: The Leeds, Barbee and W a l k e r, Christy Company, The Stormont

Single Men's Protective Association, 152-153
Sisters of the Holy Cross, 82
Six Mile Canyon, 260
Smith, Grant, 229
Smith, Harold, 314-316
Smith, Jedediah S., 10
Smith, Joseph, 16, 96, 138
Smith, Lot, 231
Snow, Erastus, 141
Snyder, Edward H., 159
Snyder, George C., 78
Snyder, Samuel C., 76, 78
Snyder, W. F. and Sons, 112
Soldier Summit, Utah, 65
Sonora, Mexico, 28
Southern Pacific Railroad, 44
Spafford Hall's Station, 259-261
Spanish Fork Canyon, Utah 9
Spaulding, Tom, 100
Spencer, Howard, 32
Stagg, Parry, 80
Standard Oil Company, 61
Stanford, Leland, 42
St. Ann's Orphanage, 87
Steen, Rector, 78-79
Stenhouse, T. B. H., 31
Stewart, Senator William, 68-69, 146, 223, 239-240
St. George Cook, Colonel Phillip, 34
St. George, Utah, 141
Stiles, George P., 23
Still, Daniel C., 148
Stimler, Harry, 298
Stokes Castle, 173
Stout, Hosea, 138
Sublette, William L., 10
Sullivan, John L., 278-279
Sutro, Adolph, 234-235
Sutter, Adolph, 15
Sutter's Fort, 15

Tabernacle, Mormon, 21
Tanner's Hotel, 73
Tannersville, Utah, 72
Taylor, Charley C. D., 300-301
Taylor, John, 17

330